TEACHING WITH
Spiritual
POWER

TEACHING WITH *Spiritual* POWER

Jerry A. Wilson

BOOKCRAFT
Salt Lake City, Utah

Copyright © 1996 by Bookcraft, Inc.

All rights reserved. No part of this book may be reproduced in any form or by any means without permission in writing from the publisher, Bookcraft, Inc., 1848 West 2300 South, Salt Lake City, Utah 84119.

Bookcraft is a registered trademark of Bookcraft, Inc.

Library of Congress Catalog Card Number: 95-83325
ISBN 1-57008-223-5

First Printing, 1996

Printed in the United States of America

Contents

Preface   *vii*

Part One: The Philosophy of Teaching

1   Establishing a Philosophy of Teaching   *3*
2   The Lord's Law of Teaching   *9*
3   A Teacher's Fundamental Perspective:
    The Restoration   *14*
4   A Teacher's Fundamental Perspective:
    The Student   *23*
5   Teaching Principles of the Gospel   *28*
6   Teaching Out of the Scriptures   *37*
7   Teaching by the Spirit   *48*
8   Teaching the Message of the Gospel   *69*
9   The Way and the Method of Teaching   *85*
10 Building Faith by Teaching   *99*

Part Two: The Methodology of Teaching

11 Studying the Scriptures as a Teacher   *109*
12 Marking Scriptures: The Teaching Text   *121*
13 Overviewing: Teaching the Context
    of the Scriptures   *136*
14 Using a Graphic Focus in the Classroom   *147*
15 The Skill of Apperception   *162*
16 Using Stories to Verify the Scriptures   *177*
17 Filing: Establishing a Scriptural Treasure   *191*

18	Preparing the Heart and the Lesson	203
19	The Grand Fundamental Principles of Teaching	209
20	The Power of Teaching unto Salvation	216

Appendix 1: Overviewing the Book of Mormon   220

Appendix 2: Grand Fundamental Principles
   of Teaching the Scriptures   222

Sources Cited   225

Index   229

Preface

This book rests on the premise that in order to teach with spiritual power in the Church, one must observe what might be termed the "law of teaching." This concept, to me, provides a sense of order to a diversity of approaches within the gospel teaching arena. I cannot go to the scriptures and see the instructions there or listen to the prophets teach without having this thought permeate my soul—that there is a pattern, or manner, of teaching, perhaps even a "law" of teaching. Sensing that the idea may reflect a true concept causes me to have a totally different perspective on the subject of teaching; it points me toward discovering what teaching ought to be. Pondering this precept alone has allowed me to carefully examine not only the teaching that I do but also the countless educational experiences I have as a student in the Church. Inasmuch as the Lord seems to have a law for teaching, I am compelled to discover what the scriptures and the prophets—and, for that matter, the Lord—have said about my task as a teacher and to comply with the instructions that thus become evident.

I am personally thankful for the teachers who have affected my life. My memory quickens as I think of a number of teachers who were monumental in my learning of the gospel, and of a profound core of teachers who, as peers within the Church Educational System, have helped me to sense the grandeur of gospel teaching.

I also thank the one mortal being who has affected my teaching more than any other—my wife, Kathy. Through thirty years of marriage she has patiently listened to my strivings to understand the sacred teaching process. Inherent in our covenants to be one, we have had a united heart on teaching. We have been a team, and from the home fires of a united purpose I have gone into a legion of classrooms with greater confidence.

My philosophy of teaching has been begotten, born, and reared out of directions from the Lord, from the scriptures, and from those in our day who have been commissioned to instruct us about the nature of teaching. This book quotes liberally and naturally from the Brethren, those spiritual conduits through whom the Lord himself has commissioned us. Their precious words have become my words, my thoughts, and my philosophy concerning the powerful role of teaching.

I love teaching the gospel of Jesus Christ. I love teaching the scriptures, which reveal the nature of God, the plan of happiness, and the very covenants that cause us to become like God.

I bear witness that there is a philosophy of teaching the gospel granted by heaven itself, and that teaching in this manner is the very way by which eternal life is fostered.

Part One

The Philosophy of Teaching

1

Establishing a Philosophy of Teaching

A number of years ago, while I was serving as an area director for the Church Educational System (CES) in the Central States Area, I asked that we, the professional, full-time CES men in that area, consider our own philosophies of education. We had behaved in our classrooms for years according to the beliefs we had about education; furthermore, we were in professional assignments in which we were responsible to hold pre-service and in-service meetings for hundreds of early-morning and home-study teachers in the seminary programs of our areas.

As we progressed, many found this to be an arduous experience, one which few of us had undertaken before. It was an experience that caused us to confront the reasons why we acted in certain ways in the classroom. It was the beginning, in many regards, of being able to articulate a philosophy, which articulation lies at the foundation of being able to teach someone else about teaching; and teaching others how to teach was a major part of our professional responsibilities.

As this experience unfolded, there were some interesting ideas about this business of having a personal philosophy of education that came to me. First, it seemed that having a philosophy of education was critical to my teaching; having such a philosophy was to have a reason for my teaching, a reason for acting in certain ways in the classroom. Second, it seemed that I needed to make sure that I had a correct philosophy of education, even the Lord's philosophy, else how could I help my students toward eternal life? Third, it seemed that if I had the philosophy so ingrained in my soul that I could explain it clearly, somehow it would help me to not be deceived as to what my methodology should be.

Therefore, I derived these conclusions:

1. We must have a philosophy that guides our practices.

2. It must be a correct philosophy, for the sake of the students.

3. We must believe and know that philosophy so well that we can articulate it to another and, more important, that we can teach our students edifyingly.

Philosophy and Methodology

A teaching methodology is really born out of a philosophy of teaching. In fact, it would seem that our methodology cannot be any better than the philosophy which gives it life. If one is ignorant of the philosophy, then at best his behavior in a classroom is only a function of copying other teachers' classroom behaviors.

Perhaps the way to begin a teacher training program would be to concentrate first on the wellsprings of the philosophy, and to allow the methodology to flow refreshingly from that source. The absolute excitement that fills the teaching arena is born out of a worthy philosophy, out of true principles of teaching. When the teacher understands them, he acts to "govern himself" according to those principles. He begins to act as a teacher, according to the philosophy, and to not be merely acted upon; or, in other words, he no longer feels the pressure to imitate the techniques or behaviors of other teachers.

Divinely Commissioned

When I held the office of teacher in the Aaronic Priesthood, my first assignment as a fourteen-year-old was to usher at a door near the front of the chapel, a door which led into the hallway and to the rest rooms. As the sacrament was being passed, a young lady came to the door, having a sufficient need to get to the rest rooms. I tried to open it but was unable. The scene became pressured as most eyes focused on my inability in the context of her emergency. She eventually turned and hurried to another door. A priest came up to me after the meeting and said with an air of disgust, "Here's how you open the door!" He grabbed the doorknob, and with a gentle pulling of the door to himself, the pressure of the latch was released and the door sprang open.

Now, I tell this simple story to illustrate a point. The door which opens our understanding to teaching has an exacting doorknob. As we gently pull the knob to ourselves, as if somehow receiving the principle, then the door can swing open. The principle we have to receive, or pull to ourselves, is: *The Lord has commissioned us as teachers and has himself given us a pattern for teaching*. The room we are to enter is spacious, beautifully decorated, well lighted, and superbly comfortable. This sacred teaching chamber will provide some of the most edifying experiences of our lives, but the room cannot be entered without our taking to our deepest selves the notion that there is a manner and order of teaching already approved by heaven. This very principle grants us entrance.

Developing a Philosophy

We often struggle through the process of acquiring a philosophy. For instance, let me share with you one person's insightful comments on how he came to a particular philosophy of teaching. This will illustrate perhaps our tendencies to labor, maybe even struggle, in obtaining the correct principles.

> My first year of seminary (full-time) was one of the worst years of my entire life. I went into the classroom with extremely high and naive expectations of what the students wanted. Some of these incorrect perspectives were a result of the artificial environment of a couple of years of early morning seminary in Southern California. That situation was so easy, because of the nature of the early morning beast, that I figured teaching seminary was a case of imparting knowledge. Boy, was I ever mistaken! Highland High in Salt Lake City was not taken into consideration by J. Reuben Clark Jr. in his classic talk, "The Charted Course of the Church in Education." These kids were definitely *not* hungering and thirsting after knowledge. If they had testimonies, it was news to them. Their priorities were not after the fashion of Saturday's Warriors.

I died one hundred and eighty deaths in that first year. *Boring* was the most descriptive word my students could use in my behalf. After the first shock wore off, it was simply a matter of survival. If they wanted the scriptures, I could not figure out how. One day, near the end of a dismal year, I lucked into a discovery. I was shooting the breeze with the class, prior to the opening bell. A story of my childhood that was brought to mind came forth from my lips. The class sat quiet and thoughtfully listening. The silence and attention were startling. I could hardly believe what was happening—they wanted more! More stories came forth during the final months of that year. Lessons were taught from them, mixed with a few scriptures. Though the year was still rough, slight improvement was noticeable.

For the entire summer, my project was to figure out why some speakers and teachers in the Church were popular, and others were not. Each speaker and teacher that was *popular* with the young people was the object of my intense study. Every talk, book, tape, article, and video that was available by or about these *great* teachers was diligently analyzed and dissected. What were the reasons for success? I was less concerned with *what* success was than with what *caused* it. I was not as much interested in their views as I was in how they communicated and why others listened.

Humor played a strong role in almost every popular talk. Without exception, every teacher in my test group made abundant use of stories and illustrations. Love, though abstract and intangible, seemed to permeate each speaker's delivery. And lastly, the audiences were constantly being made to feel good about themselves.

During the next few years, I incorporated these ideas into my teaching. Stories, humor, self-esteem, personality, and enthusiasm were techniques and traits that I tried very hard to develop. As I grew in these qualities, my "success in the classroom" became increasingly obvious. After about three years, popularity as a teacher was mine. I finally had what I wanted. The kids liked me and my class. Wow! What more could a teacher ask?

At first, I was happy. The satisfaction slowly waned as the craving for something more increased. Initially I could not figure out my problem. Why had I sensed a decrease of my commitment to teaching? Why did something feel out of place in my life?

Concurrent with my increased popularity in the "youth circuit," my need for self-respect was gratified by academic means. History, especially Church history, became my real outlet for creative growth. I could not spend much time in the seminary class teaching the stuff, but I basically thrived on my research. A gulf between two worlds began to widen: scholarship and "success in the classroom." Excited about serious scholarship in academics and in the scriptures; but knowing what it took to be "successful in the classroom," I allowed my professional life to remain compartmentalized for quite a long period of time.

Confession must here be made that I never did bridge the gap while in the seminary program. At times, I would resolve to be more academic and offer the students more substance; as soon as I could see the effect on my popularity, however, I would quickly bail out of the scriptures and add more excitement to my class.

My friend's letter illustrates how we may come upon our philosophies for teaching. Perhaps, at best, it becomes only a matter of trial and error. However bright we may be, often we can be led to accept notions which are based on matters of "popularity" or "success"—standards of the flesh.

At this point, I want to verify that there is a standard of teaching in the kingdom. There is a pattern, a manner, an order, even a law, of teaching—and the God of heaven, the quintessential teacher, approves a teaching direction. I believe it is expected of us to find and know that pattern of teaching.

When one perceives the Lord's philosophy, and feasts on its principles, then the nature of the things one seeks is simply different than popularity or success, standards that the world would establish. Going back to my illustration of the Central States Area, after having struggled to write our own philosophies of education, which philosophies were various, we began as teachers to study and assimilate the principles being taught to us as Church educators in talks given to us by the General Authorities. We also began to study the principles of teaching given us by the great prophetic teachers of the scriptures and by the Lord himself. As these principles began to distill on our souls, we also began to look at the whole matter of teaching from a different perspective.

One such perspective, again a letter from a full-time CES man, indicates how feasting on the principles of teaching given by the Lord through his servants causes us to view teaching in a much more profound way:

> A very difficult part of teaching, at this stage in my development, is imparting what I have learned in and by the same Spirit by

which I have learned it. A couple of years ago, I was not faced with such a dilemma. Now, with my learning increasingly based upon the Spirit and the word, I am confronted with many more concerns than just my own ego. How can I best teach this in a way pleasing to the Lord? How can I make a spiritual insight logical and clear? Am I teaching according to the Lord's pattern? Am I drawing attention to myself or to the principles in the word? Am I teaching what my students are able to bear? Do I have the Spirit of the Lord?

Still, I must admit, this job has never been so enjoyable. Immersing myself in the scriptures and striving to teach according to the Lord's curriculum has been spiritual high adventure. It has been what has kept me in the Church Educational System. It is what will keep me in the Church Educational System.

At the conclusion of the letter, my friend made this important statement: The "pressing of the issue of adopting the Lord's 'philosophy' of teaching has changed my life." So it has with me. I bear witness to you that the Lord does have a specific teaching commission for us. He has not left us ignorant of the principles that should undergird all of our teaching in the Church. Our posture in this matter should not be that we know more than the Lord about his gospel or indeed about how it needs to be taught. Rather we should approach this sacred task with a willingness to find out the manner, pattern, order, and law of teaching. "Remember, remember," the Lord said, "that it is not the work of God that is frustrated, but the work of men" (D&C 3:3).

2

The Lord's Law of Teaching

In the Doctrine and Covenants, there is a section that has come to be known as "The Law." In it are contained several different laws that were pertinent for the Church as it was established in this dispensation. Besides the law of teaching, a group of verses which is the point of our concern, there were various sets of verses that might appropriately be called the law of preaching, the law of moral conduct, the law of consecration, the law of administration to the sick, and the law of Church discipline. To the Saints at that time, section 42 confirmed to them not only that the Lord acknowledged them as his church but also that they needed his direction for the Church.

In verses 12, 13, and 14, we read the Lord's direction about how his gospel was to be taught:

> And again, the elders, priests and teachers of this church shall teach the principles of my gospel, which are in the Bible and the Book of Mormon, in the which is the fulness of the gospel.

That they, the teachers, were to teach the principles of his gospel was the fundamental beginning of the Lord's law. Furthermore, they were to teach those principles out of the scriptures, which for their time were the Bible and the Book of Mormon. (However, in verse 15 the Lord indicated that a fulness of scriptures was yet to be given; and then, we would assume, as the Doctrine and Covenants and the Pearl of Great Price were compiled, the commission would be to teach the principles of the gospel out of those scriptures as well.)

Continuing with the law, the Lord stated:

> And they shall observe the covenants and church articles to do them, and these shall be their teachings, as they shall be directed by the Spirit.

"They," meaning the teachers, were to keep the covenants and were to keep the church articles. The word *these* in the phrase, "And these shall be their teachings," raises some interesting questions. For instance, do the words "these shall be their teachings" refer to the principles of the gospel, or do they refer to the scriptures, or do they refer to the covenants and Church articles? And furthermore, which of all the covenants and which of all the principles shall be their teachings?

The context of the verse suggests that *these* refers to the covenants and Church articles that the teachers were "observing" and "doing." "These" shall be their teachings! They could not, in this kingdom, teach what they did not live, or that which had not been directed to them by the Spirit. Nor can we. In fact, it is those covenants that we live and do for which we receive the directions of the Spirit. I witness that sacred fact. We can teach only the principles of the gospel, the covenants and Church articles, which we live; otherwise there will be a hollowness about the message we are delivering, a void of having a witness of the Spirit in our own lives concerning that principle, and an absence of a confirming witness of the Spirit to our students while we teach.

Finalizing this three-verse law, the Lord continued by saying:

> And the Spirit shall be given unto you by the prayer of faith; and if ye receive not the Spirit ye shall not teach.

Without the "prayer of faith"—that faith which indicated that they had done their part through preparation in study and "doing" the covenants—they did not have the right to the Spirit. And in our day as well, the Lord seems to indicate by these verses to us that without the Spirit, we "shall not teach," we shall not be able to teach the principles of the gospel unto the salvation of our students without the Spirit of the Lord confirming those principles in the hearts of our students.

These are the Lord's words, his feelings, his concerns, even his law of teaching. We are, in the sense of Doctrine and Covenants 64:29, "agents . . . on the Lord's errand," doing his business, according to his will, in his way.

The essentials, therefore, out of section 42 are to
1. Teach the principles of the gospel,
2. Teach those principles out of the scriptures,
3. Observe and do the covenants and Church articles,
4. Pray the prayer of faith, and
5. Be directed by the Spirit.

A Sacred Trust

In section 3 of the Doctrine and Covenants, the Lord counseled Joseph Smith concerning his responsibility toward the plates from which would come the Book of Mormon. He reminded him, as already mentioned in chapter 1, that "it is not the work of God that is frustrated, but the work of men" (D&C 3:3). He further counseled Joseph that he had "been entrusted with these things," and that there were "promises which were made to" him if he did not boast "in his own strength" and set at "naught," or transgress or trample upon, the counsel of his director. Moreover, the Lord told Joseph that he had oft "gone on in the persuasions of men," but that he "should have been faithful" and the Lord "would have extended his arm and supported" him in this sacred trust. (See verses 4, 5, 6, 8, 15.)

This marvelous counsel to Joseph is counsel to any teacher who believes the Lord has given us a trust as well. We have been promised that if we will not listen to the persuasions of men, or boast in our own strength, or set at naught the counsel of our director in these matters, he will sustain our faithfulness in teaching as we have been commissioned.

Our charge, it would seem, is to accept the Lord's directions about teaching. It is an attitude like unto Elder Bruce R. McConkie's when he declared that teachers cannot create doctrines:

> We do not create the doctrines of the gospel. People who ask questions about the gospel, a good portion of the time, are looking for an answer that sustains a view they have expressed. They want to justify a conclusion that they have reached instead of looking for the ultimate truth in the field. Once again, it does not make one snap of the fingers difference to me what the doctrines of the Church are. I cannot create a doctrine. I cannot originate a concept of eternal truth. The only thing I ought to be concerned with is learning what the Lord thinks about a doctrine. If I ask a question of someone to learn something, I ought not to be seeking for a confirmation of a view that I have expressed. I ought to be seeking knowledge and wisdom. It should not make any difference to me whether the doctrine is on the right hand or on the left. My sole interest and my sole concern would be to find out what the Lord thinks on the subject. (*Foolishness of Teaching*, p. 8.)

Our posture ought to be one of looking, searching, and accepting the "mind of Christ" on teaching. Although the phrase "the Lord's law of teaching" has been used in this book, its use is not meant to be intimidating in any way; rather it is used in order to indicate, as was mentioned already in chapter 1, that there is an order, a pattern, a manner, and a law of teaching that governs the way we look at teaching. Our personal commitment should be to understand that the Lord is commissioning us to remember the promises and to be faithful to his counsel, not to the counsels of men. The Lord has a law of teaching, and behind that law is a God who cares about not only what we teach concerning the principles of his gospel but also how those principles are taught, that is, by covenant-keeping teachers, out of the scriptures, and by the Spirit.

Conclusion

These, then, the directions and counsel of section 42, form the core of the way we teach. As Latter-day Saints and as teachers of the restored gospel, we are to conform our philosophy of teaching to the very God of heaven whose work it is to bring about the eternal life of his children. The teaching of the gospel principles, an integral part of that work, has to be done in the way that heaven itself can endorse and confirm. Teaching in the manner that the Lord has prescribed simply allows us to be a part of that great work of God, the salvation of his children. Again, I testify to you that teaching in the Lord's way, according to the law of teaching we have begun to unfold in this chapter, is a work filled with joy, not frustration. It is a work filled with the very glory of the Father and the Son, whose glory will be the salvation not only of the students but of the teachers as well.

3

A Teacher's Fundamental Perspective: The Restoration

After having established the need to have a philosophy drive our methodology in the classroom, and having sensed from section 42 the Lord's emphasis toward having certain elements in our teaching, teachers would be benefitted by feasting on some of the great talks given by the Brethren or in the scriptures concerning the pattern and manner of our teaching. One such address is called *The Charted Course of the Church in Education.* In 1938, President J. Reuben Clark Jr., a member of the First Presidency, addressed the seminary and institute employees at Aspen Grove. Although his talk was born out of a specific need in Church education at the time, the principles that he espoused really pertain to all teachers in the Church.

The introduction to this classic talk is an experience that President Clark remembered as he heard the Webster-Hayne debate. When Webster stood to speak, he said:

> Mr. President: When the mariner has been tossed for many days in thick weather, and on an unknown sea, he naturally avails himself of the first pause in the storm, the earliest glance of the sun, to take his latitude, and ascertain how far the elements have driven him from his true course. Let us imitate this prudence, and, before we float farther on the waves of this debate, refer to the point from which we departed, that we may at least be able to conjecture where we now are. I ask for the reading of the resolution. (Quoted in *Charted Course*, p. 1.)

President Clark asked the audience if they would excuse him if he used the "same procedure to restate some of the more outstanding and essential fundamentals underlying our Church school education." He went on to emphasize that there were "two prime things which may not be overlooked, forgotten, shaded, or discarded." He began to teach the number one essential of our teaching—that Jesus Christ is the "Son of God, the Only Begotten . . . , the Sacrifice . . . , the Atoner . . . , that He was crucified . . . ; that He died . . . ; that on the third day His spirit was reunited with His body . . . ; that He was raised from the tomb . . . perfect . . . , the First Fruits . . . ; that He later ascended to the Father." (*Charted Course*, p. 2.)

The second of the two prime things was that "the Father and the Son actually and in truth and very deed appeared to the Prophet Joseph"; that there were "other heavenly visions"; that "the Gospel and the holy Priesthood . . . were in truth and fact restored to the earth"; that "the Lord again set up His Church"; that "the Book of Mormon is just what it professes to be"; and that "numerous revelations" were received by the Prophet. President Clark emphasized that "without these two great beliefs the Church would cease to be the Church." (*Charted Course*, p. 3.)

As Latter-day Saint teachers we need to accept these doctrines, even the fulness of these doctrines. In fact, President Clark was so bold as to say that if a teacher (and he was speaking specifically of CES teachers) did not have a testimony of these two fundamental truths, he should at once resign, and that "the First Presidency expects this pruning to be made" (*Charted Course*, p. 7).

JESUS IS THE CHRIST

Perhaps it would be helpful to illustrate graphically the pivotal importance of this teaching dimension. There have been six thousand years of the earth's experience during which major dispensations of the gospel have been commissioned from heaven, the heads of those dispensations being Adam, Enoch, Noah, Abraham, Moses, Christ, and Joseph Smith. Throughout all of these dispensations, the one fundamental truth that needed to be taught was that Jesus is the Christ. It was, as it were, a latitudinal position on our teaching map.

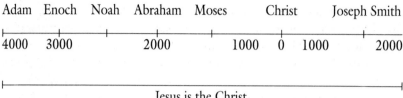

Salvation could come in no other way, could be spoken of with no other name than that of Jesus Christ. Whether a person was born in Adam's day or in Moses' day made no difference as to the testimony of Christ that was borne by the prophets or the testimony that needed to be accepted in order to have salvation. This central doctrine of Jesus Christ, the Son of God, was preached in every dispensation. It was the first and most fundamental truth upon which the gospel message was structured.

JOSEPH SMITH IS THE PROPHET OF THE RESTORATION

In each of the dispensations, the second great truth was that the prophet of that dispensation was critical to the presentation of the message. The Saints in Moses' day would have depended upon him for the true knowledge of God and therefore would have had testimony of him as the revealer of Christ to them. Had President Clark given his talk to the teachers of Moses' day, he would have emphasized that the two prime things needing to be taught were that Jesus was the Christ and that Moses was the prophet. To the Saints of Moses' day, even though they may have believed in Adam, Enoch, Noah, and Abraham, and carried the scriptures of those prophets around constantly, if they had not accepted Moses as the prophet, the true restored knowledge of God would have escaped them. Also, even more important, they would have been deprived of participation in the covenants and ordinances of the gospel, Moses having held the very keys of salvation, the keys unlocking the ordinances of eternal life for them.

So it is in our day. Joseph Smith stands as the revealer of God to us. He holds the keys of salvation for us as well. Although we may honor the prophets of the Old and New Testaments and may even be scholars in the doctrines and principles of those previous days, yet without the testimony of Joseph Smith, salvation will simply be a mystery to us. Joseph Smith, for us, is a longitudinal position on the teaching map.

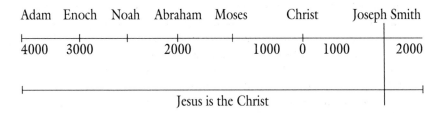

President Clark said, "I have set out these matters because they are the latitude and longitude of the actual location and position of the Church, both in this world and in eternity" (*Charted Course*, p. 3). Once we know the legitimacy of our position, then we can make alterations or changes in our bearings if they need altering. Part of the "charted course" is to have these two fundamental bearings to guide our teaching efforts.

Establishing Our Teaching Context

In our day, there are occasional voices detracting from a full acceptance of the miracles surrounding the restoration of the gospel, of the visions Joseph Smith had, or of the translation of the Book of Mormon. Yet the safety of our teaching lies in the acceptance of the context of the Restoration, where the true knowledge of God, of the gospel principles, and of the covenants and ordinances of salvation are made known to us.

As an example, during the very year that President Clark delivered his Church education message, a man by the name of LeGrand Richards, future Presiding Bishop and Apostle in the Church, was called as a local bishop of the University Ward near the University of Utah. There were some ward members who had differing views on the fundamentals of which we are speaking in this chapter. Bishop Richards had been attending the Sunday School Gospel Doctrine class, hearing doctrines that were controversial as to the role of Joseph Smith as a prophet, the Book of Mormon as the word of God, and the reality of Christ as the Savior; therefore, he stood and declared the fundamentals of a "charted course" as boldly as had President Clark:

> The things I have heard in these two weeks of free discussion are not Mormonism. Now, as long as I am bishop of this ward, we are going to teach fundamental Mormonism in this building. That means that Joseph Smith indeed received a vision of the Father and the Son (and it is provable by personal testimony), that he did indeed translate the Book of Mormon from the golden plates which he received from the Angel Moroni. In that book, we read of the vision shown to Nephi by the angel, of Mary with child, of the child growing to manhood, of his choosing twelve apostles, and of his being crucified for the sins of the world. Now, that is Mormonism.
>
> Now, if any of you do not approve of fundamental Mormonism, why don't you go and organize a church of your own and teach what you want to. There are so many churches now teaching the precepts of men that one more won't matter. (Quoted in Tate, *LeGrand Richards: Beloved Apostle*, pp. 191–92.)

Now and then there is a spirit that enters this church which, departing from the fundamentals of our theology, needs a "course correction," if you will. President Clark and Bishop Richards understood that there is a longitude and a latitude forming our position which must be maintained for the salvation of God's children. I testify, as another witness to both President Clark and Bishop Richards, that Joseph Smith is the prophet of the Restoration, and because of that, I testify that Jesus is the Christ. The testimony of Joseph Smith is the context out of which we know the true nature of God. Without these two testimonies, how could we possibly teach the truth relating to the salvation of man?

JOSEPH SMITH AND THE RESTORATION CONTEXT

Having established the necessity for both the latitudinal and longitudinal testimonies of Christ and Joseph Smith, respectively, let us consider why the testimony of the Prophet precedes the testimony of Christ—or of God, for that matter. In Moroni 7:31–32, Mormon taught that the office of angelic ministers was to

> call men unto repentance, and to fulfil and to do the work of the covenants of the Father, which he hath made unto the children of men, to prepare the way among the children of men, by declaring

> the word of Christ unto the *chosen vessels* of the Lord, that they may bear testimony of him.
> And by so doing, the Lord God prepareth the way that the *residue* of men may have faith in Christ, that the Holy Ghost may have place in their hearts, according to the power thereof; and after this manner bringeth to pass the Father, the covenants which he hath made unto the children of men. (Emphasis added.)

The order by which any of us knows there is a God is to have the veil opened by God himself, transfiguring a prophet (the chosen vessel) and bringing him into God's presence. Thereby the prophet, gaining and then retaining this knowledge of God, proclaims to mankind (the residue), by human testimony, the very knowledge on which the residue may exercise faith in God. Not only is Joseph Smith that kind of chosen vessel, but he is also a dispensational head, one who, as Elder Bruce R. McConkie stated, is pivotal to the testimony of every person in this dispensation:

> I am speaking of those great eras or periods, of those designated portions of the earth's history when the Lord, through one man, gives his word to the whole world and makes all the prophets, and all the seers, and all the administrators, and all the apostles of that period subject to, and exponents of, what came through that individual. . . .
> . . . Every prophet is a witness of Christ; every dispensation head is a revealer of Christ for his day; and every other prophet or apostle who comes is a reflection and an echo and an exponent of the dispensation head. All such come to echo to the world and to expound and unfold what God has revealed through the man who was appointed for that era to give his eternal word to the world. Such is the dispensation concept. ("This Generation Shall Have My Word Through You," pp. 4–5.)

Each succeeding prophet of this dispensation not only has had a testimony of Joseph Smith but also has proclaimed and echoed the same message of the Prophet Joseph. The testimony of this pivotal prophet is critical to the success of the restored work, in which the knowledge of God, which had been lost by an apostasy, is now revealed to man with power. Moroni stated to the young

Joseph that his name "should be had for good and evil among all nations, kindreds, and tongues, or that it should be both good and evil spoken of among all people" (Joseph Smith—History 1:33). The story that President David O. McKay told of his father's missionary experience establishes this very prophecy of Moroni. President McKay said:

> [My father] accepted a call to a mission about 1880. When he began preaching in his native land and bore testimony of the restoration of the gospel of Jesus Christ, he noticed that the people turned away from him. They were bitter in their hearts against anything Mormon, and the name of Joseph Smith seemed to arouse antagonism in their hearts. One day he concluded that the best way to get these people would be to preach just the simple principles, the atonement of the Lord Jesus Christ, the first principles of the gospel, and not bear testimony of the restoration of the gospel. It first came simply, as a passing thought, but yet it influenced his future work. In a month or so he became oppressed with a gloomy, downcast feeling, and he could not enter into the spirit of his work. He did not really know what was the matter, but his mind became obstructed; his spirit became clogged; he was oppressed and hampered; and that feeling of depression continued until it weighed him down with such heaviness that he went to the Lord and said: "Unless I can get this feeling removed, I shall have to go home. I cannot continue my work with this feeling."
>
> It continued for some time after that, then, one morning, before daylight, following a sleepless night, he decided to retire to a cave, near the ocean, where he knew he would be shut off from the world entirely, and there pour out his soul to God and ask why he was oppressed with this feeling, what he had done, and what he could do to throw it off and continue his work. . . .
>
> He entered that place and said: "Oh, Father, what can I do to have this feeling removed? I must have it lifted or I cannot continue in this work"; and he heard a voice, as distinct as the tone I am now uttering, say: "Testify that Joseph Smith is a Prophet of God."
>
> Remembering, then, what he tacitly had decided six weeks or more before and becoming overwhelmed with the thought, the whole thing came to him in a realization that he was there for a special mission, and that he had not given that special mission the attention which it deserved. Then he cried in his heart, "Lord, it is enough," and went out from the cave. (*Gospel Ideals*, pp. 21–22.)

The teaching that Joseph Smith is the prophet of the Restoration is the context for the Church's message about God, which knowledge of God and his existence, his characteristics, and his attributes brings salvation. But as has already been mentioned, one testimony precedes the other. Although some may criticize by not understanding the emphasis that is needed concerning the Prophet Joseph Smith, yet there is power in this Restoration context. For instance, Parley P. Pratt wrote of an experience that happened in Philadelphia in which Joseph Smith's and Sidney Rigdon's different teaching contexts were compared. The story verifies that the teaching of the Restoration as our context and our approach has overwhelming consequences:

> While visiting with brother Joseph in Philadelphia, a very large church was opened for him to preach in, and about three thousand people assembled to hear him. Brother Rigdon spoke first, and dwelt on the Gospel, illustrating his doctrine by the Bible. When he was through, brother Joseph arose like a lion about to roar; and being full of the Holy Ghost, spoke in great power, bearing testimony of the visions he had seen, the ministering of angels which he had enjoyed; and how he had found the plates of the Book of Mormon, and translated them by the gift and power of God. He commenced by saying: "If nobody else had the courage to testify of so glorious a message from Heaven, and of the finding of so glorious a record, he felt to do it in justice to the people, and leave the event with God."
>
> The entire congregation were astounded; electrified, as it were, and overwhelmed with the sense of the truth and power by which he spoke, and the wonders which he related. . . . Many souls were gathered into the fold. (*Autobiography of Parley P. Pratt,* p. 260.)

I bear witness in concert with Elder Pratt that the teaching of the gospel of Jesus Christ is done within the context of the Restoration, of declaring the role of the Prophet Joseph Smith, of the role of the Book of Mormon, and of the power of God that is dispensed through the order of a "chosen vessel."

Conclusion

On the day of the organization of the Church, 6 April 1830, the Lord declared concerning Joseph Smith:

> Wherefore, meaning the church, thou shalt give heed unto all his words and commandments which he shall give unto you as he receiveth them, walking in all holiness before me;
>
> For his word ye shall receive, as if from mine own mouth, in all patience and faith.

Granting promises of power to the Church, the Lord continued:

> For by doing these things the gates of hell shall not prevail against you; yea, and the Lord God will disperse the powers of darkness from before you, and cause the heavens to shake for your good, and his name's glory.

Finally, the Lord declared his testimony of Joseph by saying:

> For thus saith the Lord God: Him have I inspired to move the cause of Zion in mighty power for good, and his diligence I know, and his prayers I have heard. (D&C 21:4–7.)

I testify, along with the Lord, along with Elders Pratt, Richards, McKay, and Clark, that Joseph Smith is the prophet of the Restoration, and that through him we have received the correct knowledge of God and of the plan of salvation. The very keys to utilize the covenants and ordinances necessary for eternal life were granted to Joseph and have been passed on in our day through a line of prophets acting according to the will of God. Teaching the Restoration context brings power in our classrooms, by which the Spirit of the Lord can affect us in becoming like God himself.

4

A Teacher's Fundamental Perspective: The Student

Continuing with President Clark's monumental talk, let us consider a profound portion of his address aimed at our understanding the nature of the student in our classrooms. Often teachers are laboring under the notion that the student is fundamentally weak and ill-equipped to handle the doctrines and principles of the gospel. Feel what President Clark proposed in 1938 that we consider as teachers.

> The youth of the Church, your students, are in great majority sound in thought and in spirit. The problem primarily is to keep them sound, not to convert them.
> The youth of the Church are hungry for things of the spirit; they are eager to learn the Gospel, and they want it straight, undiluted.
> They want to know about the fundamentals I have just set out—about our beliefs; they want to gain testimonies of their truth; they are not now doubters but inquirers, seekers after truth. Doubt must not be planted in their hearts. Great is the burden and the condemnation of any teacher who sows doubt in a trusting soul.
> These students crave the faith their fathers and mothers have; they want it in its simplicity and purity. There are few indeed who have not seen the manifestations of its divine power; they wish to be not only the beneficiaries of this faith, but they want to be themselves able to call it forth to work.
> They want to believe in the ordinances of the Gospel; they wish to understand them so far as they may. (*Charted Course*, pp. 3–4.)

enter the classroom with the perspective that the stu-
"sound," "hungry," "eager"; that they are "inquirers"
cers"; that they "want," "crave," and "wish" to understand the gospel, then our teaching will be of quite a different nature than the teaching of one who feels the students don't care for
the gospel. Essentially we have the right to believe anything we
want about the student, but given the fact that an incorrect philosophy could malign our teaching approach, it seems advisable to
listen to those who have a greater vision of the plan and of the
student who participates in the grand plan of salvation.

In suggesting that President Clark has a greater vision, let me
quote two General Authorities who have consistently supported
this address. First, Elder Boyd K. Packer, who said, "I think I have
never talked to religious educators of the Church except I have
quoted some verse of scripture from the document entitled 'The
Charted Course of the Church in Education.' It was in the form
of an address given to seminary and institute leaders of the
Church by President J. Reuben Clark, Jr., and was approved by
the First Presidency." (*Teach the Scriptures,* p. 7.) Elsewhere, Elder
Packer declared, "This statement by President Clark, speaking for
the First Presidency, is to me the position paper for teachers in the
Church. Never a year goes by but that I re-read it carefully. Every
teacher in the Church should read it in its entirety." (*Teach Ye
Diligently,* p. 128.) President Ezra Taft Benson also gave strong
counsel when he said, "All of you should have a copy of this address and read it at least at the beginning of each teaching year. . . .
This counsel has not changed over the years. Its applicability is
even greater today." (*The Gospel Teacher and His Message,* p. 7.)

The Charted Course is plain and direct not only in the counsel
we discussed in the last chapter about the fundamentals of Jesus
Christ and Joseph Smith but also in the counsel about the students and how we ought to teach them:

> For example, to apply to our spiritually minded and religiously
> alert youth a plan evolved to teach religion to youth having no inter-
> est or concern in matters of the spirit, would not only fail in meeting
> our actual religious needs, but would tend to destroy the best quali-
> ties which our youth now possess.
>
> . . . I say once more there is scarcely a youth that comes through
> your seminary or institute door who has not been the conscious

beneficiary of spiritual blessings, or who has not seen the efficacy of prayer, or who has not witnessed the power of faith to heal the sick, or who has not beheld spiritual outpourings, of which the world at large is today ignorant. You do not have to sneak up behind this spiritually experienced youth and whisper religion in his ears; you can come right out, face to face, and talk with him. You do not need to disguise religious truths with a cloak of worldly things; you can bring these truths to him openly, in their natural guise. Youth may prove to be not more fearful of them than you are. There is no need for gradual approaches, for "bed-time" stories, for coddling, for patronizing, or for any of the other childish devices used in efforts to reach those spiritually inexperienced and all but spiritually dead. (*Charted Course*, pp. 9–10.)

Over the years, in a number of discussions about teaching, this counsel from President Clark has produced some really challenging thoughts about the nature of the students throughout the Church. Quite often we see the students as disinterested in the gospel, and because we do, we search for ways, maybe even inordinate ways, to spark interest and to captivate their attention; and this can cause us to err in our approach. I have wondered if this apparently "disinterested" student was simply a "malnourished" one, especially as I consider this statement by President Clark: "These students as they come to you are spiritually working on towards a maturity which they will early reach if you but feed them the right food" (*Charted Course*, p. 6).

Considering the absolute necessity for all of us to receive the right food, especially that of a spiritual nature, is it possible that for years students may have been fed only a diet of ethics, being served by an entertaining corps of cooks and waiters, and that they are suffering from vitamin deficiency or anemia? Is it possible that we have looked on their spiritually gaunt demeanor, made an improper diagnosis, and by our teaching prescribed a food that would continue to deprive them of the nourishment they need for life itself, even eternal life? Is it also possible that as teachers we have not appreciated the "right food" ourselves, having little experience with balanced, vitamin-ladened meals, full of the measure of the fulness of the gospel of Jesus Christ, having never enjoyed the taste and nourishment sufficiently to have scooped it up by double handfuls?

What we hold in our philosophy, in our teaching hearts, about the students will determine how we treat them, the kind of material we will teach them, and the dependence we will have on God to help bring about their salvation. As an example of the power of one's philosophy—a philosophy that guides our entire approach to the student—I present this story about my family's own experiences with teaching. One year as our family moved into a new ward, my wife, Kathy, was called immediately as the teacher of the twelve- and thirteen-year-old Sunday School class. Not knowing any of the students particularly, but knowing that it was a class of about fifteen (an ominous undertaking in any circle of the Church), we talked one day about how she would begin the task of teaching them. We reviewed together what we believed President Clark had said about the students. This more than casual conversation was really a reminder, a restatement to each other, not only of the potential of these students, but also of the necessity to teach them correctly.

Prepared to teach them the principles of the gospel out of the scriptures, Kathy proceeded that first Sunday to exemplify her charge. Knowing that those students needed the "right food" and that they might demand a more entertaining "dessert" portion, she taught them the food of nourishment and growth, encouraging them to bring their scriptures and to consider the grand doctrines of the kingdom.

Such a shift took time, but more important, it took trust that the students really needed and wanted the nourishment of the gospel and that the presentation of the food through the scriptures and the Spirit really was what would sustain them. Over the next few months a gradual change took place wherein the students began to bring their scriptures regularly, began to discuss the gospel more freely and willingly, and began to sense the wonder of the message.

Parents began asking Kathy what was happening in the class, why their children were insisting on taking scriptures to church, and even, kiddingly, how to answer the questions being posed by their children at the Sunday dinner table concerning the doctrines and principles of the gospel taught that day in class. The students were craving the gospel, because they had a teacher who had trusted the perspective of President Clark, who understood not only who the students were, but also what food was nourishing and the way it needed to be presented.

I testify to you, along with President Clark and the testimony and experience of my wife, Kathy, that our students in the majority "hunger and thirst . . . for a testimony of the things of the spirit" and that "they seek faith, and the knowledge which follows faith" (*Charted Course*, p. 6). I suppose that a major part of our faith will be required of us as teachers in seeing if we will hold on to the knowledge that the student wants and needs the right food, and if we will then proceed in the classroom in the way the Lord has commissioned us.

5

Teaching Principles of the Gospel

Having established the view of the student as one who hungers and thirsts for the gospel, especially as he is fed the food of nourishment, it is important to remind ourselves of the commission from the Lord in D&C 42 to "teach the principles of my gospel." The doctrines and the principles of the gospel constitute our theology, and our theology drives our religion, our ethics, and our behavior.

President Clark suggested that the students "already know that they must be honest, true, chaste," and so on; that they were taught these things since they were born; and that they ought to be encouraged to observe such things,

> but they do not need to have a year's course of instruction to make them believe and know them.
>
> These students fully sense the hollowness of teachings which would make the Gospel plan a mere system of ethics, they know that Christ's teachings are in the highest degree ethical, but they also know they are more than this. They will see that ethics relate primarily to the doings of this life, and that to make of the Gospel a mere system of ethics is to confess a lack of faith, if not a disbelief, in the hereafter. They know that the Gospel teachings not only touch this life, but the life that is to come, with its salvation and exaltation as the final goal. (*Charted Course*, pp. 5–6.)

Principles Versus Ethics

There is a fundamental difference between the principles of the gospel and the ethics of our religion. As an illustration, consider these *principles* of the gospel: creation, fall, atonement, priesthood, salvation, faith, repentance, covenant, and the Holy Ghost. Now consider these *ethics:* trustworthiness, loyalty, helpfulness, friendliness, courtesy, and kindness. Teaching which is centered on doctrines like creation and covenants will be profoundly different than teaching focused on being helpful and friendly. While the ethics and behaviors of a people are important, the emphasis of our teaching is more in the realm of principles than in the realm of ethics and practices. Also, it is not to say that we never teach ethics, but it is to say that our focus is on the theological side more than on the practical and ethical side. Again, from President Clark:

> In the first place, there is neither reason nor is there excuse for our Church religious teaching and training facilities and institutions, unless the youth are to be taught and trained in the principles of the Gospel, embracing therein the two great elements that Jesus is the Christ and that Joseph was God's prophet. The teaching of a system of ethics to the students is not a sufficient reason for running our seminaries and institutes. The great public school system teaches ethics. The students of seminaries and institutes should of course be taught the ordinary canons of good and righteous living, for these are part, and an essential part, of the Gospel. But there are the great principles involved in eternal life, the Priesthood, the resurrection, and many like other things, that go way beyond these canons of good living. These great fundamental principles also must be taught to the youth; they are the things the youth wish first to know about. (*Charted Course*, pp. 6–7.)

It is interesting to consider why the teaching emphasis is centered on the principles rather than on the practices or ethics. For instance, it seems that teaching ethics can be more difficult for the following reasons:

1. It focuses on behavior and encourages a teacher to somehow try to measure the behavior by objectives.

2. It often causes a teacher to inordinately rely on stories, especially stories from his own life, as examples of how the student should live the behavior.

3. Inasmuch as the success of behavioral teaching rests on the student actually changing and complying with the particular behavior, it tends to increase a teacher's use of moralizing and preaching, a system calculated to apply some pressure, as it were.

Teaching principles, on the other hand, can be refreshing:

1. Principles are the foundation not only of individual behaviors and ethics but also of the Church's procedures, programs, policies, and organizations.

2. The principles of the gospel remain the same throughout generations.

3. Intensive study by a teacher in the principles of the gospel is essentially more edifying to him than the study of ethics.

4. Teaching principles eliminates the need for moralizing because it does not focus on the behavior but places the emphasis on the student's understanding of the doctrines.

5. Everything we do in life is governed by principles; therefore, the teaching of principles allows a student, by his agency, to choose how he will behave in relation to these principles.

It seems that the teaching of principles not only benefits the student but also the teacher. From my own experience, I would prefer to teach the principle that God is a God of truth, from which would be derived the grand practice of honesty, than to simply teach the ethic that we should be honest; or to teach the principles of eternal marriage, procreation, and the law of chastity rather than only focusing on the behavior of morality. The wisdom of God is that "you shall teach one another the *doctrine* of the kingdom. Teach ye diligently and my grace shall attend you, that you be instructed more perfectly in theory, in *principle*, in *doctrine*, in the *law* of the gospel, in all things that pertain unto the kingdom of God." (D&C 88:77–78; emphasis added.)

I believe that our essential responsibility is not for the behavior of our students. They are ultimately responsible. As an example, my experience as a fledgling bishop with responsibility for the young women and young men of the ward caused me deep concern for their behaviors and practices. I felt it so keenly that I almost wanted to follow them around, collectively or individually, to hide behind trees, as it were, to ensure that they made the right decisions and lived a good life. That would be an unending, onerous burden upon a bishop's life, a difficult charge for any leader of youth.

Jacob, in expressing his errand from the Lord to magnify his office for the people, along with his brother Joseph, said that they would be accountable for the "sins of the people" if they "did not teach them the word of God with all diligence" (Jacob 1:19). Teaching the word of God meant teaching the principles of the gospel and allowing the people to make the decisions to live the gospel in the manner they wished. The scripture in Doctrine and Covenants 68:25, in which parents are said to be accountable if they "teach" their children "not to understand the doctrine of repentance, faith in Christ . . . , and of baptism and the gift of the Holy Ghost," is simply another indication of our responsibility to teach the principles so that others can make decisions. A teacher—or a parent, for that matter—has a responsibility to teach clearly, not to force the behavior of his students.

To teach the principles of the gospel is tantamount to honoring agency, an eternal principle which has existed with God from all eternity. Agency allows man to participate in the great plan of happiness. Stressing a particular and different behavior for each lesson may put pressure on a person to conform, whereas teaching principles allows that person, by his agency, to choose his path of religious behavior; and choosing one's own path is not only right, it enhances and contributes to the inherent power within that person to gain eternal life. We should probably conclude, as did Elder Bruce R. McConkie, that "we should teach the gospel. We should teach the gospel only. We should teach nothing but the gospel. Ethics are a part of the gospel, but they will take care of themselves if we preach the gospel. Teach doctrine. Teach sound doctrine. Teach the doctrines of the kingdom." (*Foolishness of Teaching*, p. 5.)

Imagine a small visualization created by Elder Gene R. Cook in his book *Raising Up a Family to the Lord* (pp. 19–21), in which a daughter might raise a question about the Sabbath, about why her family doesn't do certain things on Sunday.

> You might be tempted to say, "Because I said so," or "Because the Church says so." But a more inspired parent might say, "Well, you

know that keeping the Lord's day holy is not something we just made up. Let me show you something." Then you could open the Doctrine and Covenants to section 59 and read these beautiful verses [9–11 are cited].

Then you could explain, "As you can see, the Lord teaches us that Sunday is a holy day. It's not a day for us to do what we want. It's a day to rest from our labors and 'to pay our devotions to the Most High,' meaning that we should go to our Church meetings, partake of the sacrament, do our other Church duties, and visit the sick, the poor, and the needy. It's a day consecrated to the Lord, and I bear testimony to you, my dear daughter, that this is true and that the Lord has blessed us greatly for keeping the Sabbath Day. Here are some of the blessings he promises [verses 15–20 are cited]."

After the parent uses the scriptures to reveal the principles of the gospel and bears testimony to the daughter, Elder Cook said that she perhaps may say, "I never quite understood it that way. I do believe that's true. Thank you. I can see why I should keep the Sabbath Day holy." The principles, properly taught out of the scriptures and witnessed by testimony, allow a person to choose his religion, his practices and behaviors. Again, the very process of using principles to teach—that is, to feed the hungering and craving student the "right food"—is the very manner in which a person grows spiritually.

A Caution

Although I believe in teaching the principles and allowing the Holy Ghost to testify and unfold that principle in the hearts of the students, I find at times that if a class becomes a little resistant, the natural inclination is to bear down on them, urging and pressing the principle to a point of acceptance. I remember a revealing moment after an institute class when a bright and perceptive woman engaged me in this particular conversation. Said she, "Do you believe in what you teach?" Although this seemed like a genuine question, I sensed that it had an opening wide enough to consume my every hypocrisy. I carefully asked her what she meant, and she reminded me of what I had taught them, that we have a responsibility to teach the principles, not to bear down on some specific practice. She said in essence, "The principles you were teaching today can stand on their own merit. They are that good, that exciting. You didn't need to pressure us as a class to accept the principles." Her point was well made. Although it is difficult at times to remember this precept, yet when I do remember and teach the principles out of the scriptures and in a manner in which the Holy Ghost can verify their truthfulness—not with "control or dominion or compulsion," as is mentioned in Doctrine and Covenants 121:37—then the teaching is sweet and profound.

Our Right to Teach the Principles

In another talk given to Church educators in 1981 called *The Foolishness of Teaching,* Elder Bruce R. McConkie said that "we are commanded to teach the principles of the gospel." Then, after quoting our focal verses from Doctrine and Covenants 42:12–13, he said:

> We are to teach the principles of the gospel. We are to teach the doctrines of salvation. We have some passing interest in ethical principles but not a great deal as far as emphasis in teaching is concerned. If we teach the doctrines of salvation, the ethical concepts automatically follow. We do not need to spend long periods of time or make elaborate presentations in teaching honesty or integrity or unselfishness or some other ethical principle. Any Presbyterian can do that. Any Methodist can do that. But if we teach the doctrines of salvation, which are basic and fundamental, the ethical concepts automatically follow. It is the testimony and knowledge of the truth that causes people to reach high ethical standards in any event. (*The Foolishness of Teaching,* p. 4.)

Again, a host of people, from Scoutmasters to police officers, could teach ethics; but it is the teachers of the kingdom, those blessed with the Restoration's prophets, doctrines, and scriptures, who are to emphasize the grand principles of the gospel. And interestingly enough, once the principles are taught in the Lord's way, then the behavior will naturally follow, not coerced or controlled. The teaching of the doctrines allows people to reach for the eternities.

In a spirit of verification, following are statements from both

Elder Boyd K. Packer and Elder Hartman Rector Jr. that give added clarity to the notion of teaching principles. In a conference address, Elder Packer said: "True doctrine, understood, changes attitudes and behavior. The study of the doctrines of the gospel will improve behavior quicker than a study of behavior will improve behavior." (In Conference Report, October 1986, p. 20.)

Elder Rector's example, also from a conference address, is a story that illustrates the application of the principle:

> I have a very good friend who served as a Congregational minister for over 26 years. He had one of the largest churches on Long Island, New York, at one time. He became acquainted with the Mormons by visiting Salt Lake City and receiving visits from Latter-day Saint missionaries in his home. He developed a great admiration for the programs of the Church, primarily *because of* the fruits he saw that were produced by the Church. So he thought to borrow these programs and adopt them into his own church, which he tried to do. But he found that they did not work. His statement to me was:
>
> "It was somewhat of a jolt to discover that the genius of Mormonism was in its theology, not its methodology, and that the amazing vitality of the Church sprang from the commitment of its members to the Restored Gospel of Jesus Christ received by revelation. It became obvious that *one could not have the fruits of Mormonism without its roots.*" (In Conference Report, April 1975, pp. 81–82.)

I testify that the Lord has commissioned us to teach the principles of the gospel. The students we teach, who are of the lineage of God, have a hunger for the principles of the gospel because having an understanding of the principles allows them to exercise their agency better. These students thrive in a teaching environment in which the principles of the gospel are taught out of the scriptures and by the Spirit. I testify that Joseph Smith's declaration that "I teach the people correct principles and they govern themselves" (quoted by John Taylor, in *Journal of Discourses* 10:57–58) is a true teaching principle, and that there is greater progress toward salvation in teaching principles than in teaching ethics.

Teaching Principles Out of the Scriptures

In a wonderful illustration of the marriage of principles and the scriptures, Elder McConkie gave a marvelous parable:

> Hear now the parable of the unwise builder:
>
> A certain man inherited a choice piece of ground whereon to build a house to shelter his loved ones from the storms of the day and the cold of the night.
>
> He began his work with zeal and skill, using good materials, for the need was urgent.
>
> But in his haste, and because he gave no heed to the principles of proper construction, he laid no foundation, but commencing immediately, he built the floor, and raised the walls, and began to cover them with a roof.
>
> Then, to his sorrow, because his house had no foundation, it fell and became a heap of rubble, and those whom he loved had no shelter.
>
> Verily, verily, I say unto you: A wise builder, when he buildeth a house, first layeth the foundation and then buildeth thereon.
>
> Hear now the interpretation of the parable of the unwise builder:
>
> A certain Church officer was called to build a house of faith and righteousness and salvation for the souls entrusted to his care. Knowing he had been called by inspiration and having great zeal, he hastened to strengthen and build up the programs of the Church without first laying the foundation of faith and testimony and conversion.
>
> He spent his time on mechanics and means and programs and procedures and teaching leadership and never laid the great and eternal foundation upon which all things must rest in the Lord's house—the foundation of our theology and our doctrine.
>
> I am told that a high Catholic prelate said to one who held the holy apostleship: "There are two things which you Mormons have which we as Catholics would like to adopt."
>
> "What are they?" he was asked.
>
> "They are tithing and your missionary system," he replied.
>
> "Well, why don't you adopt them?" came the rejoinder.
>
> "We would except for two reasons: our people won't pay tithing, and our people won't go on missions."
>
> How often have well-meaning and sincere people in the world attempted to adopt our youth programs, our family home evening program, our missionary system, and so on, and yet have not been able to operate them in their situations!

Why? Because they do not lay a proper foundation; however inspired the programs may be, they do not stand alone. They must be built on the foundation of faith and doctrine.

The foundation upon which we build our whole Church system is one of testimony and faith and conversion. It is our theology; it is the doctrine God has given us in this day; it is the restored and revealed principles of eternal truth—these are the things that give us the ability to operate our programs and build houses of salvation.

I suggest:

1. Learn the doctrines of the gospel; ponder their wondrous import and meaning; and pray continually for wisdom and understanding. Hunger and thirst after righteousness.

2. Search the scriptures; learn the doctrines of salvation; treasure up the Lord's word. Read the scriptures daily.

3. Preach from the scriptures. Always, always, always without fail, quote or paraphrase some appropriate passage of scripture when presenting any program or procedure.

4. Get others to go and do likewise.

Remember, no man buildeth a house which will stand as a safe covert from the storms in the world unless he first lays the proper foundation. (*Doctrines of the Restoration*, pp. 226–28.)

We believe in students who crave the gospel, in principles which provide the right food, in scriptures which house those very principles of nourishment, and in teachers who have accepted the Lord's law of teaching and who have sufficient faith to act according to this flourishing philosophy within them. The Lord will, as he told Joseph Smith, sustain us, support us, and extend his arm in our behalf. He will indeed be with us if we remember that "the works, and the designs, and the purposes of God cannot be frustrated, neither can they come to naught" (D&C 3:1). I so testify.

6

Teaching Out of the Scriptures

The charge given to us by the Lord in Doctrine and Covenants 42 is to teach the principles of the gospel, the right food for the hungering student. However, the principles are to be taught in a certain manner. These principles of the gospel, in order to be nourishing in the way the Lord intends for them to be, need to be taught out of the scriptures.

Again, in a spirit of verification, I include here statements by President J. Reuben Clark Jr. and Elder McConkie from talks already introduced to establish our philosophy: "You are to teach this Gospel using as your sources and authorities the Standard Works of the Church" (Clark, *Charted Course,* pp. 10–11); "We are to teach the principles of the gospel as they are found in the standard works. . . . The scriptures themselves present the gospel in the way that the Lord wants it presented to us in our day." (McConkie, *Foolishness of Teaching,* p. 6.) Expounding on the preceding quote, Elder McConkie further added:

> But for *our* day and *our* time and *our* hour, the time of *our* mortal probation, we are to teach in the way things are recorded in the standard works that we have. And if you want to know what emphasis should be given to gospel principles, you simply teach the whole standard works and, automatically, in the process, you will have given the Lord's emphasis to every doctrine and every principle. (*Foolishness of Teaching,* p. 6.)

The scriptures have come to us under the direction of heaven. The prophets have been sufficiently moved and inspired to give us the very doctrines and principles, the very stories and experiences that are necessary for our salvation.

In fact, in 1975 a *Report on Religious Education,* the culmination of a decade of study and research by Neil Flinders, was printed and disseminated among the personnel of the Church Educational System. In it is a chapter on the scriptures which has such a fundamentally important basis that I want to quote it at some length here:

> As Latter-day Saints we have in our possession the documents which contain the precepts essential to man's eternal welfare. These special records have been prepared and preserved by inspired men who were divinely assisted in their work. In a very real sense these men were curriculum specialists. They carefully and selectively designed the housing in which these precepts have been preserved for our day. Accounts of Old Testament incidents such as Adam and Eve, Noah and the Ark, David and Goliath, and Daniel in the Lion's Den do not seem to be the consequences of chance, accident, caprice, or whimsy. They appear to be intentionally preserved accounts which safeguard and transport vital precepts from one generation to another. The experiences of the Apostles with Jesus, fashioned into stories and illustrated testimonies, were purposefully preserved by Matthew, Mark, and others. Likewise, Mormon's summation of four hundred years of history for the purpose of assisting the people in this dispensation was the product of design and careful consideration. (P. 26.)

The Prophet Joseph Smith, in Brother Flinders's words, had "spent much if not most of his time preparing and putting in order the basic curriculum for the development of the kingdom in these last days" (*Report,* p. 26). The use of the Bible (especially with the Joseph Smith Translation helps), the Book of Mormon, the Doctrine and Covenants, and the Pearl of Great Price constitutes a major responsibility we have as teachers in teaching the principles of the gospel. I testify that using the scriptures which have been granted to us in this day is the very way we are to teach the principles of salvation.

Scriptural Precepts

The scriptures are indeed the "housing in which [the] precepts have been preserved for our day." Each chapter, as it were, each setting, or each story line contains the precepts the Lord intended for us to have. As an illustration, if we were to take the first few verses of 1 Nephi 3, we would find that there are precepts couched in that story. As we teach this same scriptural story from generation to generation, the same precepts and values continue to be reinforced.

"And it came to pass that I, Nephi, returned from speaking with the Lord, to the tent of my father" (v. 1).

Precept: The Lord speaks with mankind. In fact, the language used here is much more personal than saying "praying to"; Nephi says "speaking with."

"And it came to pass that he spake unto me, saying: Behold I have dreamed a dream, in the which the Lord hath commanded me that thou and thy brethren shall return to Jerusalem" (v. 2).

Precept: The Lord is communicating by revelation with both Lehi and Nephi. The form of revelation in this verse is by way of dreams, a potentially legitimate form of inspiration.

"For behold, Laban hath the record of the Jews and also a genealogy of my forefathers, and they are engraven upon plates of brass" (v. 3).

Precept: There was a history among the people of keeping records, even or especially the family history portions.

"Wherefore, the Lord hath commanded me that thou and thy brothers should go unto the house of Laban, and seek the records, and bring them down hither into the wilderness" (v. 4).

Precept: From their position in the wilderness, many days' journey from Jerusalem, the Lord is commenting on the importance of the sacrifice that needs to be made in order for a family, a people, to have the word of the Lord in their possession.

"And now, behold thy brothers murmur, saying it is a hard thing which I have required of them; but behold I have not required it of them, but it is a commandment of the Lord" (v. 5).

Precept: If tithing, for instance, a principle commanded by the Lord, is hard to keep, it is not the bishop on whom we heap our anguish and discomfort, but it is the Lord from whom we must seek our help and from whom the blessings will come.

If this five-verse view of the story contains at least these five precepts, can we not imagine how many precepts have been carefully couched in the scriptural record, chapter after chapter? The teaching of the scriptural record, therefore, allows the precepts and principles to be transferred from one generation to another, producing the very work from which another generation will learn the same precepts. A parent teaching his children, or a teacher teaching his students, conveys by the use of the scriptures the very principles of salvation that the child and the student will pass on to the next generations as they teach the scriptures.

Our obligation is to teach the principles of the gospel as they are housed in the scriptures, records which have passed the "Lord's correlation process," as is wonderfully told by Brother Flinders, again from the same "Curriculum" chapter in the *Report on Religious Education:*

> It may be extravagant and perhaps presumptuous for religious educators today to ignore in part or in total the housing prepared by these specialists of earlier ages. Perhaps a gifted and inspired curriculum writer in our day could create an equally appropriate or perhaps better structure in which to convey some of these precepts to teachers and learners. But even if he could, one must ask if he should. It may be unnecessary to pluck these precepts out of their original housing and then hire or call a committee to create a new, "modern" story, incident, episode, etc., with which to convey honesty, chastity, courage, faith, and so forth. The creations in which these precepts are already stored may not be perfect, but they are paid for. To a large extent they have been reviewed and approved—they have already passed an important phase of the Lord's correlation process. Economy itself would suggest that continuous remodeling and totally rebuilding may not be necessary; it may be wasteful. There is the possibility that some benefits of the old structure would be overlooked and in some instances the new may be less appropriate than the old—especially for a multicultured membership.
>
> It may well be that the essential curriculum components are already prepared. Apparently, they exist in sufficient quantity, and in some important ways they are already tested; they are usable and simple. If this is the case, then the major task of the curriculum specialist today is to assist the teachers in understanding and arranging

these components in the most appropriate fashion for the particular audiences these teachers are assigned to serve—child, youth, and adult. (Pp. 27–28.)

Since the Lord has already suggested that we teach principles out of the scriptures, and since we are the agents and he is the master, not only would it seem advisable that we teach using the scriptures, but it would be helpful if we began to understand why the scriptures are so valuable in communicating the principles. One of the fine points made in the above quote is how the scriptures may be able to present the principles across cultural lines, not as coming from a "Salt Lake City-Caucasian-United States" context, but from a standard works record, directed by the Lord himself, to be disseminated among his people, born of a common premortal nature. I know that the scriptures are the precise housing we need to use in order to communicate the saving principles of the gospel to the Lord's church and people.

KNOWING THE SCRIPTURAL RECORD

One of the critical notions expressed by Neil Flinders is the need of the teacher to understand the context of the scriptures for himself, because, he said, "it seems important to teach the scriptures in ways that preserve the power and strength of the originator's intent" (*Report*, p. 28). If we believe that it is important to understand the original writer's intent, knowing that the power of the principles will be preserved by the true context, then a certain portion of our study ought to concentrate on understanding that scriptural text, perhaps more than we figured. Teachers often are so quick to identify a principle, so that they can liken it in some stimulating way, that not only is the teacher devoid of a deeper understanding of the passages himself, but the student is also left without the ability to understand the scriptural text.

There are skills that can be utilized by the teacher to see more clearly the context of the scriptures, skills that will be developed in later chapters. Our responsibility is to study intently the scriptures we will be using to present the principles. One of the marvelous fortunes of such a study is our conversion to those principles as we read of them and examine them in the context of those sacred stories. We become enlivened as the Spirit of the Lord, which is attendant with scripture study, begins to deepen our feelings, to enlarge our understanding, and to infuse us with more powerful testimony. Who would want to miss that experience by treating lightly the scriptural works? I simply attest that as we study the scriptures in their context, with some fervency, not only will we be converted ourselves, but we will teach those scriptures with an energy known only by those who have experienced the power of the word.

The Language of the Scriptures

Let us examine a primary reason why we would want to use the scriptures in presenting the principles of the gospel. When Alma concluded his powerful message to the people of Zarahemla, he emphasized in his record that he had presented the principles to them in an appropriate language. He said: "And now I, Alma, do command you in the language of him who hath commanded me, that ye observe to do the words which I have spoken unto you" (Alma 5:61).

Our charge is a similar teaching charge, to teach in the language of the scriptures, or the "language of him who hath commanded" us. The Lord has given us the principles of his gospel, expressed in scriptural language which carries a unique context, a context that puts a different set of expectations upon us.

Years ago, when Ezra Taft Benson gave the talk entitled, *The Gospel Teacher and His Message,* he addressed some concerns about the language we use to teach the gospel:

> I believe most, if not all, teachers will be in agreement with this counsel. A problem occurs on occasion when, in the pursuit of higher degrees, one becomes so imbued with the terminology and methodology of a secular discipline that, almost without realizing it, he compromises the gospel message. The simple principles of the gospel, not the disciplines of men, should always be our basis for truth.
>
> When a teacher feels he must blend worldly sophistication and erudition to the simple principles of the gospel or to our Church history so that his message will have more appeal and respectability to the academically learned, he has compromised his message. We

seldom impress people by this means and almost never convert them to the gospel. This also applies to our students. We encourage you to get your higher degrees and to further your education; but let us not forget that disaffection from the gospel and the Lord's church was brought about in the past by the attempts to reconcile the pure gospel with the secular philosophies of men. *Nominal Christianity outside the restored church stands as an evidence that the blend between worldly philosophy and revealed truth leads to impotence.* Likewise, you teachers will have no power if you attempt to do the same in your educational pursuits and classroom teaching.

Sometimes gospel principles are written with such erudition that the gospel is hardly recognizable in them. Worldly phraseology and authorities replace the scriptures and the prophets. You institute teachers need to be aware of this in teaching courses such as Courtship and Marriage, and in giving counsel on child rearing. Be careful of blending your worldly training with the gospel courses you teach lest you be guilty of diluting the pure gospel of Jesus Christ and end up teaching the philosophy of men mingled with a few scriptures. (P. 9.)

President Benson has, by this counsel, warned a person like me who has an educational background in psychology to not come into a gospel setting and teach about repentance using a concept from my field—for instance, like *catharsis*. This concept, born in a worldly setting, expresses the need for a person to purge himself of certain feelings, to vent them, to alleviate difficult emotions so that better mental health can be achieved. Although catharsis and confession are somewhat similar, the teaching of confession in a repentance context has a totally different set of expectations. In fact, one of the ways that helps the gospel message to be taught clearly is to use the scriptures, the language of which not only is approved of the Lord but, again, carries his expectation level.

Sometimes we draw into our gospel teaching certain words and phrases which, from the world's standpoint, are acceptable for them but not entirely for us. Words or phrases like *positive mental attitude* and *self-esteem* can reflect the world's expectation and could be discussed in scores of church groups without ever a mention or reference to God being made, without faith being fostered or expected. The Lord has his own principles, taught to us in his own language, a language that gives special perspective, a language that awakens us to faith and trust in him, not in the arm of flesh.

Our Context

The words we use to present the gospel message ought to be in the context of the gospel. It is difficult to come into the Church's teaching arena using the words of the world. It is equally difficult to present gospel precepts in a worldly context, in the language of that educational field. The gospel must be presented within its own context. Elder Boyd K. Packer beautifully illustrated this point in telling a personal experience that happened in an educational setting. He described what happened when he tried to take a gospel truth and put it into philosophical language.

> Let me share with you a fundamental lesson I learned a few years ago. Near the end of the course work for my doctorate, I was enrolled in an educational philosophy class with three other students. Two of us were completing our doctorates; the other two were just beginning their graduate work. An issue arose between me and the other doctoral candidate. It had to do with whether or not man is left totally to himself. Is he sufficient to himself, or are there external sources of intelligence to which he can appeal?
>
> The professor of the class . . . deftly moderated—perhaps a better word would be *refereed*—the contest without taking either side.
>
> As the debate became more intense, the other two students took sides, one on each. So there we were, two contestants, each with a "second." The issue grew more important, and each day I left the class feeling more a failure. Why should this concern me? It concerned me because I was right and he was wrong, and I knew it and I thought he knew it; yet he was able to best me in every discussion.
>
> Each day I felt more inadequate, more foolish, and more tempted to capitulate. I spent much time in the library, searched out references, and studied at least as hard as my opponent. Nevertheless, each encounter saw me that much more defeated.
>
> Then one day one of the most important experiences of my entire education occurred. As we were leaving class, his "second" commented, "You're losing, aren't you?"
>
> There was no pride left to prevent me from consenting to the obvious. "Yes, I'm losing."
>
> "Do you want to know what's the matter with you?" he asked.
>
> Interested, I answered, "Yes, I would very much like to know."
>
> "The trouble with you," he said, "is that you're fighting out of context." I asked him what he meant. I didn't know, and he didn't explain it. He just said, "You are fighting out of context."

That night I thought continuously about his comment. It wasn't the grade or the credit I would win in the class—it was much bigger than that. I was being beaten and humiliated in my efforts to defend a principle that was true. His statement stayed in my mind, and finally, in my humiliation, I went before the Lord in prayer. Then I knew!

The next day when we returned to class, I stayed in context. When the debate was renewed, instead of mumbling some stilted, sophisticated, educational jargon calculated to show I was conversant with philosophical terminology, I used the words the Lord used on the subject. Instead of saying, "The *a priori* acquisition of intelligence as though from some external source of enlightenment," I said plainly, "Revelation from God!" I talked about the spiritual in the terms that described the spiritual. Suddenly the tables were turned. I was rescued from defeat, and I learned a lesson I shall not soon forget." (*Teach Ye Diligently,* pp. 281–83.)

We sometimes find ourselves in settings where we believe in a principle, like revelation from God, but feel that we cannot say it within that religious context. When we gymnastically translate our message by rewording it into another context, it has lost its power. Teachers like Presidents Harold B. Lee and Ezra Taft Benson were particularly proficient at teaching or fielding questions using the scriptures. It was as if they wanted not to use their own words only but the scriptural words to which we already had access. In a verifying manner, President Benson, on the occasion of his previously quoted talk, said, "All of what I have to say to you tonight could be said in my own words, but I desire to do more than just speak on my own authority. I want you to understand what the Lord has said about your mission, and I wish to sustain the counsel of those, my Brethren, who have spoken to you before; therefore, I will quote liberally from scripture and from some of the Brethren's previous messages to you." (*The Gospel Teacher and His Message,* p. 1.)

Power in the Word

There is power in the word of God, the word of the prophets, the recorded scriptural word to change us, to help us toward salvation, to affect our eternal lives. There is a story told by Elder Richard G. Scott that has served to establish the scriptures' power, whether the scriptures are used in a classroom or in a host of interviewing and teaching situations.

> There is a power that can change lives in the specific words recorded in the standard works. That power is weakened when we paraphrase or alter the actual wording. I therefore suggest that you encourage students to cite scripture content with precision. All you do to encourage students to memorize selected scriptures accurately will bring to bear in their lives the power of their content. This experience illustrates what I mean:
> Some years ago, I received an assignment to go to another part of the world to investigate allegations that a Church leader had fathered a child out of wedlock. I took with me a very spiritual mission president, knowing that the assignment would be difficult. The accused was a close friend. We interviewed him, those who made the accusations, and those who supported him. After two days, I could not honestly say I had an impression of innocence or guilt. Each time there appeared to be damaging evidence, other evidence appeared to confuse or to refute it. Late into the night I continued to wrestle with the matter in prayer and meditation. I searched the scriptures and was led to some verses I felt would be helpful.
> We met with him again the next morning. This time I was impressed to take a different approach. I began, "Whoever is responsible for the act has this scripture to face. Would you read it and then explain in your own words its meaning?" He read it perfectly, but as he began to explain, he hesitated and stumbled. I continued, "This verse speaks of those sent by the servants of the Lord. Would you read it and explain its meaning?" Other scriptures followed. By then, his whole attitude had changed, and he was perspiring and nervously shifting. There came a knock at the door, and he said, "I see you have another interview. I'll just wait outside," which he did.
> About forty-five minutes later, the phone rang. It was the man. He said, "Can I see you privately?" He entered the room, sat down, and pulled from his pocket a piece of paper and pushed it across the table. It was a signed confession. How grateful I am for the scriptures that penetrated his heart and initiated the full operation of repentance, which in time has brought a full restoration of blessings.
> Teach of the power in the written word of God. ("Four Fundamentals for Those Who Teach and Inspire Youth," p. 5.)

On one occasion I remember attending a Gospel Doctrine class in a state in which I was traveling. I sat near the back of the classroom watching the members file in. Clearly half of them attended without their scriptures. Although alarmed somewhat at the scarcity, I did notice that the teacher had his lesson notes and his scriptures on the table. After forty minutes of class time, I began to understand the reason that so many perhaps had left their scriptures at home. It was a New Testament year of study, and the class was following the course outline, flowing from one scheduled weekly lesson to the other; however, never once during the forty minutes were the scriptures opened by anyone. The teacher would talk of the stories and the class would respond to the scriptural stories by paraphrasing the accounts. Never was a passage read. Never were the scriptural words taken into anyone's mouth. The teaching of the principles was informal, casual, and apparently comfortable to everyone's liking.

To one who had been schooled in the dynamics of the power of the word, to one who had been converted by the scriptural words himself, and to one who had taught them in order to establish the principles of salvation in the hearts of students—this was a moment of emptiness. To have the word of God and not use it was to have a pearl of great price and bury it.

I have taught countless hours of classes, have counseled in a multitude of settings both in ecclesiastical and Church educational matters, and have depended on the scriptures in order to answer the questions of life, to establish the principles of living. The opportunity to turn to a scripture to answer a difficult question in a class, or to open a passage to bring hope to one who has been seeking repentance and mercy, is to have a treasure lying within your hands; it is to have words approved by the Lord which bring clarity and feeling to the recipient.

I testify that the commission to teach from the scriptures is wisdom itself. There is a power in the scriptural word. There is a spirit attendant with those who read the scriptures and those who teach from the scriptures. One must discover this for himself, but the discovery again is "life," the life of teaching and the life of salvation.

7

Teaching by the Spirit

Understanding the precept of teaching by the Spirit is of no small consequence in our teaching the principles of the gospel. Knowing the dimensions and scope of the role of the Holy Ghost is crucial in our laboring with students and helping them choose the great plan of happiness. Having knowledge of the Spirit's functioning in the lives of the students and in the lives of the teachers is of paramount importance.

There are countless ways in which the Spirit of the Lord assists us in the teaching of the gospel. One classic example is demonstrated in the experience of Amasa Potter that took place in the earlier part of this dispensation:

> I was introduced to the congregation as Elder Potter, with the remark that I would continue the subject of the gospel. I arose with fear and trembling; for it was the first time in my life that I had stood in a pulpit. Before me was a large Bible and prayer book. I must say that my mind was confused; but I took a text from the Bible that lay open before me. It was from the Prophet Amos:
>
> "Surely the Lord God will do nothing, but He revealeth His secret unto His servants the prophets."
>
> After reading it I spoke a few more words and became dumb that I could not speak. I stood there without speaking about two minutes, when the words of President Heber C. Kimball came to me: He said that the time would come when I should be at a loss to

know what to say to the people, "and, at that time," he said, "if you will commence to declare the divine mission of Joseph Smith in this our day, and the divine authenticity of the Book of Mormon, the Lord will loosen your tongue and you shall say the very things that are needful to be said to the people." When this came to my mind I commenced declaring these things to the congregation. I had spoken but a few minutes, when I thought I saw several lines of large letters printed on the walls of the house, and I commenced to read them and spoke about one hour. When the letters faded from my sight I then stopped speaking. I could not tell all that I had said; but my companion told me it was an excellent discourse. ("The Lord's Blessings," p. 79.)

There have been times in my life when I have had cause to search the walls of the classroom for this very kind of help. Although the Lord has not been so obvious with me, yet my own "writing on the walls" by the Spirit of the Lord has been just as effective, though in a hundred different ways. It is our opportunity in this chapter to review the principles of receiving this help, and also to give examples showing how merciful the Lord is in granting gifts and blessings in order that salvation be fostered.

Let me use one more illustration showing the wide range of considerations we need to ponder. President Heber J. Grant, at the time when he was first called as a stake president, told of his difficulties in speaking within a seeming expectation that the amount of speaking time correlated with the quality of the Spirit's influence. Though the story is tenderly real, it reveals the concerns we all have as teachers in receiving the Spirit's help, and the obligations on our teaching hearts that qualify us for heaven to grant such gifts.

> Years rolled on, and before I was twenty-four I was made the president of the Tooele Stake of Zion. I announced in a speech that lasted seven and a half minutes that I would ask no man in Tooele to be a more honest tithe payer than I would be; that I would ask no man to give more of his means in proportion to what he had than I would give; I would ask no man to live the Word of Wisdom better than I would live it, and I would give the best that was in me for the benefit of the people in that stake of Zion.
>
> That night I heard in the dark a man say in a contemptuous way: "It is a pity if the General Authorities have to send a man out

here to preside, . . . that they could not have sent one with sense enough to talk at least ten minutes; and that they had to send a boy to preside over us."

When I heard this, I remember thinking: "The boy is the only one who has any right to complain." . . . However, I was not able during the next three or four Sundays to talk as long as I did the first one. I ran out of ideas in five, six, and six and a half minutes.

At the lunch table after my first short speech which lasted seven and a half minutes, President Smith said: "Heber, you said you believe the gospel with all your heart, and propose to live it, but you did not bear your testimony that you know it is true. Don't you know absolutely that this gospel is true?"

I answered: "I do not."

"What, you! a president of a stake?" said President Joseph F. Smith.

"That is what I said."

"President Taylor, I am in favor of undoing this afternoon what we did this morning. I do not think any man should preside over a stake who has not a perfect and abiding knowledge of the divinity of this work."

I said: "I am not going to complain."

Brother Taylor had a habit, when something pleased him excessively, of shaking his body and laughing. He said, "Joseph, Joseph, Joseph, he knows it just as well as you do. The only thing that he does not know is that he does know it. It will be but a short time until he does know it. He leans over backwards. You do not need to worry."

I went to the little town of Vernon in Tooele County, took two others with me to do the preaching, and I got up to say a few words and spoke for forty-five minutes with perfect ease under the inspiration of the Lord. That night I shed tears of gratitude to the Lord for the abiding, perfect, and absolute testimony that came into my life of the divinity of this work.

The next Sunday after speaking at Vernon, I was at Grantsville. I told the Lord I would like to talk forty-five minutes. I got up to speak and ran out of ideas in five minutes, and I was sweating.

After the meeting I walked out past the farthest house in the west part of Grantsville, I am sure nearly three miles, and I got down behind a haystack and I shed some more tears. But they were tears of humiliation. I made a pledge to God there upon that occasion that never again in my life would I stand up before an audience with the feeling that all I needed to do was just stand up and talk; but that I would get up upon all occasions with a desire to say something that might be of benefit to the people to whom I spoke, and not with the spirit of pride, such as I had that day when I stood up in Grantsville. And I have never failed from that day until now—fifty-odd years ago—to have any desire in my heart when speaking except that I might say or read something that would be of lasting benefit to those who listened to my voice. (*Gospel Standards,* pp. 191–93.)

To have the Spirit of the Lord accompany our teaching is a supreme joy. It is something for which we plead, and for which we also patiently wait, inasmuch as it is the Lord's prerogative to grant the blessings in his own way and according to his own timetable. Gaining an understanding of the rights and responsibilities of Spirit-directed teaching requires a host of personal teaching experiences in which we experiment upon the promises of the Spirit, sometimes learning as much through the failures, as did Heber J. Grant, as we do through the successes. Although our study of this principle may seem complex, with so many elements which need to be considered for the Holy Ghost to help, yet the doctrine is essentially simple, pure, and powerful.

THE DUTY AND OFFICE OF THE HOLY GHOST

In considering the words of Joseph Smith regarding the preeminent role of the Holy Ghost, we are given an overall function of the Spirit when he said, "Everlasting covenant was made between three personages before the organization of this earth, and relates to their dispensation of things to men on the earth; these personages, according to Abraham's record, are called God the first, the Creator; God the second, the Redeemer; and God the third, the witness or Testator" (*Teachings,* p. 190). This second counselor, as it were, in the eternal presidency of the heavens has the delegated responsibility of testifying, essentially of the Father and the Son. The Holy Ghost was obviously promised in all ages of the world in order that truth be established (see D&C 20:26–27), in order that the "record" of the Father and the Son be made, deep in our souls. The Spirit of the Lord is a Testator and a Revealer, critically and functionally.

The scriptures are replete with instructions and promises concerning the Holy Ghost. It will be the object of this chapter section to explore a host of scriptural notations which emphasize the role of the Spirit. At its conclusion will be a simple graphic showing the enormity of the blessings awaiting teachers and students who embark into the teaching arena with the Holy Ghost.

A Scriptural Visualization

Consider the following scriptures—though there are a host of others which complement these few—that teach us some of the dimensions of the Spirit of the Lord. Each of the passages will have certain elements and words emphasized in italics:

1 Nephi 10:22—"And the Holy Ghost giveth *authority* that I should speak these things."

D&C 6:14–15—"As often as thou hast inquired thou hast received *instruction* of my Spirit. . . . Thou hast been *enlightened* by the Spirit of truth."

John 14:26—"But the Comforter, which is the Holy Ghost, whom the Father will send in my name, he shall *teach* you all things, and bring all things to your *remembrance*."

D&C 50:21–22—"Therefore, why is it that ye cannot understand and know, that he that receiveth the word by the Spirit of truth receiveth it as it is preached by the Spirit of truth? Wherefore, he that preacheth and he that receiveth, understand one another, and both are *edified* and rejoice together."

2 Nephi 26:11—"For the Spirit of the Lord will not always *strive* with man."

Alma 11:3—"For thou hast not lied unto men only but thou hast lied unto God; for behold, he knows all thy thoughts, and thou seest that thy *thoughts* are made known unto us by his Spirit."

Galatians 5:22–23—"But the *fruit* of the Spirit is love, joy, peace, longsuffering, gentleness, goodness, faith, meekness, temperance: against such there is no law."

D&C 46:11, 26—"For all have not every gift given unto them; for there are many *gifts,* and to every man is given a gift by the Spirit of God. . . . And all these gifts come from God, for the *benefit* of the children of God."

Teaching by the Spirit

2 Nephi 33:1—"For when a man speaketh by the power of the Holy Ghost the *power* of the Holy Ghost *carrieth* it unto the *hearts* of the children of men."

D&C 100:8—"And I give unto you this promise, that inasmuch as ye do this the Holy Ghost shall be shed forth in *bearing record* unto all things whatsoever ye shall say."

D&C 50:24—"That which is of God is light; and he that receiveth light, and continueth in God, *receiveth more light;* and that light groweth brighter and brighter until the perfect day."

D&C 84:85—"Treasure up in your minds continually the words of life, and it shall be *given you in the very hour* that portion that shall be meted unto every man."

In summary, then, let us visualize through the nature of this graphic what the role of the Holy Ghost is in helping the student and the teacher.

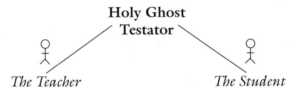

Holy Ghost Testator

The Teacher

Gives authority to speak
Gives instructions
Enlightens teacher
Teaches
Brings to remembrance
Edifies
Strives with teacher

Gives fruits
Gives gifts to teach
Bears record
Gives light
Gives in very hour what to speak

The Student

Gives instructions
Enlightens student
Teaches
Brings to remembrance
Edifies
Strives with student
Carries message to heart
Gives fruits
Gives gifts to learn
Bears record
Gives light

As the scriptures and the visualization distill on my soul and I see more clearly what the Holy Ghost is commissioned to do in the teaching arena, I am amazed at the help heaven grants us.

Who would not want the Spirit of the Lord aiding and assisting the teaching process? On the other hand, who would want to begin preparation or who would want to enter a classroom without the help of the Holy Ghost, without the assistance of a God whose purpose of eternal life is the same as that of the Father and the Son? No wonder the Lord, speaking in Doctrine and Covenants 42, said that "if ye receive not the Spirit ye shall not teach" (v. 14).

Receiving the Gifts of the Spirit

Section 46 of the Doctrine and Covenants paints a wonderful picture of the Spirit, of the gifts that are offered, and of the prescription, though brief, that qualifies us to receive those gifts:

> For verily I say unto you, they are given for the benefit of those who love me and keep all my commandments, *and him that seeketh so to do;* that all may be benefited that seek or that ask of me, that ask and not for a sign that they may consume it upon their lusts.
> And again, verily I say unto you, I would that ye should always remember, and always retain in your minds what those gifts are, that are given unto the church. (Verses 9–10, emphasis added.)

Besides sensing the absolute need of the help of the Lord in teaching, it now becomes a part of our responsibilities to qualify for the help by loving God, by keeping all the commandments—or at least "seeking so to do," another nearly quiet example of the Lord's mercy extended towards us. The rest of this chapter will concentrate on the nature of the things that either qualify us to have or disqualify us from having the Spirit's help in our teaching. The purpose of this part of the chapter is to make us aware of the delicate balance of spiritual things which beckon the Holy Ghost to help us and our students.

Grand Principles

1. *The ways of God are not the ways of man.*
The oft-quoted passage in Isaiah 55:8–9 helps us to sense an umbrella-like attitude as it relates to teaching:

> For my thoughts are not your thoughts, neither are your ways my ways, saith the Lord.
>
> For as the heavens are higher than the earth, so are my ways higher than your ways, and my thoughts than your thoughts.

Again, in the same kind of contrast between God's work and man's work, Joseph Smith was reminded by the Lord to "remember, remember that it is not the work of God that is frustrated, but the work of men" (D&C 3:3). The Lord has a way that is calculated to save his children, and the teaching we do must comply with his commission for us to have the Spirit direct our efforts. Elder Richard G. Scott reminded teachers in the Church Educational System of this necessity by describing two contrasting teaching experiences, one the work of the Lord and the other the work of man:

> This next example will further illustrate the vital importance of teaching by the Spirit. I am sure that the essence of the experience that I now relate has been felt time and again in your own life. I mention it so that you may remember that the most lasting impressions, the greatest teaching, and the most enduring effects for good will result from your ability to invite the Spirit of the Lord to touch the hearts and minds of those you teach.
>
> A few years ago, I had an experience I will not forget. It occurred during a priesthood meeting. A humble, unschooled priesthood leader in Mexico struggled to teach truths of the gospel contained in his lesson material. It was obvious how deeply they had touched his life. I noted the intense desire he had to communicate those principles. He recognized that they were of great worth to the brethren present. His manner evidenced a pure love of the Savior and love of those he taught.
>
> His love, sincerity, and purity of intent permitted a spiritual influence to envelop the room. I was so touched that, in addition to receiving again a witness of the truths that he presented, I began to receive some personal impressions as an extension of those principles taught by the humble instructor. These impressions were intended for me personally and were related to my assignments in the area....
>
> Subsequently, I visited a Sunday School class where a very well-educated individual presented his lesson. That experience was in striking contrast to the one enjoyed in the priesthood meeting. While technically correct, the lesson did not have the same spiritual

effect. The subject was Joseph Smith. The content of the lesson and the information the class would likely never otherwise hear. The instructor used his highly developed expertise, yet the message lacked spiritual power. ("Four Fundamentals for Those Who Teach and Inspire Youth," pp. 2–3.)

We do not need higher educational degrees in order to teach in the Church, nor do we need a powerful personality or exquisite charm, neither do we need money, looks, intelligence, or talents of profound artistic and creative proportions. Not only are the ways of God different than man's, but so also are the requirements he places on us to receive the Holy Ghost in our teaching, and they do not include any essentials produced or fashioned by man.

Nephi reminded us, for instance, that the Holy Ghost carried the message of the gospel "unto the hearts of the children of men" (2 Nephi 33:1), a kind of teaching which is ultimately effective and edifying. The fact that the message of the gospel delivered to a people by a man of God and by the Spirit is refused somehow is not necessarily an indication that the teacher is ineffective. The teacher who fails to have the Spirit of the Lord assist him in teaching may be doing things that offend the very nature of the role of the Holy Ghost.

Years ago, while involved in my graduate work, I did a dissertation using a "fault-tree" analysis. It is based on the notion that if we can appropriately find the reasons for failure, especially the prominent contributors to failure, and then remove them or shore them up somehow, we can enhance the probability of success. In relating a fault-tree logic to our commission that without the Spirit "ye shall not teach," it may be important to realize that inadequate preparation, improper motivation, inappropriate skills, or inadequate lifestyle may hinder the Spirit to assist; therefore, if we can eliminate those contributing areas of failure, we can enhance the success heaven desires for teacher and student.

The Holy Ghost will function in a manner different from the usual mechanics of teaching and learning to which we are accustomed as mankind. Whereas we may build into our lessons reason and logic, evidences and illustrations, so that the object of our teaching may be enticing to our students, the Holy Ghost permeates the field of learning in a different manner, bringing truths to our souls in an enlightening and feeling way that surpasses anything we can do as teachers. Comparing an approach which is basically intellectual with one that includes the spiritual dimensions engendered by the Spirit reveals staggering differences. Elder Bruce R. McConkie described such differences when he said:

> Suppose I came here tonight and delivered a great message on teaching, and I did it by the power of the intellect without any of the Spirit of God attending. Suppose that every word that I said was true, no error whatever, but it was an intellectual presentation. This revelation says: "If it be by some other way it is not of God" (D&C 50:18).
> That is, God did not present the message through me because I used the power of the intellect instead of the power of the Spirit. Intellectual things—reason and logic—can do some good, and they can prepare the way, and they can get the mind ready to receive the Spirit under certain circumstances. But conversion comes and the truth sinks into the hearts of people only when it is taught by the power of the Spirit. (*Foolishness of Teaching*, p. 9.)

Therefore, there is a fundamental difference between what man can do in the classroom and what the Spirit of the Lord can do. It is important for us to consider these differences in order that we may not fall into the trap of thinking that our abilities are what brings convincing to the souls of men. There are also certain topics which require more than we can give to them as mortal teachers, as Elder Boyd K. Packer explained:

> The gift to teach with the Spirit is a gift worth praying for. A teacher can be inept, inadequate, perhaps even clumsy, but if the Spirit is powerful, messages of eternal importance can be taught.
> We can become teachers, very good ones, but we cannot teach moral and spiritual values with only an academic approach. There must be spirit in it. (*Teach Ye Diligently*, p. 276.)

Again, the teacher in the classroom has an opportunity to prepare, to build into a lesson the necessary aspects to make it flow with evidences and illustrations, to make it interesting, as it were; but the Holy Ghost has the responsibility to assure and to certify the message we teach to the hearts of our students. Important in our thinking is the notion that we do not move into the realms of influence of the Holy Ghost—that is, to try and convince and prove the gospel to our students. Ours is a patient approach, to do what the Lord has commissioned us and then to trust that the Lord, according to his promises, will sustain the teaching process by the Spirit.

As teachers we have to sense the profound nature of the gift given to us while we are teaching in order that God's children have opportunity for eternal life. We "shall not teach," said the Lord, unless we have the Holy Ghost imbuing the process with his unique and powerful influences. Indeed, the works of God will not be frustrated if we follow the commission to teach the principles of the gospel out of the scriptures, observing and doing our covenants, praying the prayer of faith, and being directed by the Spirit.

2. A teacher must be worthy in order to have the Spirit of the Lord accompany him in his teaching.

In the revelation that contains our focal scripture which we have labeled the "law of teaching" (D&C 42), we also find a group of verses which we could call the "law of moral conduct" (see verses 18–29). It is not by coincidence, at least in my thinking, that the two segments are discussed side by side. It is as if the ability to teach in the manner prescribed by the Lord must be evaluated in terms of our being worthy of heaven's help. These verses on moral conduct indicate that as members of the Church, and especially as teachers, we should not kill, obviously, and also we should not steal, lie, lust, commit adultery, or speak evil of our neighbors.

We cannot teach while sinning knowingly, especially unrepentantly. We need to be keeping all the commandments of the Lord, as was mentioned in section 46, or be seeking so to do, in order to have the Spirit. To seek to keep the commandments—to be constantly "striving to be evermore spiritual," as quoted below from Elder Richard G. Scott—is to allow the Spirit to confirm our teachings in our students' hearts, and to also grant the teachers themselves a more powerful understanding of the gospel.

But the greatest impact of all is what they *feel* in your presence in the classroom and elsewhere. Your commitment to teach the precious children of our Father in Heaven is not alone the long hours you spend in preparation for each class, nor the many hours of fasting and prayer that you may become a more effective teacher. It is the commitment to a life every hour of which is purposefully lived in compliance with the teachings and example of the Savior and of his servants. It is a commitment to constant striving to be evermore spiritual, evermore devoted, evermore deserving to be the conduit through which the Spirit of the Lord may touch the hearts of those you are trusted to bring to a greater understanding of his teachings. ("Four Fundamentals for Those Who Teach and Inspire Youth," p. 1.)

One of the significant roles of the Holy Ghost is that of a Justifier, which allows us to have our feet planted on the covenantal path. Although we obviously are not perfect as teachers, although we may not be subject to being translated any moment, yet we need to be "justified"; we need to stand on the path, to have a forgiveness of our sins. The Holy Ghost will not dwell in an unclean tabernacle (see Helaman 4:24); therefore, if we are keeping the commandments, or seeking so to do, this becomes the very means by which the Holy Ghost can grant us this forgiveness and subsequently an array of teaching gifts.

Our ability to teach, as least as far as the world is concerned, may lack some essential characteristics or talents; however, the influence of the Spirit of the Lord on one who is deficient yet who is striving to keep the commandments will not exclude him from having an important influence on a student's life. Elder Neal A. Maxwell pointedly stated this notion with these engaging words:

Of course there are individuals who are keeping their covenants who lack teaching charisma. Of course there are those whose lives are in order who are not exciting teachers. However, the Spirit blesses the efforts of all who live worthily. It endorses what they say or do. There is a witnessing authenticity which proceeds from the commandment keeper which speaks for itself. Therefore, I prefer doctrinal accuracy and spiritual certitude (even with a little dullness) to charisma with unanchored cleverness. ("Teaching by the Spirit," p. 4.)

I remember a teaching occasion in which a student afterwards queried me, seeking answers to questions which at first seemed genuine but later revealed a uniquely distorted view of keeping the commandments. He spoke to me of his mission years, of having a driving desire to have a special revelatory experience exclaiming his surety for eternal life. He spoke of a captivating study which dominated his mission time in which he had outlined for himself an intricate set of doctrines and behaviors that would sponsor, in his mind, an angelic declaration concerning his worthiness, even while on his mission. He then rehearsed to me that specific visitation, the longed-for message, and a special charge given him by the angelic messenger to correct some doctrines being taught by the President of the Church.

Although I almost had to smile at the thought of a missionary believing an angel would come to him with a message to correct apostolic declarations, I could sense the profound difficulties which he was facing. I listened with greater intensity as to how he had been so open for the deception. True to Doctrine and Covenants 42:23—a portion of our law of moral conduct, our law juxtaposed with the law of teaching and preaching to which he had been called as a missionary—he had engaged in an intriguing system of lusting in order to someday prepare himself for plural marriage, a significant part of the doctrines and behaviors he had outlined and believed for himself. He had by his thoughts and actions verified the truth of the scripture which states that when one lusts, he "shall deny the faith, and shall not have the Spirit." Having the Spirit in his role as a teaching missionary, which Spirit had been withdrawn, was far more important for him in order to teach the gospel than he could ever have considered. The Spirit would not dwell in an unclean tabernacle, and his invitation to have the very Spirit he wanted was undeliverable through celestial mail.

I know the greatest factor toward having the Spirit is keeping our covenants, keeping our lives in order, being a commandment keeper, having spiritual certitude. We cannot underestimate the power granted to one who is keeping his covenants, who is desiring to be "evermore deserving to be the conduit through which the Spirit of the Lord may touch the hearts" of his students. I testify that living according to our covenants brings great joy, even great teaching joy. Perhaps one of the great preparation prices we pay for our students is to live according to our covenants so that the Spirit of the Lord can fully verify the doctrines, not only as to their truthfulness but also as to their joyfulness in the teachers' lives.

3. *The Spirit of the Lord is given by the prayer of faith.*

The Lord has commanded us to pray the prayer of faith in order to teach by the power of the Holy Ghost (see D&C 42:14). One of the best case studies in considering the prayer of faith is the experience of Oliver Cowdery (see D&C 8 and 9). Oliver had been instructed in section 8 that he would "receive a knowledge of whatsoever things" he should "ask in faith" (v. 1). He was to pray the prayer of faith, whatever that had meant to him. As the story unfolds in section 9 we find the Lord presenting a fuller understanding of what it means to pray in faith. He said:

> But, behold, I say unto you, that you must study it out in your mind; then you must ask me if it be right, and if it is right I will cause that your bosom shall burn within you; therefore, you shall feel that it is right.
>
> But if it be not right you shall have no such feelings, but you shall have a stupor of thought that shall cause you to forget the thing which is wrong. (Verses 8–9.)

As Elder Bruce R. McConkie used this story in an article called "Agency or Inspiration?" he said, "Now, seemingly, that's all he'd been instructed to do, to ask in faith; but implicit in asking in faith is the precedent requirement that we do everything in our power to accomplish the goal that we seek" (p. 40). Oliver was to learn that the prayer of faith required the use of his abilities to solve the problem; it required a labor on his part so that his prayer was not just a prayer but a prayer of faith.

A similar story is recorded about the brother of Jared (see Ether 2 and 3). After building eight barges, he importuned the Lord for help concerning the air and light problems he had with the vessels. The Lord, for whatever reasons, gave the brother of Jared the modifications necessary for him to correct the air difficulty and then left him to solve the other with these words, "What will ye that I should do that ye may have light in your vessels?" (Ether 2:23.)

From the scriptural footnote in Genesis 6:16 (16a) in the LDS edition of the Bible, we learn that Noah may have had "a precious stone that shone in the ark" rather than windows, and that the brother of Jared may have known this from the scriptural records. Perhaps using that as a plan of solving the light problem, the brother of Jared "did molten out of a rock sixteen small stones" which were like "transparent glass" (Ether 3:1). With a plan and much labor supporting his request, he asked the Lord to touch the stones and cause them to give light, and the finger of the Lord reached through the veil and answered a prayer of faith.

With God on one side of a continuum and man on the other, the struggle for a prayer of faith is represented by the following diagram. As Oliver Cowdery was reminded to "study it out," and as the brother of Jared planned and labored with the stones, the principle was to move toward the center of the continuum, doing their part, their precedent part, in order to be faithful.

```
                                          "study it out"
God ---------------------------◄--------------------------- Man
                                     plan and prepare stones
```

Now, from a posture on the continuum more like "a prayer of faith," one can ask the Lord to do things that he himself cannot do, that only God's powers can accommodate. And surely, as a reward of such faith, the Lord causes one's bosom to burn, or causes stones to give light. The prayer of faith is rewarded by the powers of heaven.

```
       "bosom shall burn"              "study it out"
God -------------------------►◄--------------------------- Man
       stones give light              plan and prepare stones
```

Now, inasmuch as we receive the Spirit of the Lord by the prayer of faith, how are the above continuum examples a key to understanding what is required of us in order to pray the prayer of faith in teaching? As we prepare our lessons—by studying them out, by planning and preparing—we move ourselves along the continuum sufficiently to properly pray in faith, to properly ask the Lord to "touch" our lessons somehow so that they may give "light" to our students. After all, our lessons will just be lessons (or stones, for that matter) without the Spirit of the Lord. We shall indeed learn that without the prayer of faith, without the "precedent requirement that we do everything in our power to accomplish the goal," we have no claim upon the Holy Ghost himself, nor the gifts which are given by him. We cannot be lazy teachers, as it were, as Elder Maxwell pointed out:

> Yet, when we speak about teaching by the Spirit, it is not about a mystical process. Teaching does not remove responsibility from the teacher for prayerful and pondering preparation. Teaching by the Spirit is not the equivalent of going on "automatic pilot." We still need a carefully worked out flight. Studying out something in our own minds involves the Spirit in our preparations as well as in our presentations. We must not err, like Oliver Cowdery, by taking no thought except to ask God for His Spirit (see D&C 9:7). ("Teaching by the Spirit," p. 2.)

Verifying Stories

One evening before a night class had begun, I sat chatting with a few of the early arriving students. A young married couple, whom I considered the very "salt of the earth," were talking about their teaching experiences in their ward. He was the elders quorum instructor and she was one of the Relief Society teachers. They mentioned their practice of coming home from church, having Sunday dinner, and then sitting on the couch and discussing each of their classes. He reported to this little pre-class group, I think with a slight smile of chagrin, that he had discovered that her lessons in Relief Society had invariably gone better than his lessons in elders quorum. Now, at this particular juncture of the story, it may be reasonable to assume that many of you who are readers have not discovered this really obvious fact, that in a general way Relief Society classes invariably go better than priesthood classes.

As the class continued that night, a class on teaching, she made a comment expressing the gospel brilliance had by her returned-missionary husband. Her supporting evidence of this wondrous accolade was this statement, "I get so frustrated with how easily my husband prepares lessons. He'll take twenty or thirty minutes on Saturday night reading the manual and the scriptures, and perhaps another twenty or thirty minutes on Sunday morning, and he's ready to teach. On the other hand," she said, "I have to spend hours and hours and hours in order to be prepared to teach my lessons." It was a point not to be overlooked, not to be underestimated. Here was a reason, in one innocent statement, why Relief Society meeting was invariably a better learning experience for its members than elders quorum meeting.

It reminded me of my earlier television-watching days, when the show "Name That Tune" treated us to a classic program-ending contest between two individuals who would bid each other down by saying, "I can name that tune in four notes." Then the other, to the respectful gasps of the studio audience, would say, "I can name that tune in two notes" or perhaps even "one note." Somehow we have assumed that this same game-show criterion is worthy of our acclamation, heaping our praises on one who says, "I can prepare that lesson in thirty minutes!" as if this were the summum bonum of being a teacher. This is not the object of our preparation. This is not the joy of our preparation. This supposed efficiency, this being able to spend little time in the scriptures and with the Spirit of the Lord, is not the reward we are seeking.

An important principle in understanding the process of teaching is the realization that we cannot force spiritual things; we cannot demand heaven to give help on our timetable. The Lord will grant his help, but "it shall be in his own time, and in his own way, and according to his own will" (D&C 88:68). Therefore, we should prepare early, at a time when we are not feeling the pressures of the teaching moment. Having done so, we can afford to be patient, to allow time for the inspiration of the Lord to be granted, time when we are not stressed or strained, time when we can feel the influence of the Holy Ghost without demands upon our minds and hearts.

I remember an illustration used by a temple president as he watched the morning crowd of businessmen who would come to do an endowment session before work, men whose posture was often attuned to their watches, insisting in their minds at least that the session proceed without any delays. The president suggested that he didn't feel that such individuals would receive much from the distillings of the Spirit because their minds were hampered by the pressing of their work schedules. We need time; we need opportunities in our lives to not have intrusions upon our minds so that we can then feel the Spirit of the Lord, unrestrained. Such pleasures often come as we are treasuring the word, thinking and reflecting, praying and walking, wondering and working.

Although the following story is fairly well known, it illustrates the principle of pressures excluding us from the promptings of spiritual things, from spiritual realms. This is the story of John Wells, former member of the Presiding Bishopric.

> A son of Bishop Wells was killed in Emigration Canyon on a railroad track. Brother John Wells was a great detail man. . . . His boy was run over by a freight train. Sister Wells was inconsolable. She mourned during the three days prior to the funeral, received no comfort at the funeral, and was in a rather serious state of mind.
>
> One day soon after the funeral services while she was lying on her bed relaxed, still mourning, she says that her son appeared to her and said, "Mother, do not mourn, do not cry. I am all right." He told her that she did not understand how the accident happened. . . . It was clearly an accident.
>
> Now, listen. He said that as soon as he realized that he was in another environment he tried to see his father, but *he couldn't reach him. His father was so busy with the duties in his office he could not respond to his call.* Therefore he had come to his mother. He said to her, "You tell father that all is well with me, and I want you not to mourn any more." (Harold B. Lee, quoted in Packer, *The Holy Temple*, p. 254.)

When President David O. McKay related this story to Elder Harold B. Lee and the Quorum of the Twelve, he said that "it is a great thing to be responsive to the whisperings of the Spirit, and we know that when these whisperings come it is a gift and our privilege to have them. They come when we are relaxed and not under pressure of appointments." (In Packer, *The Holy Temple*, pp. 253–54). Such is the case with our study preparations. The Spirit's influence cannot be as fully felt if we have pressures from our lives pummeling us, even the pressures of a lesson left repeatedly to the last moment of completion. It doesn't allow us to have the quietness of soul that beckons the whisperings that are also indeed quiet and sometimes subtle.

There is a joy that comes to those who persist with studying the scriptures, who continue seeking understanding from the prophets, and who bask in the powers of heaven that enlighten them with insights, revelation, and testimony. This process obviously takes time, but it is heavenly time. Our object is not to see how little time we can spend in preparing; rather it is to persist, continue, and bask in our opportunity to learn, be converted, and feel the profound nature of the Holy Ghost. Again, who would not want such a blessing? The opportunity for a teacher to prepare is the opportunity to confront the scriptures and the principles of the gospel on a regular basis, to study and be touched by their influence, to repent and be converted to a greater degree in their lives than before, and to have the Holy Ghost give its fruits and gifts in their lives. Now, someone would have to be either fairly unknowledgeable or rebellious to reject such a blessing, which blessing comes if we understand the Lord's way of teaching.

4. *We teach what has been taught us by the Comforter.*

Two of the powerful assets provided by the Lord for our teaching are the scriptures and the Holy Ghost. The reminder given in Doctrine and Covenants 52:9 states that we are to say "none other things than that which the prophets and apostles have written, and that which is taught them by the Comforter." The Spirit of the Lord, who gave the very inspiration and revelation for the prophets to write scriptures, is the very Spirit, or Comforter, who teaches the teachers. The testimony that comes to those who use the scriptures is the spirit of revelation, the spirit of testimony. Listen to Elder McConkie's sweet appraisal of true gospel teaching that utilizes the scriptures as the text and that is rewarded by the power of the Holy Ghost:

> Those who preach by the power of the Holy Ghost use the scriptures as their basic source of knowledge and doctrine. They begin with what the Lord has before revealed to other inspired men. But it is the practice of the Lord to give added knowledge to those upon whose hearts the true meanings and intents of the scriptures have been impressed. Many great doctrinal revelations come to those who preach from the scriptures. When they are in tune with the Infinite, the Lord lets them know, first, the full and complete meaning of the scriptures they are expounding, and then he ofttimes

expands their views so that new truths flood in upon them, and they learn added things that those who do not follow such a course can never know. (*The Promised Messiah*, pp. 515–16.)

These very feelings granted to teachers are the things that matter. The insights, the revelation, the testimony that come are now in our purview to use to establish the truth. We are under an obligation to testify that we know certain matters are true; for instance, we know the truth about God, his Son, the gospel, the Church, the scriptures, and particularly the principles we have personally lived and had confirmed to our souls. Again, Elder McConkie spoke plainly as he delivered this message:

There are two fields in which we are expected to bear testimony, if we perfect our testimony bearing. Of course we are to bear testimony of the truth and divinity of the work. We are to say that we know by the power of the Holy Spirit that the work is the Lord's, that the kingdom is his. We get a revelation and it tells us that Jesus is the Lord and Joseph Smith is a prophet, and we ought to say it. That is testimony bearing. But we are obligated also to bear testimony of the truth of the doctrine that we teach, not simply that the work is true, but that we have taught true doctrine, which of course we cannot do unless we have taught by the power of the Spirit. (*Foolishness of Teaching*, p. 10.)

CONCLUSION

We have discussed the role of the Holy Ghost and his responsibilities to flood the teaching process with the very powers of heaven. We have declared that the ways of God—that is, teaching by the Spirit—are not the ways of man. We have witnessed that the teacher's profound obligation is to live his covenants, to bring a measure of worthiness in order that the Holy Ghost will attend his teaching. We have focused on the preparation necessary in order that the prayer of faith can be answered. We have secured a necessary look at the right and necessity to bear a witness of that which has been borne to our souls. We have been commissioned to teach by the Spirit. Such teaching has a profound nature that will require us not only to know the powers which we are desiring but also to live commensurately as teachers in order to be worthy of the gifts.

The very notion that we are to teach by the Spirit of God opens wide the doors of eternity. This is not just a classroom situation, not just a mortal, temporal undertaking. The very fact that we have been promised the help of God the Third, the Testator, confirms that the teacher stands on an eternal threshold. We must see it, we must feel it as did President J. Reuben Clark:

> You teachers have a great mission. As teachers you stand upon the highest peak in education, for what teaching can compare in priceless value and in far-reaching effect with that which deals with man as he was in the eternity of yesterday, as he is in the mortality of today, and as he will be in the forever of tomorrow. Not only time but eternity is your field. Salvation of yourself not only, but of those who come within the purlieus of your temple, is the blessing you seek, and which, doing your duty, you will gain. How brilliant will be your crown of glory, with each soul saved an encrusted jewel thereon. (*Charted Course*, p. 10.)

We are blessed to be teachers, teaching by the Spirit. I testify that the word of the Lord is true when he said: "And again, the . . . teachers of this church shall teach the principles of my gospel, which are in the [scriptures]: . . . And they shall observe the covenants and church articles to do them, and these shall be their teachings, as they shall be directed by the Spirit. And the Spirit shall be given unto you by the prayer of faith; and *if ye receive not the Spirit ye shall not teach.*" (D&C 42:12–14; emphasis added.)

8

Teaching the Message of the Gospel

In 1987, in a talk entitled "The Book of Mormon and the Doctrine and Covenants," President Ezra Taft Benson reminded us that the Book of Mormon was referred to as the "keystone" of our religion and would bring men to Christ, while the Doctrine and Covenants was the "capstone" and would bring men to Christ's kingdom. He pointedly directed our attention to the value of those books in the teaching process:

> The words and the way they are used in the Book of Mormon by the Lord should become our source of understanding and should be used by us in teaching gospel principles. . . .
>
> I am deeply concerned about what we are doing to teach the Saints at all levels the gospel of Jesus Christ as completely and authoritatively as do the Book of Mormon and the Doctrine and Covenants. By this I mean teaching the "great plan of the Eternal God," to use the words of Amulek (Alma 34:9).
>
> Are we using the messages and the method of teaching found in the Book of Mormon and other scriptures of the Restoration to teach this great plan of the Eternal God? (P. 84.)

The phrases "the words and the way" and "the messages and the method" are an intriguing repetition, but more important, they help us to see how these scriptures of the Restoration illustrate not only *what* we are to teach but also *how* we are to teach.

At this stage of our philosophic development, this becomes a clarifying discourse.

While the object of the next chapter is to examine the way we are to teach, the importance of this chapter is to establish the message we are to teach. The Lord commissioned us to teach the principles of the gospel, and although there are a multitude of them, yet the Book of Mormon, as President Benson explained, will help us to see how certain of these doctrines and principles receive emphasis in our teaching.

GOD AT THE CENTER

The "great plan of the Eternal God," the phrase emphasized by President Benson, is only one of many used in the Book of Mormon that speak of God and his work to bring immortality and eternal life to his children. There are twenty-five such references to a "plan" mentioned in the Book of Mormon. Two examples serve to characterize the plan as "of God," such as the "the merciful plan of the great Creator" (2 Nephi 9:6) and the "the plan of our God" (2 Nephi 9:13).

God is at the center of any plan to save us, and is therefore at the center of any teaching of that gospel plan. As the Savior was instructing the Saints of the Book of Mormon lands, he gave them an extensive definition of the gospel, the first part of which centered on God and his plan to save us:

> Behold I have given unto you my gospel, and this is the gospel which I have given unto you—that I came into the world to do the will of my Father, because my Father sent me.
>
> And my Father sent me that I might be lifted up upon the cross; and after that I had been lifted up upon the cross, that I might draw all men unto me, that as I have been lifted up by men even so should men be lifted up by the Father, to stand before me, to be judged of their works, whether they be good or whether they be evil—
>
> And for this cause have I been lifted up; therefore, according to the power of the Father I will draw all men unto me, that they may be judged according to their works. (3 Nephi 27:13–15.)

God, whether it be God the Father or God the Son, becomes the center of the "words," or the "messages," of the gospel we preach. God is the author of salvation, is the very power and purpose of our becoming like him; therefore, he is at the core of our teaching the principles of the gospel. In developing a graphic for illustrating our teaching philosophy, a three-concentric-circled target would have at the center of our teaching energy the teaching of God.

Teaching Focus

CREATION, FALL, AND ATONEMENT

The next circle concentrating the teaching focus could possibly be those doctrines which Elder Bruce R. McConkie called "the three pillars of eternity,"—creation, fall, and atonement:

> Now, we are speaking of the three pillars of heaven, of the three greatest events ever to occur in all eternity, of the three doctrines that are woven inseparably together to form the plan of salvation. We are speaking of the creation, the fall, and the atonement. And these things are one. And, be it noted, all things were created; all things fell; and all things are subject to the redeeming power of the Son of God. ("The Three Pillars of Eternity," p. 31.)

In giving a reason why these doctrines are so closely tied, President Benson said:

> Just as a man does not really desire food until he is hungry, so he does not desire the salvation of Christ until he knows why he needs Christ.
> No one adequately and properly knows why he needs Christ until he understands and accepts the doctrine of the Fall and its effect upon all mankind. And no other book in the world explains this vital doctrine nearly as well as the Book of Mormon....

Are we accepting and teaching what the revelations tell us about the Creation, Adam and the fall of man, and redemption from that fall through the atonement of Christ? ("The Book of Mormon and the Doctrine and Covenants," p. 85.)

Teaching Focus

Faith, Repentance, Baptism, Holy Ghost, Endurance

In completing the definition of the gospel given in 3 Nephi 27, a third level or circle could be added to our graphic. Every person has a responsibility to God within the gospel plan. That responsibility is described best by the principles and the ordinances given in verses 16–21:

> And it shall come to pass, that whoso repenteth and is baptized in my name shall be filled; and if he endureth to the end, behold, him will I hold guiltless before my Father at that day when I shall stand to judge the world. . . .
>
> And no unclean thing can enter into his kingdom; therefore nothing entereth into his rest save it be those who have washed their garments in my blood, because of their faith, and the repentance of all their sins, and their faithfulness unto the end.
>
> Now this is the commandment: Repent, all ye ends of the earth, and come unto me and be baptized in my name, that ye may be sanctified by the reception of the Holy Ghost, that ye may stand spotless before me at the last day.
>
> Verily, verily, I say unto you, this is my gospel." (3 Nephi 27:16, 19–21.)

Teaching Focus

Summarizing our graphic: God is at the center of our teaching. Our next teaching emphasis concerns the great pillar doctrines of the Creation, the Fall, and the Atonement, followed closely by the principles and ordinances of salvation, those of faith, repentance, baptism, the Holy Ghost, and enduring to the end. As we prepare lessons, one pivotal question we ask centers around this target of teaching, "Will I be teaching so that these critical areas, leading to the eternal life of man, will be emphasized?" If we are not teaching so that these focal areas are considered and testified about repetitively, what is our purpose?

Consider for a moment the opportunity to speak in a sacrament meeting. A bishopric member has assigned you to teach the principle of tithing and given you a text in Malachi 3:8–10. Undergirding your preparation is the knowledge that tithing should be hung on the doctrinal hooks illustrated by the graphic. For instance, tithing ought to be taught to build faith in *God*, who is not only the *giver* of the commandment but also the *rewarder* of those who keep it. God, who is the *creator* of the earth and all things therein, has given us a commission, in this *fallen* world, to invest our money and our hearts in the kingdom of God. Tithing is simply a demonstration of our *covenantal* investment and, for that matter, is so organized to be an *enduring* demonstration throughout the years. It requires *faith*, and at times *repentance*, but as we live this principle the opener of heaven's windows showers upon us a multitude of gifts by the *Holy Ghost* which develop us in becoming like God himself.

Now, if the teaching of any of the principles of the gospel leaves our students without the context of the gospel, without a feeling for God, or the pillar doctrines, or the responsibilities that tie us to God, then what are we doing in the classroom, anyway?

We are involved in God's work and glory, to bring to pass the eternal life of man. Proper teaching—that is, teaching the "words" and the "messages" of the gospel—allows us to be involved in the greatest work of the eternities.

A Scriptural Verification

As an illustration of what we should be teaching, Mormon gave us the accounts of Ammon and Aaron teaching kings about the gospel. Let us consider Ammon's experience first (see Alma 18:24–35). He asked King Lamoni questions to determine the king's understanding of God. During the course of the discussion, Ammon not only declared that God existed but also taught two powerful characteristics of God—that he was the creator of heaven, earth, and man, and that he was all-knowing.

After developing that base, Ammon began

> at the creation of the world, and also the creation of Adam, and told him all the things concerning the fall of man, and rehearsed and laid before him the records and the holy scriptures of the people, which had been spoken by the prophets. . . .
>
> But this is not all; for he expounded unto them the plan of redemption, which was prepared from the foundation of the world; and he also made known unto them concerning the coming of Christ, and all the works of the Lord did he make known unto them. (Alma 18:36, 39.)

In Aaron's experience—almost as if the two missionaries had been to the same missionary training center, or were schooled in the same discussions—he began by asking King Lamoni's father whether he believed in a God. After he testified that the Great Spirit in whom the Lamanites believed was God, Aaron began

> from the creation of Adam, reading the scriptures unto the king—how God created man after his own image, and that God gave him commandments, and that because of transgression, man had fallen.
>
> And Aaron did expound unto him the scriptures from the creation of Adam, laying the fall of man before him, and their carnal state and also the plan of redemption, which was prepared from the foundation of the world, through Christ, for all whosoever would believe on his name. (Alma 22:12–13.)

Aaron continued to proclaim about the Atonement, about the principles of faith and repentance. As the king began to inquire how he could gain this eternal life, how this "wicked spirit" could be "rooted" out of his breast, he also professed his willingness to "give away" all of his sins to know God (Alma 22:15, 18).

After they heard the gospel's core message, proclaimed by witnesses themselves of its effects in their lives, the Lord granted to these two pivotal kingly potentates a powerful conversion experience like Alma's. The word had indeed contained power beyond anything man could have determined. The gospel message, "the words," had begun to change an entire people.

Alma, at a later time, spoke of this power when he said:

> O that I were an angel, and could have the wish of mine heart, that I might go forth and speak with the trump of God, with a voice to shake the earth, and cry repentance unto every people!
>
> Yea, I would declare unto every soul, as with the voice of thunder, repentance and the plan of redemption, that they should repent and come unto our God, that there might not be more sorrow upon all the face of the earth.
>
> But behold, I am a man, and do sin in my wish; for I ought to be content with the things which the Lord hath allotted unto me. (Alma 29:1–3.)

"The things" which the Lord had allotted to him, and also to the sons of Mosiah, to preach "the words" and "the message" of the gospel, were sufficient to change the hearts of men, to profoundly affect the lives of nations of people. They would "sin" somehow in their wish to be more angelically powerful as teachers. Their realization must be our realization. We have a "lot" given to us, to teach the principles of the gospel out of the scriptures and by the Spirit. The power promised from heaven is ours as well, if we teach the message of the gospel and in fact do it in "the way" and using "the method" which President Benson proclaimed. I verify from my own teaching experience that there is such power.

A Latter-day Verification

In April 1990 conference, Elder M. Russell Ballard quoted a letter from a sister missionary in South America relating her introspections concerning "the Church" and what constitutes the Church. It is a verification to our consideration about the target of teaching. It helps me to sense what the Lord commissioned us to do when he asked us to teach the principles of the gospel. Her letter read:

> It's really interesting with the people from the country—they are so quiet, timid, shy, and embarrassed. You are never sure exactly how much they understand. They will live and die in this small town. They are so poor and so simple and so childlike. They may never see a General Authority, never attend general conference, never go to BYU. They'll never be Boy Scouts, never play basketball in a huge church gym, never drive a car to stake conference, regional basketball finals, or anywhere. Many of the things we think about when we think of the Church—and take for granted—they may never see. [Now, the point.] But they have faith, they repent, they are baptized, they receive the Holy Ghost, and they renew their baptismal covenants each week when they partake of the sacrament. They pray and read the scriptures daily. They know God lives and that Christ is our Savior. And, I believe, they are going to the celestial kingdom. I do all the things they never will, but I'm not so sure about my own salvation.
>
> At first glance, the Church here looks absolutely nothing like the Church in downtown Orem, Utah. I have to keep reminding myself it is the same church and we all follow the same prophet. We have a sacrament meeting in the country each week because the members there really can't afford to come into town. And as I sit there outside on a wooden chair on the plain ground, with the sun setting and the six people in attendance, as we sing hymns, pray, and partake of the sacrament, I wonder if that isn't closer to Christ's church than at home. But I guess it is really the same. The things that matter, the true elements of the gospel as Christ taught in 3 Nephi 11, are the same here as they are in Orem, Utah. ("Small and Simple Things," p. 6.)

If we miss the point of what the gospel is, or what the Church is, then we are subject to miss the *what* of the message we are to teach. I testify that the scriptures of the Restoration will provide us with a clear example of the doctrines and principles which should be at the core of our message. In fact, there is a subject matter about which the prophets seemed to feel strongly, that of teaching us the nature of God; that is so fundamental to the gospel message that I will develop this subject in greater detail so that we may understand its profound importance in our teaching.

Teaching the Nature of God

In a bold and declarative talk given eighty-one days before the Prophet Joseph's martyrdom, he repeatedly emphasized the necessity to know the nature of God:

> It is necessary for us to have an understanding of God himself in the beginning (*Teachings*, p. 343).
>
> There are but a very few beings in the world who understand rightly the character of God (*Teachings*, p. 343).
>
> If men do not comprehend the character of God, they do not comprehend themselves (*Teachings*, p. 343).
>
> My first object is to find out the character of the only wise and true God, and what kind of a being he is (*Teachings*, p. 344).
>
> It is the first principle of the Gospel to know for a certainty the character of God (*Teachings*, p. 345).

Joseph Smith, as a contributor to the Lectures on Faith (3:4), also suggested that one of the three things necessary for faith unto salvation was "a correct idea of his character, perfections, and attributes." A number of years ago, as a result of some powerful teachings of fellow Church educators and an intense pondering of the Lectures on Faith, I began to realize how important it was to understand God's nature in order to exercise faith. In analyzing the characteristics and attributes contained in both Lectures 3 and 4, I used the computer to assist my study, to make lists and printouts of the characteristics attributed to God in the scriptures.

In deciding on a way to verify that particular learning found on the scriptural pages, I further chose and utilized a particular color, a light green shade, and began marking each of the attributes according to the scriptural references from my lists. A host of hours and weeks later, and a number of lists later, I realized that I didn't need these mechanical means any longer, that I had discovered a sensitivity beyond the task. The scriptures were a record from the prophets of the nature of God. Like Nephi they were persuading me to "come unto the God of Abraham, and the God of Isaac, and the God of Jacob" (1 Nephi 6:4) by teaching me of his nature. I had realized it with great feeling.

The Lectures had led me to the importance of knowing the nature of God. My knowledge had led me to an overviewing of the specific characteristics of God within the scriptures. My desire to mark not only had led me on a profound discovery of the attributes but also had now become a record from the scriptures, splashed in light green, of the reason the prophets were persuading me to come to God.

The Apostle John declared that "we love him [God], because he first loved us" (1 John 4:19). The scriptural record manifests to us this profound characteristic of God, that of love for his children, as well as the other characteristics. Perhaps one of the teacher's most important roles is to help the student realize the nature of God, that it is demonstrated on the scriptural pages. It is possible that a natural-flowing love for God begins with the repeated message of God's love for us, so adequately indicated within the scriptural record.

We need to hear, perhaps we even crave it, that God, in every dispensation, cares for his children and utilizes his attributes to work for their eternal life. Stories from our own day simply verify the scriptural stories of former days. For instance, Elder James M. Paramore, in a speech given in 1989 at Brigham Young University, indicated the importance of knowing God's love by relating a story of how God's omniscient mercy was extended toward a wayward son:

> I would like to share with you an experience I had with one small dimension of his [Jesus'] efforts to lead a wayward son. A year and a half ago, I was assigned to go to a stake conference in New Mexico. The normal route would have been to fly to Albuquerque, rent a car, and drive to Grants, where the conference was to be held. But for some reason I was impressed that I must go to Gallup and get a car there. It had meant taking a little tiny plane. I was the only passenger on the plane with two pilots. It was a terribly windy day, and I wasn't sure we were going to arrive.

When we arrived safely at Gallup, I was very, very happy to land. I went into the airport, took out my driver's license, and put it on the desk to pick up my car. The gentleman there said, "Mr. Paramore, I'm sorry, I can't let you have a car."

"Why not?" I asked.

"Your driver's license has expired."

It had expired a week earlier on my birthday! What was I going to do? I picked up the phone and called the local bishop. He was on his way out the door to perform a marriage ceremony. I told him I was Elder Paramore, and he said, "Who?"

I told him again and I'm not sure he believed it.

He replied, "I'll see what I can do."

But I knew he didn't believe that I was there because he said, "We don't have a conference here today. What are you doing in Gallup?" I was out of my pattern; I was out of the route that I should have taken.

Sitting over in the corner of the room was a young man with his teenage son. He was dressed in tank top and construction clothes and had long clean hair. He came over to the desk, and he said, "I understand you are in a little trouble. I just came by to get some applications to take flying lessons, and I couldn't help hearing that you need help. Could I take you somewhere?"

I said, "You would be a great Christian if you could." I explained my dilemma.

"You buy my gas," he said, "and I'll drive you over." We had sixty miles to go. So we got in his old, old worn-out car, filled with junk, and we started toward Grants, New Mexico.

On the way, I asked what every Latter-day Saint would ask:

"What do you know about the Mormons?"

"Have you ever been to Salt Lake City?"

"Have you ever read the Book of Mormon?"

To all of them the answers were affirmative. When I asked him if he knew the Book of Mormon was true, there was a long, long pause. Finally he responded by saying, "I'm an elder in the Church, and two years ago my wife left me and my two children for another man. I was a member of the branch presidency where I live. The members of my branch cut me off and blamed me for the departure of my wife. We've never been able to go back to church because of those feelings.

"Do I know if the Book of Mormon is true, Brother Paramore? (I knew who you were.) I've read the Book of Mormon many times, and I know it's as true as anything on this earth."

In the hour and a half that passed as I rode with him to Grants, I began to see that I was sitting in the presence of a great man of God; that he knew the gospel is just as true as I did; that he had been deeply hurt by some of the members, and he hadn't been back among them. We had a wonderful conversation, including a discussion of his son some day going on a mission. I've written him every week, sent him copies of the *Church News* every week, and given him other things to read. He is making great progress. Now, think about it. There are five billion people upon the earth, and here was one man out in the wilderness about whom the Lord was concerned. So he sent a General Authority, all unknowing, out of his way, redirecting his path. It could have been anyone, but it happened to be me. And when I came home that day, I knew that God loves all his children. ("Leadership—Jesus Was the Perfect Leader," pp. 3–4.)

This is the core of our teaching message: God is our Father; Jesus Christ is the Son; their work is to bring to pass the eternal life of God's children; and by their natures they are empowering us to gain eternal life. Whether it is taught from the scriptural page or from the pages of our day, it is the same message. Furthermore it is our responsibility to "see" it written on the scriptural pages, our commissioned teaching text, so that we have greater power to persuade the children of men to come to God.

A Scriptural Illustration: Mosiah and His Missionary Sons

In the book of Mosiah, we read that the Lord responded to King Mosiah's anguish about his sons going on missions to the Lamanites, which Lamanite nation had collectively been a threat to the lives and peace of the Nephites. The Lord, however, comforted this father by speaking promises to his heart: "And the Lord said unto Mosiah: Let them go up, for many shall believe on their words, and they shall have eternal life; and I will deliver thy sons out of the hands of the Lamanites" (Mosiah 28:7).

In green in my scriptures are the phrases "many shall believe on their words" and "I will deliver thy sons." The first shows the omniscient nature of God, who, knowing the resultant powers of the conversion that would take place in the kingdom of the Lamanites, encouraged the father to exercise faith. Second, the promise of protecting his sons was given to the father by a God of power, one who could certainly shield or deliver them from dangers. A further characteristic revealed within the verse is the notion that Mosiah could believe in the promises made by God because he, according to the Lectures on Faith, is a "God of truth and cannot lie" (Lectures on Faith 3:16).

As a teacher, having realized the attributes being illustrated within this scriptural story, I find it easier to see the magnitude of why Mormon gives us the missionary experiences of Ammon and Aaron. This is not just the story of a couple of missionaries entering new and dangerous mission fields; this is the story of God, whose life and purpose runs concurrently with the story of the sons of Mosiah. If our study or teaching of the story is fixed only on the mortal level, and is oblivious to the level on which God operates, then the knowledge base on which faith in God is fostered will be lacking critically. Being sensitive to the nature of God, perhaps even marking those characteristics, may help a teacher to sense the power level on which God is central to our faith.

In an effort to confirm to our students that a God of truth has spoken promises which will certainly be fulfilled, which the Book of Mormon prophets labored to do as well, we see that our teaching can help the students focus on God. The omniscience of God, for instance, regarding the conversion of the Lamanites and the promises of a God of power are recorded by Mormon in specific and separate incidents. In each of the following passages, which I have marked in light green in my scriptures, Mormon seems to make a point of drawing our attention to God. Furthermore, I make it a point in the teaching of these chapters to draw my students' attention to these passages, even encouraging them to mark their scriptures as well, giving them a knowledge base whereby they too can trust in the attributes of God in their own lives.

Omniscient Evidences

Alma 19:13	Ammon: King Lamoni converted
Alma 19:29	Ammon: Queen converted
Alma 19:31–34	Ammon: Many Lamanites converted
Alma 19:35	Ammon: Many others subsequently converted
Alma 21:17	Aaron: Many brought to the truth
Alma 22:23	Aaron: King and household converted
Alma 23:5	Aaron: Thousands brought to believe
Alma 25:6	Aaron: Many converted in wilderness

Omnipotent Evidences

Alma 17:20–21	Ammon: Protected from king
Alma 17:37–38	Ammon: Smote arms, cast stones
Alma 19:22–23	Ammon: Man falls dead
Alma 20:2	Ammon: Voice of Lord warns
Alma 21:14	Aaron: Delivered from prison
Alma 22:22	Aaron: Raised king, protected from harm
Alma 23:1	Aaron: King's proclamation a protection

The prophets have persuaded us to come to God when they revealed to us not only that God existed but that his nature was something on which we could depend. We, the teachers, persuade our students when we help them to see the purposes of the prophets, which we ourselves have seen in our study and which we have felt as we have drawn closer to God. We then teach with a greater fervency, an energy that enlivens our teaching and produces not only the knowledge base that they need for their faith but also the feeling from us that this is "verily" important.

A Scriptural Verification: The Anointing Woman

A further illustration of a scriptural story which needs to be seen on more than just a mortal level is found in the New Testament. Three Gospel writers relate a similar experience of a woman who anointed Jesus (see Mark 14, Luke 7, and John 12). It could easily be viewed as a record of the goodness of a woman only. However, I remember one year at a CES symposium when I heard a superb teacher use this story. He carefully read with us the accounts from the three Gospels, showing how precious and sacrificial the woman's worshipful actions were in paying sacred homage to the Christ, which the Savior exclaimed would be known from generation to generation (see Mark 14:9). And then, as carefully as he had revealed the woman's wonders, he began to teach about the story of God, which had been running concurrently with her story on the scriptural page. He showed how the Son of God, who has the same nature as the Father, had continually defended the woman's actions in the midst of those, especially Church members, who were criticizing her for what they termed a "waste of the ointment" (Mark 14:4).

> And Jesus said, *Let her alone; why trouble ye her? she hath wrought a good work on me.*
> For ye have the poor with you always, and whensoever ye will ye may do them good: but me ye have not always.
> *She hath done what she could:* and this which she has done unto me, shall be had in remembrance in generations to come, wheresoever my gospel shall be preached; for verily she has come beforehand to anoint my body to the burying. (Mark 14:6–7; JST, Mark 14:8; emphasis added.)

The italicized words in this scriptural quote are rendered in light green in my scriptures, indicating that they reveal the nature of God. One of the important points of the story is how God, who is merciful and just, becomes a mediator for the woman, which woman is representative of any of us who need such a mediator and defender when others may be criticizing us for the very actions accepted of heaven.

Our needs in mortality are many and varied, but can be met when, in our study of God in the scriptures, we begin to exercise faith in him. As a final confirmation to sense our need for God, I conclude this chapter with a poignant story that Elder Marion D. Hanks told about a child's need for his father, and about a father's need for his Father.

> A grieving young father and his two children sit before a television set in their home after a makeshift dinner. The children have been staying with Grandmother while their mother has slowly slipped

away in a lingering illness; now they and their father are home again after her funeral. The little girl drops off to sleep and is carried to her bed. The little boy fights off sleepiness until he finally asks his father if tonight, just tonight, he can sleep with him in his bed. As the two lie silently in the dark, the lad speaks: "Daddy, are you looking at me?" "Yes, son," the father replies, "I am looking at you."

The boy sighs and, exhausted, sleeps. The father waits a time and then, weeping, cries out in the dark, in anxious anguish: "God, are you looking at me? If you are, maybe I can make it. Without you, I know I can't." ("Changing Channels," p. 39.)

I testify that the scriptures are a record of God, not only of his existence but, more important, of his nature. We make it, I suppose, through a difficult mortal experience by holding on to the knowledge that God is working for us, that it is indeed his work and glory "to bring to pass the immortality and eternal life of man" (Moses 1:39). The admonition that we teach from the scriptures as teachers, and that as students we search from them daily, reflects the need to be in constant touch with God, being reminded of his work to save us.

God is working for us. I witness this sacred fact. Knowing this allows us not to feel alone during this probationary time. Our teaching can make a difference in giving to our students "the words" and "the message" that the God of creation is a God of atonement, and that by observing our covenant of salvation with him by faith and repentance, the Spirit of God will change our natures until we have endured mortality faithfully, sustained and protected and saved by God himself. Who wouldn't want to teach this message?

9

The Way and the Method of Teaching

The way that we teach the gospel must be worthy of the very gospel itself. The beauty of teaching about God and the gospel principles which tie us to God must be set in a delivery system that enhances the presentation of that gospel. Again, in the words of President Ezra Taft Benson, "Are we using the messages and the method of teaching found in the Book of Mormon and other scriptures of the Restoration to teach this great plan of the Eternal God?" ("The Book of Mormon and the Doctrine and Covenants," p. 84.) The method and the message must be harmonious with each other in order that the teaching of the principles of eternal life may be enhanced.

A number of years ago I used the computer to help me search out words that described the teaching process. It began with a passage in the Book of Mormon in which Moroni explained the nature of church meetings in his day:

> And their meetings were conducted by the church after the manner of the workings of the Spirit, and by the power of the Holy Ghost; for as the power of the Holy Ghost led them whether to preach, or to exhort, or to pray, or to supplicate, or to sing, even so it was done (Moroni 6:9).

As I considered the simple differences between praying and supplicating in that passage, I was also led, from a teaching standpoint, to consider the differences between *preaching* and *exhorting*. Looking at other scriptures as well, I began to widen my understanding of the subtleties of this teaching process. For instance, in the Doctrine and Covenants, section 20, additional words expanded my consideration:

> The priest's duty is to *preach, teach, expound, exhort,* and baptize, and administer the sacrament,
> And visit the house of each member, and exhort them to pray vocally and in secret and attend to all family duties (verses 46–47; emphasis added).

Examining that section further, in verse 59 I found words like *warn* and *invite,* adding to my growing list. These words describing the various teaching responsibilities of the priesthood opened a broad scriptural search. With each word identified, I would search the scriptures, again by use of the computer, for each occasion in which it was used, and then run a listing of each essential passage. Not a few weeks later, I had compiled a host of print-outs containing various but specific words describing teaching. As each new word was examined, newer possibilities, words, and searches continued. Not a few lists later, I had thrilled at the expanse of the teaching arena that was contained within the scriptures. I was nearly reeling from the multiplication of considerations, but was lacking an understanding of any kind of a structure or bigger picture.

One day, in an elemental desire for finding some organization for the ever-growing material I was collecting, I spread the lists on my desk and on the floor, wherever I could find a place. I looked, thought, gathered, stacked, pondered, and reshuffled, and . . . after many hours a formation of ideas slowly took place. Combinations of lists, having common purpose, began to take shape; furthermore, these areas began to suggest, at least in my mind, a larger organization of principles regarding teaching. Three major categories of teaching stood out: "the word," "the teacher," and "the Spirit."

Without the word of God (or the scriptures), without the Spirit of the Lord, could the prophets have taught the gospel? Both of these areas are what we could term "non-negotiable" as far as teaching goes. They cannot be excluded from our discussion concerning the way, or the method, of preaching the gospel of Jesus Christ.

Let me here suggest that the teacher, the third category, is also non-negotiable in this process, especially in a church in which the Lord has commissioned us to "teach one another the doctrines of the kingdom" (D&C 88:77). This is not simply a home-study church in which we are "hermitized" into little enclaves of monastic study. Part of the perfection process is being teachers, wherein the study and presentation of the gospel message causes us to come face-to-face with the principles of the gospel, to live them, to have the Spirit of the Lord testify their truthfulness to us.

Breaking down this larger area of "the teacher" into five sub-areas, it became easier to see how groups of words had common purpose.

1. It seemed to me that the prophets and teachers of the scriptures were using the word of the Lord to teach by reading, rehearsing, preaching, declaring, writing, publishing, and imparting the scriptures.

2. After presenting the word of the Lord, they took on the teaching responsibility to expound, explain, unfold, liken, reason, and give meaning concerning the scriptures.

3. A further obligation involved verifying, signifying, showing, proving, convincing, and establishing the word once it had been presented and expounded.

4. In an additional way, they established the word by testifying, manifesting, ascribing, esteeming, and witnessing.

5. At certain times, in an effort to encourage the living of the principles, the prophet-teachers exhorted, stirred, admonished, and persuaded their patrons.

The Book of Mormon prophets, from whom the majority of the items listed in the accompanying chart come, were exemplifying a pattern and manner of teaching. They were using the *word* of God from which to teach the gospel; and they then *expounded* the word, *verified* the word, *testified* as to the truthfulness of the word, and *exhorted* those they taught to live the gospel, all the while depending on the Lord that the *Spirit* would manifest the truth of these matters unto the people.

A "Holy Order"—Teaching

Word		Teach				Spirit
	Read	*Expound*	*Verify*	*Testify*	*Exhort*	
Word	Read	Expound	Verify	Testify	Exhort	Spirit
Word of Lord	Rehearse	Explain	Signify	Manifest	Stir	Holy Ghost
Word of angels	Preach	Unfold	Show	Ascribe	Admonish	Spirit of prophecy
Word of prophets	Declare	Meaning	Prove	Esteem	Tell	Spirit of revelation
Voice of Lord	Write	Liken	Establish	Witness	Remember	Power
Lord spake	Publish	Reason	Convince	"I saw"	Hearken	Discern
Prophecies	Impart	Suppose	"Thus we see"	"As the Lord liveth"	Cry	Perceive
Scriptures		Ask (Q's)	Wherefore		Convince	Converted
Records		Plainness	Therefore		Persuade	Convinced
Plates		"Somewhat to say"	Fulfilled		"See that ye"	Constrained
Book		"For this intent"			If	Prepared
					Choose	Inquire
					Except	Pray
					Wo	Cry
					"O my brethren"	Fast

In a wonderful talk given by Elder Neal A. Maxwell called "Those Seedling Saints Who Sit Before You," he summarized a portion of this chart by using a simple play on words. "As you teach the precious gospel, your task is to clarify, to verify, and to testify. For doing each of these there is a season, time, and place in your classroom. Finally, you are to exemplify by your lives something which is never out of season." (P. 1.) Although the word *clarify* is not a scriptural word, yet it captures the essence of the word *expound*, which is scriptural.

Therefore, in a very succinct way, remembering initially the essential non-negotiables—the word, the teacher, and the Spirit—it may be easier to remember our teacher responsibilities to "clarify," "verify," and "testify" concerning the word. This is a critical part of the "way" and the "method" that the prophets were exemplifying for us.

Establishing the Word: The Law of Witnesses

When Alma and Amulek were preaching in Ammonihah, at a certain stage Alma followed up Amulek's teaching when he "opened his mouth and began to speak unto [Zeezrom], and to establish the words of Amulek, and to explain things beyond, or to unfold the scriptures beyond that which Amulek had done" (Alma 12:1). In three of the four other passages in the scriptures which use the phrase "establish the word," each of them has the context of utilizing the law of witnesses, which Alma was doing in conjunction with Amulek:

> And my brother, Jacob, also has seen him as I have seen him; wherefore, I will send their words forth unto my children to prove unto them that my words are true. Wherefore, by the words of three, God hath said, I will establish my word. Nevertheless, God sendeth more witnesses, and he proveth all his words. (2 Nephi 11:3.)
>
> Wherefore, the Lord God will proceed to bring forth the words of the book; and in the mouth of as many witnesses as seemeth him good will he establish his word; and wo be unto him that rejecteth the word of God! (2 Nephi 27:14; same wording as JST, Isaiah 29:19.)

The law of witnesses—"in the mouth of two or three witnesses shall every word be established" (2 Corinthians 13:1)—is employed by those who teach in the manner of the Lord. It is a verification method. It is a way, or a pattern, of teaching. It allows the word to be taught, and then allows sufficient evidences to be given so that the word can distill on the soul of the student. The prophets, therefore, clarified the word by expounding on the principles of the gospel, and they verified the word by utilizing a law of witnesses. Now, we must consider their role to testify in establishing the word.

Testifying:
The Spirit of Prophecy and Revelation

While Alma, as recorded in chapter 33 of the book of Alma, was teaching the Zoramites, he employed a verification technique in teaching about the Son of God. He quoted from his own scriptural records the words of Zenos (see verses 3–11); then he quoted a short passage from Zenock (see verse 16), and then he concluded by mentioning Moses' experience with the brazen serpent. As Amulek stood (see chapter 34), he reminded them how Alma had employed the scriptural law of witnesses:

> And ye also beheld that my brother has proved unto you, in many instances, that the word is in Christ unto salvation.
>
> My brother has called upon the words of Zenos, that redemption cometh through the Son of God, and also upon the words of Zenock; and also he has appealed unto Moses, to prove that these things are true. (Alma 34:6–7.)

And then, in the spirit of the law of living witnesses, Amulek bore testimony confirming the teaching of his companion, Alma, and of the word of the Lord himself:

> And now, behold, I will testify unto you of myself that these things are true. Behold, I say unto you that I do know that Christ shall come among the children of men, to take upon him the transgressions of his people, and that he shall atone for the sins of the world; for the Lord God hath spoken it. (Alma 34:8.)

These ancient missionary companions had used the witnesses of their scriptural records to verify the word; and then, as those who bore the message of the scriptures to the people, they employed their own testimonies as living witnesses. The word had been "established."

Let me illustrate the point from President J. Reuben Clark, from whom we have quoted frequently. He gave strong counsel concerning the possession of a testimony and the courage to so bear it:

> The first requisite of a teacher for teaching these principles is a personal testimony of their truth. No amount of learning, no amount of study, and no number of scholastic degrees, can take the place of this testimony, which is the *sine qua non* of the teacher in our Church school system. . . .
>
> But for you teachers the mere possession of a testimony is not enough. You must have besides this, one of the rarest and most precious of all the many elements of human character,—moral courage. For in the absence of moral courage to declare your testimony, it will reach the students only after such dilution as will make it difficult if not impossible for them to detect it; and the spiritual and psychological effect of a weak and vacillating testimony may well be actually harmful instead of helpful. (*Charted Course*, p. 7.)

So there you have it, a manner of teaching exemplified in the scriptures. Alma and Amulek, companions and witnesses, preaching the word of God, establishing the truth of the word by utilizing the scriptural law of witnesses, and then employing a seal of testimony from the very spirit of prophecy and revelation which was in them.

VERIFICATION OF THE PATTERN

Let's consider five scriptures which establish the truths we have been considering. Showcased are the three non-negotiable areas which form the basis of our philosophy about the way we ought to be teaching—that is, the word, the teacher, and the Spirit. If we were to chart our core scripture, Doctrine and Covenants 42:12–14, which we established in chapter 2, it would look like this:

Scripture	The Word	The Teacher	The Spirit
D&C 42:12–14	Bible and Book of Mormon	Teach principles of gospel; observe and do covenants; prayer of faith	Directed by the Spirit

The teacher has the responsibility to teach principles and to use as his sources the scriptures which house those principles. He also is to observe his covenants and pray the prayer of faith, so that he can be directed by the Spirit of the Lord. In one regard he uses scriptures which have come about because of the spirit of prophecy and revelation, and in another regard he has to be able to bear witness of the truths in the scriptures by the very spirit of prophecy and revelation which is "in him."

Another powerful yet succinct scripture, found also in the Doctrine and Covenants, is that recorded in Doctrine and Covenants 52:9, which reads:

> And let them journey from thence preaching the word by the way, saying none other things than that which the prophets and apostles have written, and that which is taught them by the Comforter through the prayer of faith.

The charting of this scripture follows the same pattern of section 42:

Scripture	The Word	The Teacher	The Spirit
D&C 52:9	Prophets and Apostles have written	Preaching the word	Comforter teaches teacher

Inasmuch as we have been counseled that the Book of Mormon would give us the way and the method of teaching, consider now these three powerful examples of prophets and teachers who not only taught the gospel out of the scriptures but also were able to verify the scriptural word by the witnesses they had received by the power of the Holy Ghost:

And Alma went and began to declare the word of God unto the church which was established in the valley of Gideon, according to the revelation of the truth of the word which had been spoken by his fathers, and according to the spirit of prophecy which was in him, according to the testimony of Jesus Christ, the Son of God (Alma 6:8).

And now, my brethren, I would that ye should hear me, for I speak in the energy of my soul; for behold, I have spoken unto you plainly that ye cannot err, or have spoken according to the commandments of God.

For I am called to speak after this manner, according to the holy order of God, which is in Christ Jesus; yea, I am commanded to stand and testify unto this people the things which have been spoken by our fathers concerning the things which are to come.

And this is not all. Do ye not suppose that I know of these things myself? Behold, I testify unto you that I do know that these things whereof I have spoken are true. And how do ye suppose that I know of their surety?

Behold, I say unto you they are made known unto me by the Holy Spirit of God. Behold, I have fasted and prayed many days that I might know these things of myself. And now I do know of myself that they are true; for the Lord God hath made them manifest unto me by his Holy Spirit; and this is the spirit of revelation which is in me.

And moreover, I say unto you that it has thus been revealed unto me, that the words which have been spoken by our fathers are true, even so according to the spirit of prophecy which is in me, which is also by the manifestation of the Spirit of God. (Alma 5:43–47.)

Now these sons of Mosiah were with Alma at the time the angel first appeared unto him; therefore Alma did rejoice exceedingly to see his brethren; and what added more to his joy, they were still his brethren in the Lord; yea, and they had waxed strong in the knowledge of the truth; for they were men of a sound understanding and they had searched the scriptures diligently, that they might know the word of God.

But this is not all; they had given themselves to much prayer, and fasting; therefore they had the spirit of prophecy, and the spirit of revelation, and when they taught, they taught with power and authority of God. (Alma 17:2–3.)

Charting our three Book of Mormon and two Doctrine Covenants passages allows us to see the pattern, the manner, and the order of teaching. God seems to care about how his gospel is taught, inasmuch as there is so much commonality in the prophets' approach to teaching:

Scripture	The Word	The Teacher	The Spirit
D&C 42:12–14	Bible and Book of Mormon	Teach principles of gospel; observe and do covenants; prayer of faith	Directed by the Spirit
D&C 52:9	Prophets and Apostles have written	Preaching the word	Comforter teaches teacher
Alma 6:8	Spoken by the fathers	Declare the word	Spirit of prophecy in him
Alma 5:43–47	Spoken by the fathers	Stand and testify; fasted and prayed	Spirit of revelation in him
Alma 17:2–3	Scriptures	Searched diligently; prayer and fasting	Spirit of prophecy and revelation

The manner in which the Book of Mormon prophets taught was no different than the instructions the Lord gave us for our day in the Doctrine and Covenants. The scriptures—or that which was spoken by the fathers, or what the Apostles and prophets have written—are to be our source for teaching the principles of the gospel. However, that is not enough. Each teacher must have within himself the witness of the truth of these principles. The spirit of prophecy and revelation is not relegated only to the Quorum of the Twelve Apostles, or to those who are designated as prophets, seers, and revelators. Each teacher must have the witness of the gospel message. Each teacher must be a prophet himself, not in the terms of being called as a prophet or being in a leadership quorum of the Church, but in his ability to receive that witness of truth and to declare it in concert with the teaching of the principles of the gospel from prophetic works.

It is not always an easy task to be the kind of teacher for which the Lord is asking. The third column in our chart is suggestive of a great deal of work, the work of prophets themselves. Such work as preaching, teaching, and declaring the word must be complemented by the work of observing and doing the covenants, of praying the prayer of faith, of searching the scriptures diligently, and of fasting and prayer. The spirit of prophecy is not easily earned. The spirit of revelation, so necessary for edifying teaching, cannot be bought with money or any other worldly currency, but exacts an important spiritual price from any of us. Yet, the promises and rewards of edifying teaching are precisely that, edifying to us and to our students.

A Sacrament Talk

Let's suppose for a moment that we have been asked to give a talk in sacrament meeting, and that the bishopric member responsible to assign us to speak has asked that we speak on the principle of revelation, specifically that it comes "line upon line." He has further suggested that we use as a scriptural text the passage in 2 Nephi 28:30, which we will quote here:

> For behold, thus saith the Lord God: I will give unto the children of men line upon line, precept upon precept, here a little and there a little; and blessed are those who hearken unto my precepts, and lend an ear unto my counsel, for they shall learn wisdom; for unto him that receiveth I will give more; and from them that shall say, We have enough, from them shall be taken away even that which they have.

Delighted that we have the opportunity to teach a principle of the gospel, we prayerfully begin our preparation, asking that the Lord help us not only to teach the "message" but also to do it in the "way" that would best present that particular principle. As we begin our study of our scriptural text, which houses the principle we are to teach, we sense that there are footnote helps regarding that specific "line upon line, precept upon precept" principle. Those scriptural references are Proverbs 2:9, Isaiah 28:13, and Doctrine and Covenants 98:12.

In examining each of these references, we find that two of them use the same phraseology of "line upon line, precept upon precept" but within their own context, helping us to see the principle with some additional light. Furthermore, the footnotes in Isaiah 28 and Doctrine and Covenants 98 lead to many more passages of scriptures which do not just use the same terminology but help us to see the principle within a host of different settings.

As an illustration, there are a host of stories housing our very principle in the scriptures. For instance, in Judges 7, as Joshua pleads before the Lord to understand why Israel had been defeated at Ai, the Lord explains to him the revelatory procedure by which the man who had taken the accursed thing would be made known. All of the tribes would be marched by, and the Lord would indicate which one. Then that particular tribe would be marched by, and the family indicated, then the household, and then the man. The manner of revelation used by the Lord to assist Joshua simply verifies our teaching text, allowing us to see the principle of "line upon line" revelation in action.

Other stories might also be considered; for instance, 1 Samuel 16, in which Samuel finds the new king of Israel. Instructed to go to Bethlehem to the house of Jesse, Samuel is given no foreknowledge as to who the king is. He simply enters the city and begins the process of examining the boys of Jesse's lineage. In conjunction with the Lord's denials, which is part of the revelatory "line upon line," Samuel is led to the selection of David.

The manner in which the Liahona (see 1 Nephi 16) operated in the wilderness is also a working example of orderly revelation. The ball, or director—having "things which were written" on it which changed from day to day depending on the "faith and diligence and heed" which were given unto those writings—served Lehi's people in a "precept upon precept" manner. The pointers operated in showing them the way to the promised land on a daily, "line upon line" basis.

Now, in the spirit of a diagram, for illustration's sake, the organizing of a talk begins with the principle and the scriptural text which are our central focus, and from there we begin to clarify and verify the word:

Principle: Line upon Line Revelation
Text: 2 Nephi 28:30

Theological Verifications	*Scriptural Story Verifications*
Isaiah 28:10, 13	Joshua 7
Alma 12:9	1 Samuel 16
D&C 42:61	Matthew 13
D&C 50:24	Luke 2
D&C 93:20	1 Nephi 16
D&C 98:12	D&C 93
D&C 128:21	JS-H 1

Although there are many more passages which would theologically verify our scriptural text in 2 Nephi, and many more stories from the scriptures that could exemplify our principle, yet we now have an adequate knowledge base from which we can begin to organize our talk. Hypothetically, we begin our talk perhaps by using our scriptural text, and then in the spirit of clarifying the principle that has been made known to our listeners from the text, we begin to use a reference or two to establish the theological soundness of that principle; in other words, we allow the principle to distill upon their souls by a law of witnesses. In helping our audience to see the applicability of the principle, we may use a reference or two from the stories list that would allow them some sufficient time to assimilate the value of the principle, again by way of the law of witnesses. As our presentation reaches a conclusion, or at particularly important junctures along the way, we will want to personally testify of the principle, to witness of its truthfulness, to help establish the truth.

In summary, we have taught a principle of the gospel, teaching it from the scriptures, verifying the principle through sufficient witnesses and examples so that the people could see the principle more clearly and convincingly. And finally we have testified to the principle, just as Amulek "established the word" of Alma. We have sealed, as it were, a jar of precious fruit, having heaped the scriptural principles to the brim. We have verified and testified sufficiently that the sealed jar will produce nourishing fruit for many months and years into the future.

Conclusion

Obviously, this is a simplified way of addressing teaching. Whether we are speaking for fifteen minutes in a sacrament meeting or giving a forty-minute Gospel Doctrine lesson, we are utilizing the same procedure, manner, pattern, and way of teaching. We are teaching principles of the gospel from the scriptures. We are employing the law of witnesses as we clarify and verify the principles by using examples. We are sealing and establishing the entire message as we bear testimony concerning our teaching. Although the process is not a rigid step-by-step method, yet the elements of the "way" can wonderfully flow through the teaching moment. We are to establish the word of God in the manner he has commissioned.

> And the Lord said unto them also: Go forth among the Lamanites, thy brethren, and establish my word; yet ye shall be patient in long-suffering and afflictions, that ye may show forth good examples unto them in me, and I will make an instrument of thee in my hands unto the salvation of many souls (Alma 17:11).

The Lord fulfilled his word unto the sons of Mosiah. As they established his word, he showed them as good examples and made an instrument of them in bringing salvation to his children. I witness, as one teaching in this day, that the Lord is the same as he was with Ammon and Aaron. We are made instruments in his hands to bring salvation, as we teach to "establish the word" of the Lord in the hearts of our students. I testify there is a way and method of teaching that complements the words and the message.

10

Building Faith by Teaching

Building faith unto salvation is the ultimate reason we teach. Helping our students receive the message of salvation, and in a way in which the Spirit of the Lord can confirm the principles, will contribute to helping the students exercise faith unto eternal life. Elder Boyd K. Packer has, on a number of occasions, addressed issues related to faith-promoting teaching. In one address called "The Mantle Is Far, Far Greater Than the Intellect," he said:

> In the Church we are not neutral. We are one-sided. There is a war going on, and we are engaged in it. It is the war between good and evil, and we are belligerents defending the good. We are therefore obliged to give preference to and protect all that is represented in the gospel of Jesus Christ, and we have made covenants to do it. . . .
>
> And I want to say in all seriousness that there is a limit to the patience of the Lord with respect to those who are under covenant to bless and protect His Church and kingdom upon the earth but do not do it. (*Let Not Your Heart Be Troubled,* pp. 110, 111.)

The language of Elder Packer is strong, but it is a consistently strong message from the Brethren when our teaching is missing the key ingredients to building faith. For instance—and we dealt with this in chapter 3—President J. Reuben Clark warned Church educators that if they did not have testimonies of Joseph Smith and Jesus Christ, they should at once resign, that "the First

Presidency expected this pruning to be made" (*Charted Course,* p. 7). President Ezra Taft Benson, in quoting *The Charted Course* on this issue, verified and punctuated this message in an equally strong manner when he said: "We assume that every one of you, without any equivocation, has such a testimony; otherwise, you are flying under false colors and your teaching is a sham—a pretense" (*The Gospel Teacher and His Message,* p. 2).

Teachers are covenant defenders of the faith. Again, from Elder Packer, "Those of you who are employed by the Church have a special responsibility to build faith, not destroy it. If you do not do that, but in fact accommodate the enemy, who is the destroyer of faith, you become in that sense a traitor to the cause you have made covenants to protect." (*Let Not Your Heart Be Troubled,* p. 112.)

It seems to me that if we develop our philosophy of teaching by using the Lord's commission from section 42, then the directions to teach principles out of the scriptures, to observe and do the covenants, and to pray the prayer of faith will have enabled our teaching to have the Spirit's direction. Such a philosophy will have established us as teachers within some pretty sound covenantal parameters in order to build faith. The Lord will simply have prepared us, by his commission, to be faith-promoters.

We will now examine three addresses from which we have been quoting as to directions given for promoting faith. There are a host of phrases which these leaders have used for our consideration. President J. Reuben Clark told us: "I repeat again for emphasis, your chief interest, your essential and all but sole duty, is to teach the Gospel of the Lord Jesus Christ as that has been revealed in these latter days. You are to teach this Gospel using as your sources and authorities the Standard Works of the Church, and the words of those whom God has called to lead His people in these last days." (*Charted Course,* pp. 10–11.) He further stressed the following ideas (the numbers have been added here):

> 1. You are not, whether high or low, to intrude into your work your own peculiar philosophy, no matter what its source or how pleasing or rational it seems to you to be.
>
> 2. You are not, whether high or low, to change the doctrines of the Church or to modify them.

Sacrament Service

Presiding .... Bis[...]
Conducting .... Bish[...]
Organist .... Cheryl [...]
Chorister .... Terri Lanham

Welcome

Opening Hymn No. 230
"Scatter Sunshine"

Invocation .... Terry Bussard

Ward Business

Sacrament Hymn No. 177
" 'Tis Sweet To Sing The Matchless Love"
Sacrament Administered
By The Aaronic Priesthood

Speaker .... Catie Linfesty
"Special Music"
Lani Hersom and Becky Schwendinger

Speaker .... Leslie Hersom
Congregational Hymn No. 60
"Battle Hymn Of The Republic"

Speaker .... Karen Lanham
Closing Hymn No. 136
"I Know That My Redeemer Lives"

Benediction .... Ray Garcia

...NARIES IN THE FIELD

- A. Clark Gunnerson
  67 Rue Furtado
  33800 Bordeaux
  France

- Elder Rene Bueno
  Casilla 70
  Antosgasta, Chile

- Sister CharlyAnn Mary Chun
  Salt Lake Temple Square
  Mission
  P.O. Box 112110
  Salt Lake City, UT 84147-2110

El Cajon Fifth Ward of the Church of Jesus Christ of Latter-Day Saints

Primary Scripture: I Nephi 19:23 "I did liken all scriptures unto us, that it might be for our profit and learning."

June 5   Last day of seminary
June 7   Seminary Graduation
June 10   Stake Merit Badge Night (EC4)

"And thou shalt love the Lord thy God with all thine heart, and with all thy soul, and with all thy might.
And these words, which I command thee this day, shall be in thine heart: And thou shalt teach them diligently unto thy children, and shalt talk of them when thou sittest in thine house, and when thou walkest by the way, and when thou liest down, and when thou risest up."
Deuteronomy 6:5-7

3. You are not to teach the philosophies of the world, ancient or modern, pagan or Christian, for this is the field of the public schools. Your sole field is the Gospel, and that is boundless in its own sphere. (*Charted Course*, p. 11.)

"A . . . responsibility I name," said Ezra Taft Benson in our second address, "is that you teach only the gospel of Jesus Christ." He further emphasized (again, numbers have been added below):

1. Doctrinal interpretation is the province of the First Presidency. The Lord has given that stewardship to them by revelation. No teacher has the right to interpret doctrine for the members of the Church.

2. There have been and continue to be attempts to bring [a humanistic] philosophy into our own Church history. We must never forget that ours is a prophetic history. Our students need to understand this prophetic history, but this can be done only by teachers who themselves possess the spirit of prophecy and revelation.

3. We would hope that if you feel you must write for the scholarly journals, you always defend the faith.

4. We are entrusting you to represent the Lord and the First Presidency to your students, not the views of the detractors of the Church. (*The Gospel Teacher and His Message*, pp. 10–12.)

And in the third of our quoted talks, Elder Bruce R. McConkie emphasized this:

Let me say just a word about false doctrine. We are supposed to teach. Pitfalls we are supposed to avoid are the teaching of false doctrine; teaching ethics in preference to doctrine, compromising our doctrines with the philosophies of the world; entertaining rather than teaching, and using games and gimmicks rather than sound doctrine, coddling students, as President Clark expressed it. (*Foolishness of Teaching*, p. 11.)

A Dedication to Faith

The following is an extensive quote from a talk given at Brigham Young University at the dedication of one of its buildings.

Elder Packer, in giving the talk, tried to stress the uniqueness of BYU as an institution with a purpose. Everything that is stated here could be used to designate the unique purpose of the Church and of the teachers who teach within its classrooms.

> Brigham Young University is unique among all universities. It is a private school and it is established for a special spiritual purpose.
>
> Last year in Boston I heard Dr. Christ-Janner, president of Boston University, describe that school in these words, "We can best serve as a neutral territory—a kind of arbiter where people can come to reason."
>
> This could not be said of Brigham Young University. For this University is not neutral; it is committed; it is one-sided; it is prejudiced, if you will, in favor of the gospel of Jesus Christ.
>
> This is not a playing field where good and evil can come and joust with one another until one may win. Evil will find no invitation to contest here. This is a training ground for one team. Here you are coached and given signals preparatory for the great game, and we might say the great battle, of life. The scouts and the coaches of the opposing team are not welcome here. (*A Dedication—to Faith,* pp. 3–4.)

As a student steps into a Church Educational System setting—or, for that matter, a Primary class or an Aaronic Priesthood class—he is entitled to know that in the classroom he will have an experience that will foster faith. He should stand assured that the enemy of righteousness, in any of his forms or formats, has not been invited to either defame his faith or even hinder it in the slightest. Continuing with Elder Packer, he said:

> And as we add buildings as we do today, we are conscious of the fact that never can all of the disciplines adequately be found here. There are other things that you will not find here. There are philosophies and ideologies which are not taught here. There are associations and environments and expressions, some of which may be all right elsewhere that are not welcome here. There are some voices that cannot be heard here. This school is maintained as a forum for faith. It is perhaps a last citadel. Faith in the world is fading. Its voice grows feeble. In almost every institution of higher learning faith is closed out by court edict. Do not press to have this last platform of faith

shared with the atheist, the skeptic, the destroyer of faith. If these are the voices you would hear, one is free to go where they speak. (*A Dedication—to Faith*, p. 4.)

A BYU student with his own agenda could possibly see the wisdom in going to a host of other universities where he could have the freedom to express his purposes rather than stay at BYU hypocritically. So should we as teachers in the Church realize that we do not provide every environment for every Church member. Some of our students with their own agendas may need to sense that the Church has a monumental mission and cannot be dissuaded from that mission. Elder Packer went on to say:

> Thank God for the faculty of this institution—men and women full of faith. Theirs is the voice of faith, the voice to trust. They know that one would hardly go to an ice cream parlor to order a bag of insecticide; then to be upset and abusive if the proprietor explains that not only is there none in stock, but that he has never carried it nor does he intend to. If it is insecticide you want you must go elsewhere.
>
> Sillier yet, would it be, if the clerk hired to dispense ice cream should be critical of the proprietor and argue that insecticide is useful to some; a customer may request it. And, where is the morality of the clerk who in defiance of his employer's instructions would presume himself to carry a secret stock of it and subtly to do business in it?
>
> Have you ever thought how intemperate you could become if you went to an ice cream parlor for pistachio nut, later to learn that by some inadvertence they had served you insecticide! Now there is a protest for which I think I could find some enthusiasm!
>
> This University is like a specialty shop. It is a very large specialty shop. It is endowed to dispense the commodity, faith. Packaged in a hundred ways, in dozens of disciplines—the product is faith. Other universities are like variety stores. Faith is a product that has been taken from the shelves of the variety store. Unfortunately, even most shops which pretend to specialize in the product, faith, market only a man-made synthetic—a product which will not last and when analyzed turns out to be nothing more than the philosophies of men mingled with scripture. (*A Dedication—to Faith*, p. 5.)

I echo the words of Elder Packer. We are commissioned. We are charged to dispense the purity of the principles of the gospel within a delivery system of the scriptures and the Spirit, which will make it enticing and delicious. Our teaching is part of the mission of the Church, part of the work of God. His glory will come with those who inherit eternal life. Our glory, in mortality and in the eternities, will be dependent on the same results. Teaching should be a continual process for fostering faith.

A Case Study

One year when I was teaching the Old Testament in a Gospel Doctrine setting, we were studying the first two chapters of 2 Kings. The story contained in chapter 1 was of Ahaziah, the king of Samaria, who fell and was sick. Inasmuch as he was not a believer in the God of Israel, he sent his messengers to seek help from the God of the Philistines. Elijah, being warned by an angel, intercepted the king's party and told them to return and tell the king that he would die no matter what. When the king realized it was Elijah who had interfered with his healing, he sent a captain with his fifty to demand that Elijah come with them. In response to Elijah's prophetic words, the heavens opened and fire consumed the fifty. A second fifty, equally as demanding as the first, approached Elijah and the same heavenly fire consumed them as well. There began in the classroom a slight wave of laughter, having seen the prophet defended so adamantly by heavenly powers. It was, as it were, what we may have hoped would happen, a providential judgment from heaven supporting the righteous against those who provoke them.

We continued with the story of chapter 2, where Elisha was mocked by a host of taunting youth. Again, in response to the curse which Elisha leveled against them, two she bears came from the woods and "tare" them. Here were two stories in as many chapters in which the prophet's words were vindicated and the consequence was to the hurt or consumption of 142 individuals. Now, some in the class were exulting in the defense of the prophet. But some others were offended by the seeming lightheartedness by which these events were being considered by fellow class members. There were some who felt that God was the problem. He it was who was vengeful, full of anger, and more than unfair. We had read the scriptural account together, and by some, God's nature was found wanting.

While reading the scriptures, it is easy for some to have misgivings about what God is doing. However, if we start right, start with what we already know about God given us by the prophets of the Restoration, then our understanding of the scriptures, and God particularly, will not be found deficient.

As was mentioned in chapter 8, in the third and fourth Lectures on Faith a list of characteristics and attributes of God was given to us. In fact, Lecture 4:2 suggested that the Lord, knowing our weaknesses here in mortality, granted to us what we needed to know about his nature. Hence, we have been given insight into God by knowing the following characteristics he has in perfection: He is a God of creation, mercy, truth, love, justice, judgment, knowledge, power, who is also unchangeable, and no respecter of persons. The prophets, knowing God more intimately than we, have given us these characteristics so that we, holding to this knowledge, can exercise faith in God.

Knowing this nature of God before I go into the scriptures helps me not to misinterpret what is happening in 2 Kings 1 and 2. Knowing these characteristics allows me to draw different conclusions. For instance, rather than concluding that God was unfair, vengeful, and full of anger, I could draw a host of faith-promoting conclusions from our stories:

1. Without question, God had shown his power.

2. God supported the prophetic word of Elijah and Elisha, showing that he is a God of truth who cannot lie.

3. God must have had sufficient cause to issue into the spirit world one hundred of his own children, or to allow forty-two youth to be injured.

4. If I believe, as is stated in Moses 1:39, that God's work is to bring to pass the eternal life of man, then I must believe that all were benefitted somehow by God's actions—Elijah, Elisha, the 142 dead or injured, the people who remained to view and know of these experiences, and the millions upon millions who have read or will read the accounts and come to know of God.

The conclusions we have reached because of restored knowledge, and our desire to consider that knowledge, allow the God of heaven to be viewed in the classroom by our students with greater faith. We have, as covenant defenders of the faith, protected our students from a harsh and maybe immature view concerning the scriptural accounts.

Conclusion

We are covenant defenders of the faith. We are teachers with a commission to teach by the Spirit, which Spirit can accompany only those who are teaching the message of the gospel, and in the way it has been prescribed. In the host of circumstances that come in a classroom moment, questions can arise which need a teacher who has faith, a teacher who can promote faith. We are in the classrooms of the Church in order to help the students come to know and love God, to help them to honor their covenants by learning to feast on the scriptures and to enjoy the Spirit of the Lord, who is attendant with earnest scripture study.

Part Two

The Methodology of Teaching

11

Studying the Scriptures as a Teacher

In the beginning ten chapters we established a host of principles in the "law of teaching." We now consider certain methodologies that naturally come out of our philosophy, out of our principles of teaching.

The Lord commissioned us in Doctrine and Covenants 42 to teach the principles of the gospel out of the scriptures. The Brethren in this day have counseled us along that same vein; therefore, it seems appropriate that a focal methodological skill would be to have an affinity for—a comfortableness with, if you will—the scriptural word. One of the behaviors a teacher exemplifies in the classroom is the simple use of the scriptures while teaching.

Years ago, while studying in the field of educational psychology, I read an experience of a professor trying to increase the learning experiences of his counseling practicum students. In an extemporaneous and experimental way he asked one of the secretaries in his department to interview a student, a skill required of the psychology students he was supervising. He brought her into an interviewing room where they taped her initial experience. During this first interview she exemplified many of the beginning counselor behaviors; for instance, she looked away, shifted nervously at times in her chair, and panicked slightly when she couldn't think of additional questions. After the session, the professor, in an attempt to help her to be a better interviewer, tried to teach her what he called the "attending behaviors" of a good counselor. Three skills were taught the secretary. He taught her how to have attentive posture, taught her how to maintain eye contact, and then taught her a simple skill called verbal following, a skill that allows the counselor to think of continuing questions based on what the person being interviewed is saying presently. When they sent her back for another interview she had improved dramatically. Simple behaviors, simple attending behaviors, had brought some profound results. (See Ivey, *Microcounseling*, pp. 45–47.)

By the same measure, there are simple "attending behaviors" of a good gospel teacher. For instance, this kind of teacher has a piece of chalk in one hand and an opened set of scriptures in the other. The scriptures are opened in his hand because that is the focus of his teaching. (The manual is not in his hand, because he has not been commissioned to teach from the manual. The manual is given to provide correlated direction, and should be used to prepare the lesson, but it is not the teaching focus once the teacher is prepared.) The chalk is in his other hand so that he, in a normal classroom situation, can clarify the message of the scriptures and the principles by illustrating these principles on the board (which skill will be discussed in chapter 14).

Furthermore, there are even "attending behaviors" of a good gospel student. This student is one who has his scriptures with him in class, opened, and he is ready to make notes or to mark verses according to the direction of the teacher or to the impressions brought to his own mind. He also has pencil and paper in order to capture the flow of the points of the lesson for that day. Can you imagine a classroom full of students exemplifying these kinds of behaviors? These are the very dreams that make a teacher subsequently wake up refreshed and hopeful.

Both the teacher and the student realize that the teaching or the learning of the gospel have the scriptures as the core documents by which the principles of the gospel will be manifest. As we use the scriptures in the classroom pointedly, the students sense their need to have their own scriptures with them, prepared for learning.

Let us accept that the scriptures are an absolutely critical resource in teaching the gospel, and develop the skills necessary to use them. Therefore, consider five areas that will help us establish the scriptures as our focus, both for teaching and studying.

READ THE SCRIPTURES

Elder Bruce R. McConkie, in preparing Church educators to teach the Old Testament, described different techniques of helps for studying, and then ranked them from one to ten in their importance. His first help was simple but profound:

> *Key One: Read the Bible*
> Could any key be more obvious than this? Simply read the book itself. Unless and until we do, nothing else will fall into place. We cannot do other than rate this key as a ten on our scale. All biblical scholarship and understanding begin with reading the basic source material.
> One of our problems is that we read what others have said about the Bible; we read a book of Old Testament stories; we get something the *Reader's Digest* publishes under the biblical name that leaves out the genealogies and supposedly hard parts.
> Read the book itself. "Search the scriptures" (John 5:39). Treasure up the Lord's word. Go to the source. The words are sacred. Insofar as they have come down to us as originally penned, they were inspired by the Holy Ghost. They are to be read over and over again as long as we live. ("The Bible—A Sealed Book," p. 3.)

In the same vein, but in an interview years before, Elder McConkie was quoted by the *Church News* staff. He addressed the importance of utilizing the scriptures in his own study and, for that matter, in our study.

> "It would be a great surprise to most people, I think, to know that the very large percent of any study I do is on the scriptures themselves."
> He said, "I think that people who study the scriptures get a dimension to their life that nobody else gets and that can't be gained in any way except by studying the scriptures.
> "There's an increase in faith and a desire to do what's right and a feeling of inspiration and understanding that come to people who study the gospel—meaning particularly the Standard Works—and

who ponder the principles, that can't come in any other way." (*Church News,* January 24, 1976, p. 4.)

It would seem that the great majority of the study we should do in preparation for teaching would be within the domain of the scriptural pages, reading the text, studying the "words of eternal life." Though a teacher is tempted to find a quicker understanding of the scriptures by seeking words of commentary from a host of sources, yet if he will discipline himself in the beginning of his study, he will develop an ability to make the scriptural word come alive. By his own study and by the spirit of prophecy and revelation that is due him as a teacher, he will find there is indeed power in the word.

USE THE RIGHT SCRIPTURES

We have been given a great gift in the scriptures we use in the classroom. In 1979 and 1981, the Bible and the triple combination, respectively, were published anew for our use. In them were contained not only a correlated testimony of the Savior but also a host of helps allowing us to use the scriptures more wisely, helps like the Topical Guide, the Bible Dictionary, chapter headings, maps, index, and an extensive footnote system.

Elder Packer helped us to see the importance of the scriptures we now use by establishing two key points. First, he said that the prophecy of Ezekiel 37, that the record of Judah and the record of Joseph would be one in our hands, has now been accomplished by the utilization of the footnotes ranging back and forth between the Bible and the Book of Mormon, establishing these two scriptures as one witness of Christ. Second, he said that the crowning achievement of President Spencer W. Kimball would be the scriptural work that was produced during his administration. As I think of the profound revelation concerning all worthy males holding the priesthood, and also the importance of the reorganization of the seventy, both given during President Kimball's presidency, I am quietly reminded of the great scriptural gift we received. (See *Let Not Your Heart Be Troubled,* p. 9.)

When I was called to be the bishop of a ward in 1982, three years had transpired since the introduction of the "new Bible," and one year since the publication of the triple combination. For a person at that time to give up his old set of scriptures—the ones that he had taken on a mission, the ones that had all the markings and notes—was a monumental sacrifice. Even understanding the value of the new scriptures did not make the transition any easier. The reverence people had for their personalized scriptures, as well as the economics of buying a new set, made for a sluggish changeover. However, without attempting any compulsion or haranguing techniques, we simply tried in our ward to have the teachers in the organizations use the scriptures in a way that would entice the members to buy them and to use them.

As an example, in the normal flow of teaching, the teacher would call attention to an excellent footnote leading from the Bible to the Doctrine and Covenants, a help that the ward members with their old scriptures would not have. Or, the teacher would utilize a Joseph Smith Translation (JST) reference in the footnotes that clarified a difficult passage. Or, the Bible Dictionary would be opened to give background to a passage or book of scripture, something the members would not have in such clarity in their old scriptures. This simple technique, that of realizing the power of the helps, worked mightily on the class members. As a ward, we became converted to the new scriptures more quickly than if we had not seen their beauty and power.

The work that the Prophet Joseph Smith did with the Bible, and which we now have as a powerful aid known as the JST references, was as much a part of the doctrinal restoration as was the Book of Mormon, the Doctrine and Covenants, and the Pearl of Great Price. Having the JST references in our footnotes allows us to have a theological brilliance we could not otherwise have.

The reason that I am establishing this point is perhaps there will come a time in the future when a newer set of scriptures will be produced. Instead of "JST" references in the footnote sections of our Old and New Testaments, what if there were "BPL" or "SP" references? What if the Lord granted to the prophets of the future additional helps from the "Brass Plates of Laban" or the "Sealed Portion" of the Book of Mormon, which we now do not have? Would we be first in line to purchase the new set, or would we hold on to our old set, the one we had taken on our missions and had "bronzed" for our memories? How could we be teachers in the kingdom at that time and not use the scriptures for our day, the ones giving evidence of the new materials the Lord had chosen to share with us? Would we continue to be brilliant theologically without those current helps?

Our responsibility is to study the word of God as found in the scriptures. It is to study the word of God in the scriptures prepared and approved for our use. I testify that the scriptures which we now have are a profound work, unlike any other scriptures given to a people in this dispensation.

Use the Study Aids

In 1984, five years after the new Bible came out, Elder McConkie said he received a letter from a teacher criticizing all the helps that were included. "He argued that these were crutches which kept people from that intensive study in which they would make their own cross-references. Well," emphasized Elder McConkie, "I for one need these crutches and recommend them to you." ("The Bible—A Sealed Book," p. 5.) I also think these helps are intended to keep us within the text of the scriptures, not only searching the word of God but also searching materials that will help us understand the word of God.

One of the remarkable benefits of these study aids is the extensive cross-reference system which ties us to other scriptures within the four standard works. Elder Harold B. Lee, a prophet whose ability with the scriptures was legendary, said:

> I have had a little experience reading some lessons for the various organizations. The First Presidency has a publications committee charged with the responsibility of looking over all the lessons prepared. In reading them over, I have been amazed to see how many of our writers fail to have sufficient understanding when they are making interpretations of scriptural teachings. They often fail to realize that the very interpretation that they are straining for is spelled out clearly in the Book of Mormon, the Doctrine and Covenants, the Bible, and the Pearl of Great Price. We have what no other church has: four great books, the truth of which, if we would read them all, is so clear that we need not be in error. For instance, when we want to know about the interpretation of the parable of the tares as the Lord meant it, all we have to do is read the

revelation known as the 86th section of the Doctrine and Covenants and we have the Lord's interpretation. If we want to know something as contained in the teachings of the Beatitudes or the Lord's Prayer, we can read the more correct version in Third Nephi. Many concepts that otherwise would be obscure are made clear and sure in our minds. (*Ye Are the Light of the World*, pp. 108–9.)

If we assume from Elder Lee's remarks that the scriptures are a powerful commentary on the scriptures themselves, then the cross-referencing system becomes an essential system to enlarge our study. Consider how they might help us understand a text in Numbers 21:8–9:

> And the Lord said unto Moses, Make thee a fiery serpent, and set it upon a pole: and it shall come to pass, that every one that is bitten, when he looketh upon it, shall live.
> And Moses made a serpent of brass, and put it upon a pole, and it came to pass, that if a serpent had bitten any man, when he beheld the serpent of brass, he lived.

Our key to utilizing other scriptures for commentary is found in the footnotes. The reference in 9a directs a further study to 1 Nephi 17:41 and Alma 33:18–22. In examining the Alma 33 passage, the cross-reference of 19b gives a further reference in 2 Nephi 25:20, which gives us another reference in John 3:14 and also in Helaman 8:14. This particular search of the footnotes has led us from Numbers 21, the passage of our study, to a reference help from the New Testament and four other excellent passages out of latter-day scriptures, passages which years ago in our old scriptures we would not have had but which give us enormous help with the meaning of the original passage.

Looking at just one more example, consider the verses in Doctrine and Covenants 88:96–99. Herein are recorded two groups who will be resurrected, those who are celestial, called "Christ's, the first fruits," and those who are terrestrial, called "Christ's at his coming." Those two phrases, unusual somewhat for description, show the order of the resurrections. In fact, the cross-reference in verse 98 leads us to 1 Corinthians, chapter 15, verse 23:

> For as in Adam all die, even so in Christ shall all be made alive.
> But every man in his own order: Christ the firstfruits; afterward they that are Christ's at his coming."

Section 88 helps us understand the biblical verses, giving commentary directly on the description of those who will be resurrected and in what order. Inasmuch as there was no footnote leading from the Bible to the Doctrine and Covenants, we can help ourselves by putting a note in the margin of our scriptures, causing us to see that the Doctrine and Covenants is a direct and viable commentary.

STUDY THE PROPHETS CONCERNING THE SCRIPTURES

We have in our footnotes the ability to sense how the prophets of other scriptures clarify the passages we are studying. However, another perspective helping us to use our scriptures is to find commentary from the prophets of this dispensation. As we try to hone our understanding of the gospel by using the commentaries of the prophets, we are adhering to a caution given to us by Elder Jeffrey R. Holland. While serving as the commissioner of education in 1978, he gave some poignant remarks as to our responsibility as teachers in this kingdom:

> As professional employees, we are teachers of the gospel, not preachers. "Again I say unto you, that it shall not be given to any one to go forth to preach my gospel, or to build up my Church, except he be ordained . . . " (D&C 42:11). "We believe that a man must be called of God, by prophecy, and by the laying on of hands . . . to preach the Gospel . . . " (Fifth Article of Faith). Brethren, in our classroom work we are not ordained. . . .
> With this appropriate restraint, what we then teach must be in harmony with the prophets and the holy scriptures. We are not called upon to teach exotic, titillating, or self-serving doctrines. Surely we have our educational hands full effectively communicating the most basic and fundamental principles of salvation. You will all know more than you can teach. You can hardly be called a religious educator if that is not so. Continue to study for the rest of your life, but use caution and limit your classroom instruction to what the Brethren prescribe. Listen carefully and see what they choose to

teach at general conference—and they are ordained. ("Pitfalls and Powder Sheds," p. 1.)

Since there are so many commentaries printed, so many books of potential help, let me suggest that some of the finest resources given to us as teachers in the Church are the institute student manuals designed as scripture study aids. There are two covering the Old Testament, and one each for the Book of Mormon, the Doctrine and Covenants, and the New Testament. For very little cost, the manuals present us with the scriptural references and then provide us with commentaries by leading authorities, particularly General Authorities in this dispensation. These manuals have passed an important correlation process, and they give us an opportunity to study and teach what the prophets, or "preachers," have taught. From this secure starting place, one can begin to build a library of books that would help in the study of the scriptures.

In paraphrasing the kernel of Elder Holland's caution, we might conclude that teachers teach what preachers preach—not a bad watch-phrase for ensuring safety in our teaching. We need to understand the gospel in the way that the Lord has provided, utilizing prophecy to understand prophecy, prophets to understand prophets.

As an example of this kind of help, consider a passage of scripture in Doctrine and Covenants 124:15–16. These verses record some interesting counsel given to John C. Bennett. In two brief verses the Lord mentions the word *if* three times. On one occasion President Harold B. Lee made a statement that has forever helped me to understand this *if* type of warning. He said:

> Now, just one final thought. I sat in a class in Sunday School in my own ward one day, and the teacher was the son of a patriarch. He said he used to take down the blessings of his father, and he noticed that his father gave what he called "iffy" blessings. He would give a blessing but it was predicated on "if you will not do this" or "if you will cease doing that." And he said, "I watched these men to whom my father gave the 'iffy' blessings, and I saw that many of them did not heed the warning that my father as a patriarch had given, and the blessings were never received because they did not comply."

> You know, this started me thinking. I went back into the Doctrine and Covenants and began to read the "iffy" revelations that have been given to the various brethren in the Church. If you want to have an exercise in something that will startle you, read some of the warnings that were given through the Prophet Joseph Smith to Thomas B. Marsh, Martin Harris, some of the Whitmer brothers, William E. McLellin—warnings which, had they heeded, some would not have fallen by the wayside. But because they did not heed, and they didn't clear up their lives, they fell by the wayside, and some had to be dropped from membership in the Church. (In Conference Report, October 1972, p. 130.)

Not only does a copy of this quote find its way into my filing system, but I try to make a note of it in the margin of my scriptures, so that I can remember it and can teach the principle more clearly. President Lee made another statement, on another occasion, which also helps us understand the value of the "iffy" revelation:

> What is the most important of all the commandments of the gospel? If you will think about that rather carefully and thoughtfully, you will see that the most important of all the commandments for you at this moment is the one you are having the most difficulty keeping. If it's dishonesty, that's your problem, and yours is the task to overcome dishonesty. If it's falsehood, if it's betrayal of your friends, if it's unchastity, today is the day for you to consider that as the most important of all the commandments of the gospel of Jesus Christ. And when you have successfully mastered that particular problem, then you should select the next one you are having trouble with and so on until you have conquered them all. ("A Sure Trumpet Sound," p. 78.)

These two statements by President Lee have helped me to understand a host of verses in the scriptures, and subsequently to teach them with greater clarity and purpose. Studying the prophets and what they have said about the scriptures has been joyous. Who doesn't want, for instance, to have help seeing the meaning of the scriptures? We are constantly, as teachers, reading the *Ensign* and other Church organs, reading the conference addresses and books of the prophets that will help us to teach more edifyingly. Our privilege to study their words, from a host of sources, is part of the joy surrounding our preparation.

Below is a graphic summary of the preceding points. It is important to remember that our responsibility is, first, to study the scriptural word of God; second, to find scriptural commentary helps listed in the cross-referencing and study aid segments of the scriptures; and third, to seek prophetic and inspired commentary outside the scriptures.

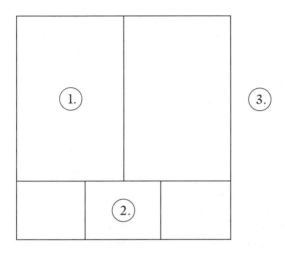

1. The scripture text
2. Other scriptures
3. Prophetic and inspired commentary

Treasure the Word

Study also requires that we meditate on and ponder the word. Such study is not always an active, "book-learning" matter. There are other elements of study which are particularly unpressured, activities that can sponsor a furtherance of the spirit of prophecy and revelation.

I have long enjoyed physical activities that keep me fit, none of which has been more rewarding than walking. Because I love to walk and study at the same time, the fitness I receive from walking is compounded by the joy of receiving inspiration and testimony from my pondering. Such feelings come from thinking about the scriptures while my mind is clearer, less harried. I have a set of scriptures that I have purposely dismantled so that I can take a few pages with me at a time. I have learned to read while I walk, to ponder and pray as I walk. I have also learned to give "great" discourses, talks, and lessons while I walk. Some of my greatest feelings associated with teaching have been on quiet country roads, even on early-morning city streets. I have had powerful flashes of inspiration, profound feelings of testimony, and great strokes of ideas.

Carrying a card and pencil whenever I walk, I am inclined to stop for a few brief seconds and jot down the ideas that come to me. Ideas which come by inspiration need to be recorded or they are easily lost. There are ideas that come about the meaning of doctrines or how to teach a particular principle. These common experiences during my "road study" are essentially a treasuring experience, calculated to keep me thrilled with being a teacher. Teaching is not simply a grind of study and preparation turned by arduous labor into a presentation. It is obviously diligent study, but it is also combined with the showering of feelings and insights, with sensations and testimony about principles and truths. This kind of treasuring is, in reality, a bonding with heaven's promises to have the spirit of prophecy and revelation, which is given every teacher who would so claim it.

Conclusion

Using the scriptures while we teach is more than just an attending behavior; it is also one of the grand secrets of how to teach the principles of the gospel. We must learn to do a concentrated study in the text of the scriptures themselves, to feast on the words of God in their pure form. We are aided immensely in our study by using the composite power contained in the scriptures published for us as a people in 1979 and 1981. We are given powerful helps by the multitude of talks and commentary that have come from the authorities of the Church. And finally, we are personally imbued with the Spirit of the Lord as we treasure the word, seeking to have the testimony and insights sufficient to teach our students.

12

Marking Scriptures: The Teaching Text

One of the attending behaviors of a good gospel teacher is to have a set of scriptures in his hand so he can teach the principles of the gospel contained therein. If his scriptures contain his notes and markings representing his learning and study, then holding the scriptures in his hand has even greater meaning. There may come a time when, with the use of laptop computers, we will study the gospel in a classroom with high-tech finesse. However, in the meantime, given what has been published for our use, we can make our scriptures a storehouse for learning.

There is much in our study that can be placed on the scriptural pages as a reminder to us. There are notes that can help make a principle clearer. There are authoritative references which, written in our own margins, are a quick resource to supply to our students. There are colors and markings to help organize the content of the records of these prophetic authors. Marking is an active study skill which, while we are learning, provides us with many clarifying ways to teach.

While my family and I lived in Indiana, where the weather in the winters was particularly cold, I purchased, with thoughts of a fireplace insert filled with blazing hot logs, a sixteen-inch gas-powered chain saw in order that I might be a firsthand woodsman. It was a wonderful activity to be out in the woods on a crisp, sunny fall afternoon, empowered with a saw which had a newly sharpened chain. The saw would effortlessly fling the cuttings into the air, bringing that fresh-cut wood smell while dividing the wood with precision. It was a manly activity and I loved it.

However, one needs to have only a few experiences with a chain that is not sharp to sense the difficulty and frustration of cutting a log when the chain is so dull it has to burn its way through the wood. Equally difficult is trying to maintain a straight cut through wood when the chain is not sharp. The frustration level is sufficient to necessitate carrying an extra chain or two, sharpened and ready to be used.

Marking our scriptures is like sharpening the chain of our scriptural teaching instrument. The power of the scriptures is made more effective when our chain is adapted for more efficient use. Having the right notes in the margins of the pages can be as wondrous as newly sawn wood. Having a system of colors which organizes the scriptural author's intent is like cutting through a log with precision.

Marking Footnote Helps

Shortly after the new scriptures were published, Dan Ludlow, who had been connected with the work of their preparation, printed a little book called *Marking the Scriptures*. One aspect of his book involved a system of coloring that can capture the power of the study helps in the footnotes. For instance, there are four kinds of language helps which could be marked—that is, the "HEB," "GR," "IE," and "OR" footnotes (check the "Explanation Concerning Abbreviations" page opposite Genesis, chapter 1). There is also the doctrinal restoration help labeled "JST" in our footnotes. Brother Ludlow suggested that the "GR" could be colored green, the "OR" orange, the "IE" yellow, the "HEB" blue, and the "JST" red. (See pp. 34–36.)

Taking these five colors in hand, one begins to read one's scriptures from the footnotes up. For instance, finding an "HEB" in the footnote, one marks the "HEB" in blue. Then he marks that same color on the corresponding superscript in the text of the scriptures. A "JST" reference is marked in red in the footnote and then again up in the text of the scriptures. Proceeding through both the Old and New Testament requires perhaps twenty to twenty-five hours of marking. However, imagine the help those markings provide for one's future study in the Bible, and especially while teaching. A glance at any verse indicates a language or a JST help below, a help that is now more easily examined in the footnotes.

JST Footnotes

The language helps are obviously important. However, they are not nearly as important as the JST helps that may add clarity to a doctrine or principle of the gospel. I have sat in a host of classes since the arrival of the new scriptures. There have been many times when a doctrine or precept has been taught incorrectly or incompletely because the teacher—and, for that matter, the students who were listening—never checked the JST reference which lay below like an uncovered treasure. Having one's JSTs marked is a way to make the teaching of the Bible precise and true. Can you imagine how paranoid you could become, having not marked the JSTs but now worrying sufficiently that there was one below that you have to look at every footnote every time you read those passages? It is simpler to pay the price, to get the chain sharp, and to more fully enjoy every future study and teaching moment.

Marking Parables and Miracles

A number of years ago, I chose a simple organization for marking miracles and parables. I placed a slanted *M* at the beginning of each miracle in the Gospel accounts. For a parable, I used a system of making an indented box within the verses, showing where a parable began and ended, and then I labeled the parable with a title.

Both of these methods are quite simple. When I open my scriptures and see these two major items organized already, it helps me to remember more quickly what I have already studied and logged on the scripture page. One can easily refer to the list of miracles and parables in the Bible Dictionary or in the New Testament institute student manual, and in only a short time the two areas can be marked.

Identifying Large Patterns

One of the important insights a teacher gains is to somehow sense the organization of the scriptural pages. The great prophetic writers—like Mormon and Moroni, for instance—spent exacting time organizing the stories and the teachings for our eternal benefit. As I study the scriptures and see the way they put the material together, and as I realize the beauty of a theme or recognize a pattern that they employed, I come to sense the great value of the work they so ardently prepared. I find myself saying, "I give you an A for that, Nephi. That was profoundly written. Not only do I recognize what you were doing, but it has also affected me wonderfully."

Doctrine and Covenants 1

Examine the first section of the Doctrine and Covenants. Besides being the Lord's preface to his revelations and being filled with important doctrines, there is a subtlety of testimony that can be picked up in that section. In verse 17 the Lord, although not in formal testifying language, indicates that Joseph Smith is his prophet. He also bears witness for the Doctrine and Covenants and the Book of Mormon in verses 24 and 29, respectively. In more formal language, his feelings for the Church are given in verse 30, and for the Doctrine and Covenants in verse 37. In verse 38, there is a subtle but sure testimony of Joseph Smith and all the prophets of this dispensation, including he who is the prophet today. Concluding the section, the Lord testifies of himself and of the record that the Spirit of the Lord bears. All in all, testimonies are given by the Lord for Joseph Smith, the Doctrine and Covenants, the Book of Mormon, the Church, the prophets, and the Godhead.

Marking these testimonies is a way to identify the pattern, a way to remember the pattern as you teach. The Lord actually exemplifies, on these pages, his commission to teach using testimony. Section 1 not only helps me to teach with testimony myself but also prepares me to rejoice in the language of the Lord when he formally bears witness of the Book of Mormon in a later section: "And as your Lord and your God liveth it is true" (D&C 17:6).

Doctrine and Covenants 20

As another illustration, notice one aspect of organizing section 20 of the Doctrine and Covenants. Inasmuch as this section is like a priesthood handbook of instructions, it is possible to mark some breakdown areas almost as if you were tabbing a larger handbook of instructions today. The markings simply allow you as a teacher to see the organization more clearly and quickly. If one would shade the following words in the following verses, then section 20 would be more easily utilized for teaching:

verse 1	Church of Christ
verse 2	Joseph Smith
verse 3	Oliver Cowdery
verse 8	Book of Mormon
verse 17	God
verse 21	Only Begotten Son
verse 26	Holy Ghost
verse 29	Repent and believe
verse 37	Manner of baptism
verse 38	Elder
verse 46	Priest's
verse 53	Teacher's
verse 57	Deacon's
verse 61	Conference
verse 63	Licenses
verse 65	Vote
verse 68	Duty of the members
verse 70	Children
verse 72	Baptism
verse 75	Bread and Wine
verse 80	Transgressing
verse 83	General Church record

It is also a helpful teaching tool to show your students the markings you have done, and to encourage them to mark similarly so that the beauty of the organization can be helpful to them as well.

Alma 37

In the same vein as section 20, but much simpler, Alma gave to his son Helaman in chapter 37 of the book of Alma five things that we'll call the "paraphernalia of a prophet." He gave to him:

in verse 2	the plates of Nephi,
in verse 3	the plates of brass,
in verse 21	the twenty-four plates,
in verse 21	the interpreters, and
in verse 38	the Liahona.

Marking or shading these five areas brings a simple organization to the chapter. Knowing that these prophetic furnishings were also given in Mosiah 1:16 (from King Benjamin to his son Mosiah) and in Mosiah 28:20 (from King Mosiah to Alma) helps us to see that Alma was transferring to Helaman the same things that had been passed on to him in the past. However, in this chapter, instead of just listing the plates and instruments, Alma gives commentary to Helaman as to the value of the plates, the interpreters, and the Liahona—powerful instructions that we can use in the classroom. Identifying the basic outline of this chapter, and marking it, helps us to teach in a clarifying manner.

1 Corinthians 12

Let's examine one more chapter for its organization. In trying to sense the outline of Paul's writings in 1 Corinthians 12, I have marked or shaded three areas: the "Spirit" in verse 7, the "body" in verse 12, and the "church" in verse 28. Under each of those headings is a listing of the different gifts, different members, and different positions or callings—which I have also marked, this time by underlining.

Paul seems to be teaching that as the Church has its different members, who will in turn have different positions and different responsibilities, so will the Spirit of the Lord be given to them as to their different needs and gifts. What a wonderful way the Lord provides for our salvation as a church!

Using Colors

A very complicated system of colors could be utilized in marking, depending on how extensively one wants to be involved in organizing the scriptures. However, as an illustration of using just a few colors, let me suggest an idea that has been of help to me in my study as a teacher.

Orange

In chapter 9 I explained how, with the aid of the scriptures on computer, I made lists of words describing teaching. Because it was such an extensive project, I felt it would be helpful to choose a color that would represent the study. Choosing the color orange, I began shading every time the word *expound,* for instance, appeared on the scriptural pages, and then methodically proceeded through my scriptures until I had marked each of the lists of each of the teaching words in orange as well. Although it was massive work to do, marking all the lists of about fifty words, the nature of teaching began to open up and the marking of these characteristics organized them for my future considerations. A whole host of teaching characteristics were recorded for me to review every time I opened my scriptures. As a full-time teacher in the Church Educational System, I found that this had proved to be most valuable.

Yellow

A second color, and really more helpful than the orange, was the use of yellow to illuminate whenever the Lord was speaking, or an angel was conversing with a prophet, or for that matter, when one prophet quoted another prophet through scripture. In other words, I tried to mark in yellow "the word of God," whether from heaven or from the scriptural record. This was another extensive project because it ran throughout the entire scriptures.

Now, imagine for a moment that your scriptures showed you this revelatory pattern. Imagine yellow marked down the marginal side of every verse in which the word of God was identified in

Abinadi's experience with King Noah. In Mosiah, chapters 11 through 16, Abinadi not only receives revelation from the Lord (which is marked in yellow) but also uses the scriptures of other prophets from which to teach (also marked in yellow). It is instructive to see the way in which Abinadi uses the scriptures for his texts, and then expounds and testifies in teaching. The following verses are marked with yellow in my scriptures:

Mosiah 11:20–25	Lord's commandments to Abinadi
Mosiah 12:1–8	Lord's commandments to Abinadi
Mosiah 12:21–24	Scriptural quote from Isaiah 52 used by the priests of King Noah to bait Abinadi
Mosiah 12:34–36	Abinadi quotes portion of Ten Commandments
Mosiah 13:12–24	Abinadi quotes rest of Ten Commandments
Mosiah 14	Abinadi quotes Isaiah 53
Mosiah 15:6	Abinadi quotes Isaiah 53:7
Mosiah 15:10	Abinadi quotes portion of Isaiah 53:8, 10
Mosiah 15:14	Abinadi paraphrases Isaiah 52:8
Mosiah 15:29–31	Abinadi reiterates Isaiah 52:8–10
Mosiah 16:1	Abinadi uses phrase from Isaiah 52:10

Using the yellow to mark the scriptural passages that Abinadi read helps me as a teacher to understand the necessity to use scriptural texts when I am teaching. It further helps me to sense the need to clarify the scriptures when teaching, as Abinadi had done. The pattern of teaching, that of using the scriptures, is quite evident when one marks his pages in this manner. Not only does it give meaning to teaching from the scriptures, but it also gives credence to the necessity for teachers to have the spirit of prophecy and revelation, as Abinadi did, in order to teach in a clarifying manner.

One interesting way to see this pattern in the New Testament is to turn to the "Quotations" entry in the Bible Dictionary. Contained are three-plus pages that include some passages in which the New Testament writers have "clearly been under the influence of the Old Testament scriptures." The process by which one could utilize this chart would be to turn to the first New Testament passage listed, that of Matthew 19:4. Marking yellow down the side of the verse and writing Genesis 1:27 in the margin would allow you to know that this particular verse is being quoted or paraphrased. Although the project of marking in yellow each of the New Testament verses which quote or paraphrase from the Old Testament is a task of some hours, the reward of seeing more clearly how our teaching mentors taught is well worth it. As one examines the completed project, specifically in the book of Hebrews, it is a little startling to see how Paul so freely quoted from the Old Testament in the first few chapters. And again, the marking technique serves to sharpen the chain, making our use of the scriptures all the more powerful.

Light Green

My absolutely favorite color, a light green, I have used to mark the nature of God. Chapter 8 in this book describes why knowing the characteristics and attributes of God is important to the message of the gospel. The Prophet Joseph Smith and others taught, as recorded in the Lectures on Faith, that we need to know not only that God exists but also the correct characteristics and attributes of God, or, in other words, his nature.

If we seek an obvious example of a prophet identifying the nature of God, it probably would be 2 Nephi 9. There are passages here in which Jacob, for emphasis' sake, started with a declarative "O." These particular verses stand out as bold testimony concerning God's nature:

verse 8:	"O the wisdom of God, his mercy and grace!"
verse 10:	"O how great the goodness of our God, who prepareth a way."
verse 13:	"O how great the plan of our God!"
verse 17:	"O the greatness and the justice of our God!"
verse 19:	"O the greatness of the mercy of our God, the Holy One of Israel!"
verse 20:	"O how great the holiness of our God! For he knoweth all things"

Words like *wisdom, mercy, grace, goodness, plan, justice, holiness,* and *knoweth* are marked in green. They help me to sense what the prophet is declaring about God and all his perfections. This process of identifying the nature of God is important to me in realizing who the God of heaven is. It is a part of what draws me to him and causes me to be faithful. We have a scriptural record which witnesses that we can trust in him and depend on him for our salvation. The light green markings become a powerful record, colored on the pages, as a testimony that Nephi and the rest of the prophets were correct; they write "to persuade [us] to come unto the God of Abraham, and the God of Isaac, and the God of Jacob, and be saved" (1 Nephi 6:4).

It should be pointed out that the scriptures contain more than bold and obvious words describing God's nature. There are many more passages in which the characteristics are subtle. Consider 2 Nephi 26:1–7.

> And after Christ shall have risen from the dead he shall show himself unto you, my children, and my beloved brethren; and the words which he shall speak unto you shall be the law which ye shall do (verse 1).

The phrase "Christ shall have risen from the dead," although not a complete subtlety, shows that God is a God of power. Continuing, the statement that "he shall show himself unto you" not only shows that he has the power to do so, but also indicates the love that God has for his children in making sure they have the needed witness of his resurrection.

> For behold, I say unto you that I have beheld that many generations shall pass away, and there shall be great wars and contentions among my people (verse 2).

The only way that Nephi can behold the future is that God, who is omniscient, allows him to see as He sees. A simple shading of the word "beheld" identifies that God is all-knowing, and furthermore it reminds me of that characteristic every time I return to my scriptures.

And after the Messiah shall come there shall be signs given unto my people of his birth, and also of his death and resurrection; and great and terrible shall that day be unto the wicked, for they shall perish; and they perish because they cast out the prophets, and the saints, and stone them, and slay them; wherefore the cry of the blood of the saints shall ascend up to God from the ground against them (verse 3).

The "signs" expressed here, to someone who is sensitive that the scriptures are a record of God, show that his work is the eternal life of man. Signs are given that man may prepare, and God is desirous that we not be caught unaware of certain great events. The word "perish" indicates that God is a God of judgment, something which will be not only "great" for the righteous, but "terrible" for the wicked. The use of the word "because" and the phrase "the cry of the blood of the saints" both show God as a God of justice, showing that matters will not be unfair but will be according to the laws of heaven.

Some of the words in the following verses of our text are italicized as if they were shaded in green. They represent the characteristics of judgment and of truth that are found in God in perfection:

Wherefore, all those who are proud, and that do wickedly, the day that cometh shall *burn* them up, *saith the Lord of Hosts,* for they shall be as *stubble.*

And they that kill the prophets, and the saints, the depths of the earth shall *swallow* them up, *saith the Lord of Hosts;* and mountains shall *cover* them, and whirlwinds shall *carry* them away, and buildings shall *fall* upon them and *crush* them to pieces and *grind* them to powder.

And they shall be *visited* with thunderings, and lightnings, and earthquakes, and all manner of destructions, for the fire of the *anger of the Lord* shall be kindled against them, and they shall be as stubble, and the day that cometh shall *consume* them, *saith the Lord of Hosts.* (Verses 4–6.)

As Nephi beheld the scenes of death and destruction, it pained his soul. Yet because he had also seen the generations of prophets preaching the truth, had seen the signs given, and had witnessed the subsequent rejection of the truth and the blood of the saints, he cried before the Lord, "*Thy ways are just*" (2 Nephi 26:7). The God of heaven, he who works for our salvation, is a God of perfect characteristics. He it is who invites us by covenant to become like him. Our desires to keep those covenants are greatly enhanced as we see the nature of God in our daily study of the scriptures. We aid our own salvation as we sense the reason for the scriptures. We aid our memories and understanding each time we return to the scriptures, especially if we have marked the nature of God in our study.

Helping Our Students Mark Their Scriptures

Knowing that the marking of our own scriptures helps us to understand the material better should serve as an impetus for us in helping our students to mark their scriptures as well. Often they do not sense in the classroom, while we are reading passages of scriptures as a part of the learning process, that certain words and phrases are as important as they are. We sense their importance because we have been earnestly studying the material and know how they fit in with a clearer understanding of the principles. We should—and this takes a little practice on our part—encourage or suggest that they "underline this phrase," or "circle that word," or "write this explanation in your margins."

We can encourage them to "mark this JST reference," or "circle that superscript in this verse, and then circle it down below in your footnotes, and underline this particular scripture reference listed there." We can suggest that they mark the following verses as a parable, or "put a slanted *M* by these verses" representing a miracle. Or we can say, "Write *BD* for Bible Dictionary, p. 740, by that verse and you will have a help for understanding that passage."

As we bring in statements from the Brethren that help us understand a passage of scripture better, we can say to our students, "Write this reference in your margin by verse 34. Write *TPJS* (for *Teachings of the Prophet Joseph Smith*), page 190. Now write very neatly this short note of explanation." The student will come to trust you as he sees the value of having marked his scriptures, of

Marking Scriptures: The Teaching Text 133

having made notes that will clarify the passages, and for having material that he can use as a student in a future class, or as one who is to give a talk or lesson.

In a videotaped presentation made in the summer of 1988, at a New Testament CES symposium, Todd Parker taught a group of his students in front of hundreds of CES teachers. As he taught he employed his normal teaching methodology, that of having the students mark their scriptures. As the presentation concluded, a review took place in which some questions were asked of the students. One particular question centered on the students' involvement in the learning process, and the question was, "To you students, there are probably a thousand teachers who think they have just watched the biggest setup in the world, you all with pencils, diligently marking your scriptures, actually looking like you are having fun doing it. Would you respond as to what Brother Parker does with you in your scriptures?"

The students responded freely and convincingly. They had experienced something in the classroom which had helped them immensely, and they were willing to express it with some conviction. Here are five such explanatory testimonies to having marked and been involved with their scriptures:

Student no. 1: "Actually we do that every day in seminary, and we mark with pens. I mean, if you want to see my scriptures for proof . . . " (At this stage they scanned the students' scriptures, showing that they had indeed been marking their pages, some with great creative flair.)

Student no. 2: "I do enjoy marking the scriptures because then I can get something in the margins I can take home with me after my seminary years are over. I like to go home in the summer and reread the book we studied in seminary, and with the markings in the scriptures it helps me to understand it better and I get more out of it."

Student no. 3: "I just want to say something about marking in the scriptures. Brother Parker has us mark all the time. I've probably worn out twelve or thirteen pens this year, and it's neat for me because when I go home, like in Sunday School last week, I had a whole bunch of answers to the lesson we were participating in and it was so fun because I knew what we were talking about. I had input and it was just from Brother Parker's class. I had all these facts and doctrine in the margins that I could relate. That's what's neat for me."

Student no. 4: "And also when we mark the scriptures, when you go home and read it just at nights and read in your scriptures, it's really nice because you remember so much more of the lesson when you have just a piece of it here. You can remember a lot more of what you learned, generally, and not just what you have written down."

Student no. 5: "He doesn't let you fall asleep in class, we're doing something . . . I fill up my margins. I never have enough space to write what he brings to us and it is helpful. It always provides insights into something. The class is not a song-and-dance routine, but it's lively, and we always have our fun to do it."

The videotape was a powerful illustration of students who enjoyed being in the scriptures, actually "hungering and thirsting" for the gospel, as President J. Reuben Clark had so indicated. These students had acquired the very "attending behaviors" of good gospel students, prepared with their scriptures, prepared with pencils and paper, and eager to transpose their learning onto their scriptural pages and into their eager hearts.

Conclusion

The scriptures have come to us at great price. The prophets have sacrificed that we may have the very documents necessary for our salvation. The scriptures will aid us commensurate with the price we have paid to understand and live the doctrines and principles of the gospel, and perhaps in some part by the way we have sharpened our chain. Marking is more than making marks. It is an active learning process to identify matters of importance and to mark and organize them. It is also a powerful teaching help to have our scriptures already marked, available to yield some of the knowledge we have gained in our study.

Not only is marking a valuable study help, it is a bonus to students. To have a teacher who has already paid a price to see the organization of the scriptures, and marked them appropriately, is to have a fountain of help as he shares it in the classroom. To have the scriptures in our hands while teaching is certainly one of the attending behaviors of a good gospel teacher, but to have them also organized, annotated, and marked is to have a profound resource, more than just an attending behavior while we teach.

13

Overviewing: Teaching the Context of the Scriptures

The scriptures contain the precepts and principles necessary for our salvation. These documents, written by the prophets whom the Lord inspired, are the very housing for transporting important principles to each successive generation. As teachers we should find ways to preserve the power of the word, to preserve the intent and purpose of the prophetic writers.

We have the opportunity to study and teach the scriptures from beginning to end. We see what principles the Lord has included in the scriptures, and also how often we ought to be teaching those principles. For instance, how often should we teach about the lost ten tribes in our classes? Well, how often is that subject contained on the scripture pages as a whole? How often should we be teaching the subjects of faith, or repentance, or covenants, or the nature of God? How often are those principles repeated for us over and over again? As we teach the scriptures as a whole, we sense the Lord's emphasis on the very principles he inspired his prophets to record.

Part of our responsibility as teachers is to regard the standard works for what they are, the very means by which we teach the everlasting gospel, the gospel that is standard in its requirements for salvation. Studying the scriptures intently causes us to be converted to those principles and to sense the power of the word ourselves. We cannot be ignorant of the context of these prophetic writers, as to why they included what they did, why they put their materials together in the manner they did. Again, as was mentioned in the last chapter, as I study and overview the organization of writers like John, Nephi, or Mormon, I often find myself basking in the beauty of their work and exclaiming, "Not only was that magnificently sculpted, but it touched my soul!"

OVERVIEWING: A PERSPECTIVE SKILL

In an effort to see this bigger picture, to sense the organization of the writers, there is a skill in the educational world known by words like *scaffolding, framework, skeleton, organizers,* and *overviewing.* Elder Boyd K. Packer, in writing of this teaching precept, said:

> I have always thought it helpful to the student to have an overview of the entire course to begin with. If he has an overview of the course or of the subject, then the teacher can go back and fill in the details and a lot more will be taught.
>
> For instance, in teaching Church history there is a great advantage in giving what might be called a "mini course" in Church history the first few class periods. In brief overview form, with a map included, the apostasy might be discussed, the restoration of the gospel, the organization of the Church, the movement of the Church from place to place, and the establishment of the Church headquarters in the Salt Lake Valley. All of that could be briefly covered as an overview of Church history.
>
> Then the teacher can start over again and go over the same material, but this time take the full time of the course to develop it. The students then know where they are going and will be collecting information along the way. The class will be much more meaningful to them. They will, in other words, have an objective in mind.
>
> There is a tendency on the part of speakers, and sometimes of teachers, to assume that since an idea is clear to them, it is clear to the audience or class. There is the tendency also to assume that the student is learning, putting each piece in place, because the teacher has a plan. (*Teach Ye Diligently,* p. 119.)

Not only is this type of preview used at the beginning of a course, but this notion of an overview is referred to *during* the course to make sure the students—and, for that matter, the teacher—

repeatedly see the context and do not miss the originator's intent. Quite often teachers, given several chapters to teach, center their attention on only a couple of verses, passages that have become important to them. When they teach those verses only, leaving the class in ignorance as to the larger context out of which those verses are formed, the students are not as prepared to use the scriptures themselves in the years to come.

As an illustration of the skill of overviewing and its potential to help us see more clearly the original writer's intent, let me tell you an experience. A number of years ago, during an Old Testament Gospel Doctrine year, I had the assignment to teach Genesis 37–50, the story of Joseph in the scriptures. I had already done a great deal of study in the text, and was nearly completed with the way I was going to teach the principles in those particular scriptures. It was Saturday afternoon and I was pondering particularly why these chapters were given to us. I decided to take out a piece of paper and list the fifty chapters of Genesis. Looking basically at what was recorded in the chapter headings, I wrote a few key words to remind me what was covered in each chapter. After lumping chapters together in a very simplified manner, I discovered the following breakdown:

2 chapters	on the Creation
1 chapter	on the Fall
2 chapters	transition from Abel to Noah
4 chapters	on Noah
2 chapters	transition from Noah to Abraham
12 chapters	on Abraham
4 chapters	on Isaac
9 chapters	on Jacob
14 chapters	on Joseph

I then jotted down on another paper a brief overview of the major gospel dispensational heads in the Old Testament so that I could see more graphically how Moses, living around 1500 B.C., had the responsibility of writing the book of Genesis, a book covering twenty-five hundred years of history. The fact that the remainder of the Old Testament books (thirty-eight in number) covered an eleven-hundred-year portion made the book of Genesis look like a unique offering.

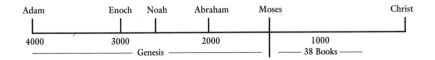

Why had Moses—who probably had many records on which to draw, who had seen the world from beginning to end—include only fifty chapters' worth for our study? And why would he include them in this particular apportionment, at least as I organized them on my study sheet? Why were there only two chapters on the Creation? Why were there twelve chapters assigned to Abraham, and fourteen assigned to Joseph alone?

Having my teaching appetite whetted, I then decided to break down the fourteen chapters of Genesis 37–50, my teaching assignment, into one more list, a list of what each of the chapters on Joseph contained:

37	Dreams of Joseph
38	Story of Tamar and Judah
39	Story of Joseph and Potiphar's wife
40–41	Dreams of butler, baker, Pharaoh
42–45	Story of brothers buying grain
46–47	The family of Jacob established in Egypt
48–49	Blessings of Jacob on his sons
50	The great prophecy of Joseph

More questions needed to be asked, simply because I began to see the context of Moses' writings in a new way. Why did Moses include a story of adultery, the story of Tamar and Judah, in the midst of telling the story of Joseph? Why is Judah's experience juxtaposed with Joseph's experience with Potiphar's wife? Why did Moses give us four chapters of an intricate story of the brothers buying grain from Joseph, when he gave us only four chapters on Noah, or four chapters on Isaac? The overviewing method led to asking questions. The potential answers caused me to prepare more deeply, to present more widely, and certainly to help the student use the overviewing skill in his own study.

Developing the Skill of Overviewing

The original writers, inspired of God as to the things they gave us scripturally, organized the material to house the precepts necessary for our salvation. As teachers who are primarily students of the gospel, we make a purposeful effort to sense the organization of the scriptures, to see the wonder of the housing, and to bask in the clarity it gives us as students in understanding and living the gospel principles.

Consider this illustration from the Book of Mormon, particularly the book of 1 Nephi. There are twenty-two chapters in the book. However, as it was originally written, the book did not have chapter or verse breakdowns. Although they were subsequently provided to aid us in our study, the making of the verses and the chapters may hinder our understanding of the context or of the bigger organizational picture.

If we examine the makeup of the twenty-two chapters, looking for specific helps from the chapter headings, and then form them into larger blocks, the book of 1 Nephi looks like this:

1   2——7   8——10   11——15   16——18   19——22

The question might be asked, why? Why this breakdown? What is there about each of these sections that would cause one to place these chapters together? Complementing our diagram with the following headings, the book of 1 Nephi begins to take on a clearer organization, not twenty-two different chapters but six subject areas. Six areas are easier for a teacher to understand than twenty-two separate chapters, and subsequently easier for the students as well.

1	2——7	8——10	11——15	16——18	19——22
Lehi's vision	Journeys in the wilderness	Lehi's dream and vision	Nephi's prophecy	Journeys continued	Nephi using Isaiah and commentary

The teacher now has a greater grasp of this particular part of the small plates on which Nephi masterfully constructed "the things which are pleasing unto God." (1 Nephi 6:5). One first begins to see the absolutely profound nature of chapter 1, viewed on its own, as a reason for the Book of Mormon, for the calling of a dispensational leader of a people of prophetic prominence. The journey chapters, 2–7 (2—into the wilderness; 3 and 4—return for the plates; and 7—return for Ishmael's family) and 16–18 (16—the Liahona; 17—building the ship; 18—crossing the ocean), are interrupted in the small plates by the record of Lehi's dream and vision, and Nephi's prophecies.

Our understanding of the flow of the book is aided when we see the "prophetic parentheses" of 1 Nephi 8–15, a demonstration of the prophetic power which undergirded this unique family in their journeys to the promised land. The concluding chapters, 19–22, show us how Nephi used Isaiah to teach us concerning the promises of the Lord, and how one prophet, filled with the spirit of prophecy and revelation himself, aids us in understanding other prophets and their writings.

Overviewing allows the teacher to more confidently approach his teaching task, sensing more clearly himself the organization that Nephi may have been giving to the book. In fact, as we continue our study into the book of 2 Nephi, analyzing and grouping the chapters, we see quite a different book presented to us by Nephi.

1——4	5	6——10	11	12————24	25————33
Lehi's blessings	N/L split	Jacob—Isaiah and commentary		Nephi using 13 chapters of Isaiah	Nephi's commentary on Isaiah

Lehi's blessings and instructions to his family, and Nephi's Psalm at the conclusion of chapter 4, are priceless in their doctrines. The Nephite and Lamanite split recorded in chapter 5 is particularly instructive for the context of the rest of the Book of Mormon. However, after examining these five chapters, thinking more in terms of a historical context, we find that the rest of the book is the recording of two monumental addresses. One is given by Jacob almost like a conference talk, and the other is a written address given by Nephi. Both of these brothers, leaders of the fold, speaking by the spirit of prophecy within them, quote extensively from the prophet Isaiah and then give commentary that enriches our understanding not only of Isaiah but also of the great doctrinal principles which will provide salvation for us.

Chapter 11 is positioned sacredly between these two addresses and becomes, in my opinion, the focal chapter in the entire book, testifying of Christ.

> And now I, Nephi, write more of the words of Isaiah, for my soul delighteth in his words. For I will liken his words unto my people, and I will send them forth unto all my children, for he verily saw my Redeemer, even as I have seen him.
>
> And my brother, Jacob, also has seen him as I have seen him; wherefore, I will send their words forth unto my children to prove unto them that my words are true. Wherefore, by the words of three, God hath said, I will establish my word. Nevertheless, God sendeth more witnesses, and he proveth all his words. (2 Nephi 11:2–3.)

Nephi, characteristic of his editing ability, organized this record as a book of witnesses, meeting the requirement of the law of witnesses, establishing the divinity of Christ as the Redeemer. Three prophets had seen Christ. Three witnesses were recorded and organized, and if a teacher in our day should so sense it, he could teach it to his students with greater clarity and witness himself. I am thankful to the prophetic writers like Nephi who wrote with such skillful organization. And I am grateful for a simple study and teaching skill that helps me to appreciate their monumental record.

Once a teacher understands by precept and experience how to overview a particular book of scripture, then given enough time and motivation, he can overview any of the scriptural books. The appendix at the end of this book contains overviewing examples for all fifteen books of the Book of Mormon. As you practice the skill yourself, you may organize the chapters in a different way than I have, but remember that the process of doing the overviewing is nearly as important as the finished product, as it is a process of assimilating the wonder of the scriptures in our own hearts.

Overviewing Chapters

A great deal of work produced the chapter headings we have in our scriptures and which overview briefly the content of the chapters. Not only can we effectively help our students by overviewing books of scripture, but it is a boon to our students when chapters are occasionally organized as a help and clarification. Moses chapter 1 is a powerful beginning to the Pearl of Great Price, and is seen more clearly when it is overviewed:

```
1————11      12————24       25————39         40——42
Vision of God  Encounter with  Vision of God,   Conclusion
and earth      Satan           earth, and other
                               worlds
```

The student, having a simple chapter organizer to help him, is made a better student. He begins to see the pages covering chapter 1 in a more distinct and organized fashion.

Consider a more complex chapter, like Moses 7, and how the same benefit is granted to a student and a teacher through overviewing:

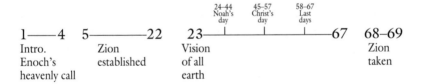

```
                                  24-44  45-57   58-67
                                  Noah's Christ's Last
                                  day    day      days
                                    |     |        |
1——4   5————————22   23———————————————————————67   68-69
Intro. Zion          Vision                        Zion
Enoch's established  of all                        taken
heavenly call        earth
```

Enoch's call is recorded, Zion is established, and a vision is had of the entire earth from beginning to end. In a world of extreme wickedness (see Moses 7:36), Enoch's record then gives us the three great periods of wickedness, three great ghettos of iniquity—Noah's day, Christ's day, and our very own "last days." As soon as one is introduced to a breakdown of the chapter, as it is graphically done above, it begins to help the student, especially in the longer chapters, in sensing the relationships of the parts.

Overviewing: A Pacing Technique

One of the purposes of overviewing is to help the teacher and the student realize the grand design of the record's organization, because out of that housing come the principles that offer salvation. Another powerful purpose is to help a teacher pace the lesson material. We have to remind ourselves as teachers that we can never teach everything. Therefore, as we are choosing what to teach as far as the doctrines and principles, we should not leave the student without the context of the whole record, which record gives birth to the specific verses and passages and principles we may be teaching that day.

A Gospel Doctrine teacher, for instance, assigned to teach during the New Testament year, and coming to those series of lessons that cover the last week of the Savior's life, puts a chart on the board overviewing the last week:

Saturday	Anointing of Jesus
Sunday	Triumphal entry
Monday	Fig tree; cleansing of temple
Tuesday	Questions and answers; confrontations
Wednesday	No record
Thursday	Passover; Gethsemane; betrayal; trials
Friday	Cross; death; burial; spirit world
Saturday	Spirit world
Sunday	Spirit world; resurrection

As the weeks progress, it is helpful for the class, which is meeting only weekly, to have a reminder of what they have covered, where they will be heading, and what their present assignment is, given the context of the "Last Week." Furthermore, as each lesson is developed by the teacher, he utilizes a brief overviewing technique and, at the beginning of class, diagrams the nature of that particular lesson. For instance, if the lesson for that week is Matthew 21–23, then the teacher visually outlines the organization of Matthew's chapters as follows:

Tuesday—Matthew 21–23

Confrontation:	"By what authority"	Chief priests and elders
	Parable: Two Sons	
	Parable: Wicked Husbandmen	
	Parable: Royal Marriage Feast	
Confrontation:	"Tribute to Caesar"	Pharisees and Herodians
Confrontation:	"Marriage"	Sadducees
Confrontation:	"The great commandment"	Pharisees

Knowing that the class period is only forty minutes in length (on a good day), and even though this particular assignment is only three chapters long (while many Gospel Doctrine assignments range much longer than that), the teacher knows that he cannot teach everything. The value of the overview is to aid the class in seeing the whole organization, knowing that they will not possibly be able to discuss all of the items listed. But particularly, the overview is to aid the teacher in trying *not* to teach everything, and *not* having to do it superficially. If every course we take in Gospel Doctrine is simply a survey course, then much will be missed.

The teacher's role, in my opinion, is to organize the scriptural material for the class, even diagramming it for clarity's sake, and then pointing out what they might be able to cover during that class period. Given our illustration, maybe all that can reasonably be taught and discussed are the first and third confrontations. The others will not be studied this particular year, nor will it be necessary to carry over the lesson for two or three weeks. However, given the overview, the teacher now begins to open the scriptures to more depth, and the student not only is given an appreciation of the overview and the context but also begins to taste the wonder of the principles delicately couched within the scriptures.

Conclusion

Overviewing is first a study skill, calculated to help the teacher, as a student, understand the scriptures better. It is also a presentation skill that the teacher uses to help the students see the organization of the scriptural record, while not having to miss the nourishment in the principles of the gospel, which principles most often take time to develop in a teaching experience.

14

Using a Graphic Focus in the Classroom

We have a responsibility as teachers to help our students better understand gospel principles, and graphics are a powerful way of increasing understanding. Whether we use pictures, objects, transparencies, or our own drawings on a chalkboard, we are incorporating a graphic focus calculated to help the students see the principle more clearly.

There are many people who have difficulty with learning that is simply verbal. I have a child, for instance, who finds it painful to follow an intricate number of directions or instructions. He can, however, act out what he sees, with great flair. He can, after watching shows about heroes and superheroes, emulate and act out their characters and roles with preciseness.

I have labored with a similar difficulty, a challenge in following a set of directions or comprehending a host of facts in a classroom. Unless there is some way of organizing those directions and facts in my mind, as we did in the last chapter on overviewing, or perhaps visualizing the entire process in my mind, as we will discuss in this chapter, then I probably will continue in my difficulty.

Such is the case with many in our classrooms. Many need visualizations to aid their learning, or graphic organizations to propel their understanding. One of the vital roles of a teacher, then, is to have not only a sensitivity to the students who need this kind of help, but also a determination to provide some graphics while teaching.

Research Studies

Research in the field of education reveals that there is an important value of pictures in the learning process. Such research helps us to see that graphics, in so many different forms, can help us to clarify our teaching message. Pictures, with text or with instructions, help all students to learn better, not just those who, like me and my son, need specific visualizations to bolster our learning.

For instance, it has been observed that pictures are "easier to remember than words" and are "more easily processed by the brain than words." Pictures have an enduring quality as well, allowing the student to remember details for years. They can be used to organize and clarify facts, and if used along with text or the spoken word, they can enhance the learning capabilities of our students. It is believed that "pictures add another dimension to learning, and that teaching people with words and pictures is the most effective way to teach certain subjects." (See Doyle and Dunnit, "More Than Just a Pretty Slide," pp. 10–16.)

Using some form of graphics along with the scriptural words, or along with instruction from the teacher, increases the ability of the students to understand, process, and remember the message. A vital dimension to learning is having graphics and words being used simultaneously. It is somewhat like the phenomenon of our ability to remember a host of words, in lyric form, when we hear a tune we haven't heard for ages. The words, which were processed years ago within the context of the music's power, are given birth again in our minds when the music is replayed. Such is the power of graphics to process the principles of the gospel, and to resurrect them at a future time with greater wholeness.

In not a few classes, instructors produce various "decorations" which, though they may be considered graphics and beautify a sterile classroom atmosphere, do nothing to enhance the understanding of the gospel message, a primary reason for teaching. And also, a host of teachers, determined to have a chalkboard in the classroom, then use it only to remind the class members of next week's reading assignment, whether it be in Gospel Doctrine, priesthood, or Relief Society. There are students who need this visualizing help.

Interestingly, a teacher who prepares graphic help for his students will often find that the very process of thinking, pondering, and creating a graphic to clarify the lesson has given him a greater understanding of, and greater energy about, the truth of the principles he is teaching. Therefore, both teacher and student benefit in the process.

Scriptural Illustrations

Dream of the Tree of Life

Consider for a moment the wondrous vision given to Lehi by way of a dream. The message of 1 Nephi 8 contains powerful principles on Christ, the word of God, and people's progression, distractions, and reactions in coming to Christ. These principles are not given to Lehi simply in words of instructions. They are given as a dream, full of visualization. This powerful graphic not only benefitted Lehi's learning but also has benefitted the whole Church. Everyone who is a member of the Church knows the dream, and everyone who relates the different dimensions of the vision can talk with greater understanding and feeling concerning the principles. All this because the principles were housed in a graphic format. The dream and the principles are more easily remembered, more easily processed and discussed in classrooms because they were given in the form of visualization.

A teacher can easily draw a visualization of the dream on the chalkboard, showing the relationship of the different elements and at the same time focusing a discussion based on the scriptural story.

As a further verification of this visualization precept, consider also the experience of the angelic tutor, three chapters later (see 1 Nephi 11), who is sent to help Nephi understand the dream. Again, rather than using only words of explanation and commentary, the angel employs a series of visualizations. In helping Nephi to understand each dimension of the dream, he grants a series of mini-visions by saying, "Look" (see verses 8, 12, 19, 24, 26, 30, 31, 32). Each time he says "Look," the vision changes, specifically illustrating and clarifying another aspect or principle of the dream.

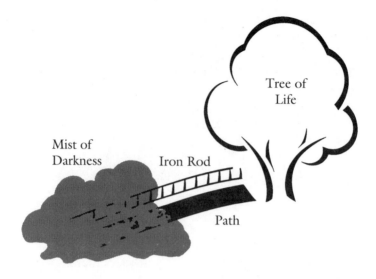

So, here we have the Lord, our preeminent teacher, granting to Lehi profound teachings wrapped in the housing of a visualization, and furthermore we have a heavenly teacher, educated in schools beyond the veil, teaching important principles to Nephi while using visions, like graphics. The principle of the condescension of God is clarified for us by a vision of the tree, the iron rod, the path, and a subsequent host of visions about the Savior's mission.

THE CHALKBOARD, KING OF THE GRAPHICS

In chapter 11 we introduced the idea of the "attending behavior" of a good gospel teacher. In one hand are his scriptures, opened and readied to aid him in the presentation of the gospel, and in the other hand, a piece of chalk, positioned eagerly to become a tool of clarification. The chalkboard is a universal instrument, as Elder Boyd K. Packer reminds us with this counsel:

> On balance I think that no teaching aid surpasses, and few equal, the chalkboard: first, because it is simple to use, and next, because it is universally available—everywhere in the world you can get a chalkboard. You can use it to focus the eyes of your students while

the main lesson is presented audibly. As you talk, you can put just enough on the board to focus their attention and give them the idea, but never so much that the visual aid itself distracts them and becomes more interesting than your lesson. (*Teach Ye Diligently*, pp. 224–25.)

Making diagrams and overviews is a demanding yet creative task for the teacher. After preparing his study on the principles of the gospel, he now begins to bring life to the principles by the way he clarifies their vibrancy and importance. Although it may take sheets of "preparation" paper in order for the right graphics to be planned, organized, and developed, there is in the mind of a "clarifying teacher" a way in which he can make this principle more plain, more clear, and, therefore, naturally more profound.

Actual Chalkboard Demonstrations

Priesthood

Teaching some of the priesthood sections of the Doctrine and Covenants (20, 84, and 107) is an exhilarating and powerful doctrinal experience. As we use a graphic or two that will help our students see the relationship of the two priesthoods, the different offices in those priesthoods, and the keys given to the presidents of the quorums, we enliven our students' understanding of those scriptural sections. Consider Elder Bruce R. McConkie's suggestion in *Mormon Doctrine* (p. 595) in which he wrote, "This principle may be diagramed by dividing a circle into segments. The priesthood is the circle; the segments of the circle are the callings or offices in the priesthood." Using that idea, we can begin our diagram by drawing two circles, and labelling them Aaronic Priesthood and Melchizedek Priesthood. After drawing the four segments of the Aaronic Priesthood and labelling the offices of deacon, teacher, priest, and bishop, we then draw the segments of the Melchizedek Priesthood with its five offices of elder, high priest, patriarch, Seventy, and Apostle.

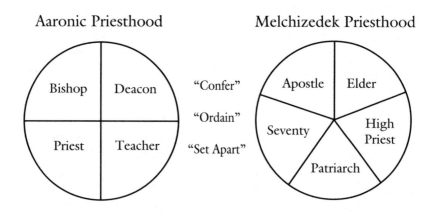

Our graphic is simply a tangible way of making the scriptural verses more workable in the minds of our students. And our students may find that as the drawing takes place on the board, they can focus better on the relationships between the two priesthoods, and can ask even better questions for clarification. As a result, the teacher can then expound more clearly on the principles. At this stage of teaching, with the graphic already displayed, a teacher may introduce a furthering principle related to the giving of the priesthood and its offices to an individual. Not only are the words *confer, ordain,* and *set apart* placed on the board, but explanations are given as well.

As a priesthood leader I have found that the using of this simple graphic, either on a chalkboard or on a piece of paper, helped other priesthood holders to see more clearly what the priesthoods are, and how they "confer" the whole priesthood on an individual, and then "ordain" them to a specific office in that priesthood, and how presidents are "set apart" in order to give them keys. In fact, there is rarely a time when I have laid my hands on an individual to grant some authority of this priesthood that I have not visually seen the two circles, and sensed the various segments and offices, and visualized the words that needed to be said. The graphic has not only served to clarify this whole priesthood process in my own mind but also been a valuable teaching demonstration.

Garden of Eden

One of the powerful doctrinal segments of the scriptures is the account of our first parents, Adam and Eve, in the garden. The doctrine of the Fall, made so clear by the surrounding doctrines of the Creation and the Atonement, is made even more clear in the classroom by a simple use of graphics to help the student understand the scriptural account. A drawing of the two trees, with Adam and Eve nearby, and a listing of the conditions of the garden make for a helpful analysis of a somewhat difficult to understand event. For emphasis' sake, given the conditions which we have listed from the writings of Joseph Fielding Smith (see *Doctrines of Salvation* 1:107), it is clarifying to label the two trees as, contrastingly, the "Tree of Life," and the "Tree of Death"; the "Tree of Immortality," and the "Tree of Mortality"; the "Tree of Innocence," and the "Tree of Knowledge of Good and Evil."

The Garden of Eden

As we list the commandments given to Adam and Eve—that is, to multiply and replenish the earth and also the "forbidding" them to eat of the tree of mortality—we sometimes feel that the Lord was giving conflicting commandments. However, by combining a graphic focus of the Fall with the following commentary by Joseph Fielding Smith, the teaching of the Fall becomes quite clear:

> Well, it wasn't a shameful fall. What did Adam do? The very thing the Lord wanted him to do, and I hate to hear anybody call it a sin, for it wasn't a sin. Did Adam sin when he partook of the forbidden fruit? I say to you, no, he did not! . . .
>
> Now this is the way I interpret that [having quoted Moses 3:16–17]. The Lord said to Adam, here is the tree of the knowledge of good and evil. *If you want to stay here* then you cannot eat of that fruit. *If you want to stay here* then I forbid you to eat it. But you may act for yourself and you may eat of it if you want to. And if you eat it you will die. . . .
>
> Mortality was created through the eating of the forbidden fruit, if you want to call it forbidden, but I think the Lord has made it clear that it was not forbidden. He merely said to Adam, *if you want to stay here* this is the situation. If so, don't eat it. (Institute address; emphasis added.)

Our ability to have a doctrinal discussion from the scriptures is aided immensely when we utilize a developing graphic on the board. A clearer understanding comes to the students who can see the differing elements of the doctrine within the context of a bigger picture. Their attention is focused more on the scriptures and the board in trying to understand the doctrine than it is on just you as the teacher.

A Scriptural Verse—Joshua 1:8

One of the powerful verses of scripture about organizing our scriptural study duties in relation to the Lord's promises of success is found in the beginning chapter of Joshua.

> This book of the law shall not depart out of thy mouth; but thou shalt meditate therein day and night, that thou mayest observe to do according to all that is written therein: for then thou shalt make thy way prosperous, and then thou shalt have good success (verse 8).

One of the key words in the passage, *then,* is a flag word showing that there is a cause-and-effect force at work within the verse. *Then* is almost an equation mark showing that the Lord's promise of success will be granted if we meet certain requirements. It could be diagrammed as follows:

Using a Graphic Focus in the Classroom 155

A +	B +	C	= ("then")	D
Book of the law	*Meditate day and night*	*Observe to do what is written*		*Success and prosperity*

Now that the graphic is on the board and we have organized a visualization from the words on the scriptural page, our teaching expands by understanding the graphic better. Questions can be asked. For instance: "Do you think that having a set of scriptures will in and of itself produce the promised blessing of success; in other words, do you think that A could equal D?" "Do you feel that if we meditated on our scriptures day and night, that the Lord would bring us success and prosperity; or, in other words, could A and B equal D?" The questions, while the graphic is in full view, help the student to sense that perhaps the prosperity from God comes when we "observe to do what is written," and nothing else.

There is another flag word in that verse that helps us understand the value of the scriptures and meditating therein day and night. The word *that,* as in "that thou mayest observe to do according to all that is written," is an indication that the A and B parts of the equation actually lead us to C; in fact, my own experience would indicate that having the scriptures and meditating on the principles therein continually is perhaps the greatest force enabling me to observe what is written therein, and therefore to receive the promises.

As we are teaching the precept taught in Joshua 1:8, the chalkboard work helps us to focus our discussion, and particularly to have a better understanding of the scripture itself and its meaning. Our principles are naturally verified and expanded as we enlarge our graphic with other scriptures, like the one in Mosiah 1:7, used to illustrate the same principles.

> And now, my sons, I would that ye should remember to search them [the scriptures] diligently, that ye may profit thereby; and I would that ye should keep the commandments of God, that ye may prosper in the land according to the promises which the Lord made unto our fathers.

A	+	B	+ ("that")	C	= ("then")	D
Book of the law		Meditate day and night		Observe to to do what is written		Success and prosperity
Scriptures		Search them diligently		Keep the commandments		Prosper in the land

This simple technique of using the board to illustrate while we use the scriptures and discuss the principles is valuable to more students than just those like me who have a need for a visual aid.

QUESTIONING: A STUDY SKILL

There is a naturalness about using the chalkboard in a classroom, almost as if the chalk were an extension of the words you speak. One doesn't have to always prepare elaborate types of drawings, as simple diagrams flow in every class period. For instance, when I teach a series of lessons about asking questions of the scriptures, I put a very basic organization on the board showing what will unfold in those two or three days.

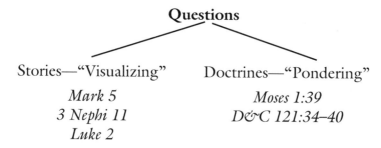

As I draw the diagram, I explain that the skill of asking questions of the scripture stories helps us to visualize those stories. I then list two or three examples of stories in the scriptures that we will examine, that will help us to learn how to ask questions better. Furthering the drawing, I explain that the asking of questions of doctrines in the scriptures helps us to ponder those principles.

After again listing two or three examples, I have completed in just a couple of minutes the overview of the skill we will be learning.

Remember, Elder Packer said: "There is a tendency on the part of speakers, and sometimes of teachers, to assume that since an idea is clear to them, it is clear to the audience or class. There is the tendency also to assume that the student is learning, putting each piece in place, because the teacher has a plan." (*Teach Ye Diligently,* p. 119.) Not only are we employing a simple overviewing skill, which we discussed in the last chapter, but we are employing a graphic skill as well. To all students, whether they have a learning deficiency in this regard or not, this ability to put a graphic on the board is a blessing, helping them to see the bigger picture, to see the organization of ideas, and to see a purpose in the things they are studying.

THE GREAT PLAN OF HAPPINESS

Probably the most important overview and graphic we can understand ourselves, and then produce for our students, is the "great plan of happiness," the plan of salvation. Elder Packer gave all CES teachers an assignment in 1993, asking that we "prepare a brief synopsis or overview of the plan of happiness." He cautioned us not to think of this as a simple assignment, and not to include too much in this overview, that it was to be designed "as a framework on which your students can organize the truths you will share with them." Using the scripture in Alma 12:32, in which it is said that "God gave unto them commandments, after having made known unto them the plan of redemption," Elder Packer emphasized:

> Young people wonder "why?"—Why are we commanded *to do* some things, and why we are commanded *not* to do other things? A knowledge of the plan of happiness, even in outline form, can give young minds a "why.". . .
> Providing your students with a collection of unrelated truths will hurt as much as it helps. Provide a basic feeling for the whole plan, even with just a few details, and it will help them ever so much more. Let them know what it's all about, then they will have the "why." (*The Great Plan of Happiness,* p. 3.)

When I served as a missionary in England in 1962, we taught a fifth discussion which was entitled "The Law of Eternal Progression," a lesson on the plan of salvation which we demonstrated from our portable, umbrella-like flannel board. It would have been extremely difficult to teach such a lesson without the ability to show the pre-existence, mortality, spirit world, judgment, to visualize the celestial, terrestrial, and telestial kingdoms.

By the same measure, over the years in a classroom, it would be equally difficult to try to teach the plan of happiness without some form of representation on the board. This kind of lesson lends itself well to a continual development where the student can see the relationship of the parts to the whole plan. As the teacher continues to add to the chart, again the focus of the student is toward the drawing, allowing him to sense the overview, to ask questions, and to make more important comments than if our discussion were simply words in the air.

The plan of happiness represented here in the accompanying graphic is in large part a synthesis of the principles from the Lectures on Faith. I will list some ideas in order of their being drawn on the board, so that you may see the development of the graphic.

1. The circles represent mortality, premortality, and the celestial, terrestrial, and telestial kingdoms. A male and a female figure are representative of all mankind.

2. A box containing the word *Faith* is drawn over a box containing the word *Knowledge*. Faith, which represents action on our parts, has to have preceding knowledge, has to have an object. Whether faith is simply a principle of action or the power of salvation depends on the knowledge base which gives it life. The knowledge of God must be within the knowledge base of anyone who desires salvation.

3. Three kinds of knowledge are important for us to receive salvation—(1) the knowledge that God exists, (2) the correct knowledge of the characteristics and attributes of God, and (3) the knowledge that one's course in life is agreeable to God (see Lecture 3).

4. The knowledge that God exists is given to us by prophets, chosen vessels who have seen God and who by "human testimony" establish a knowledge base on which we can then exercise our faith (see Lecture 2).

5. The knowledge of the correct characteristics and attributes is also given to us by the prophets, who know his nature. Lectures 3 and 4 include the following characteristics and attributes of God: that he was God before and after the Creation; that he is the same from everlasting to everlasting; that he is no respecter of persons; and that he is a God of love, knowledge, power, justice, judgment, mercy, and truth. In order to lay hold on eternal life, it is important that we know these characteristics specifically.

6. Lecture 5 is a declaration that the Father, the Son, and the Holy Ghost are one God, and that we can become like God ourselves. The context of the Lectures confirms that the oneness of the Godhead relates to the characteristics and attributes they share. They are, as a Godhead, the demonstration that salvation can happen to any of us. We can become like God, as the three of them are one.

7. The sacrifice of earthly things is the price necessary for us to know that our course in life is agreeable to God and also to have our natures changed to become like God's (see Lecture 6).

8. The pathway leading to the celestial kingdom is really a figurative progression of taking on the nature of God. The pathway is essentially covenantal, moving from the beginning covenant of baptism, to the reception of the Holy Ghost, sacrament, priesthood, endowment, and temple marriage. The Holy Ghost's function, in response to our faithfully honoring our covenants, is to change our natures by dispensing the fruits and gifts of the Spirit in our lives, which fruits and gifts are essentially the characteristics and attributes of God.

9. The promise of eternal life, exaltation, or salvation, is to be like the Father, to be assimilated into his likeness as the Son and the Holy Ghost are (see Lecture 7).

10. The great plan of happiness is precisely that, a happiness that comes from becoming like him who is a God, who is offering us everything that he has and is working to bring to pass our immortality and eternal life.

The accompanying graphic is illustrated in my own chalkboard handwriting, so that you may see the drawing as it would appear in the classroom.

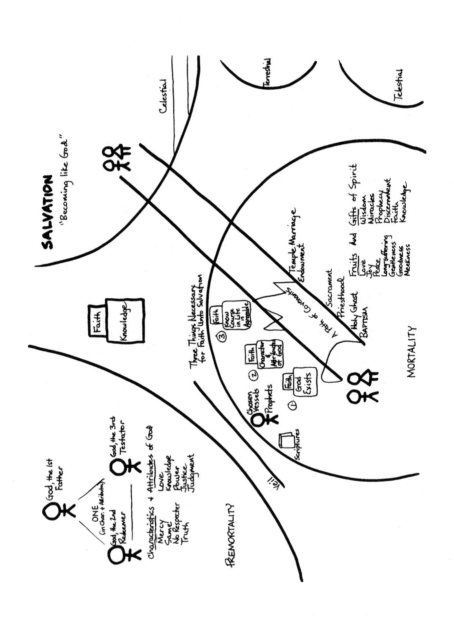

Such a diagram can foster the very understanding the student needs. The development of this overviewing plan not only aids the teacher in deeper and more joyous comprehension, but also provides for the student the same kind of awareness and excitement about the gospel principles.

Conclusion

Our philosophy is to teach the principles of the gospel out of the scriptures. Having the attending behaviors of a good gospel teacher in mind—that is, having the scriptures in one hand and a piece of chalk in the other—we are prepared to teach the principles in the most clarifying way possible.

Our preparation time as a teacher is to study the scriptures—the doctrines, principles, and stories within those records. Part of that study, a part which can make them come more alive to us, is to think through ways in which those scriptures and principles can better be visualized for the student. Knowing that the Lord and his heavenly host have taught us so profoundly in this manner is really a beginning incentive for us to do so as well. Realizing also that there are students who need such help is a complementary motivation. Spending time developing graphics not only brings the "life" of the principles to us as teachers, but also conveys to our students an understanding of the principles on a more profound level.

15

The Skill of Apperception

Clarifying the word of God for the benefit of our students is one of our chief responsibilities as teachers. This is not just a home-study church in which everyone is independently and exclusively responsible to study and research and determine the course and pathway of happiness. We are—as a church, that is—interdependent on each other to teach and to receive the word, to proclaim and to hear. According to our discussion in chapter 9, in which the method of teaching is examined, we have clarifying rights to expound, explain, unfold, liken, and give meaning to the word of God.

In developing this responsibility to clarify, it is important for a teacher to think through an educational process called apperception, defined in one dictionary as the "process of understanding something perceived in terms of previous experience." Elder Boyd K. Packer, in explaining this process, said: "This means that if we have something difficult to teach, such as honesty or reverence or love, we should begin with the experience of the student and talk about the things he already knows. Then when we make a transfer or comparison with what we want him to know, he will perceive the meaning." (*Teach Ye Diligently*, p. 20.)

Other authors in writing of this teaching opportunity describe the process as that of making "metaphors" ("Understanding a thing is to arrive at a metaphor for that thing by substituting something more familiar to us") or "analogies" ("In simple terms, analogizing means describing one thing by comparing it with something else"). (Stepich and Newby, "Analogizing as an Instructional Strategy," p. 21.)

The ability to take a subject which is new, or which may be difficult to understand, and help the student in the learning process to comprehend something better is the very nature of teaching, and forms a bond between the student and teacher. We regard the Savior as the master teacher, whose teachings of eternal life were declared in such a manner that those who cared about the gospel could understand more and, therefore, more clearly. For instance, in the account in Luke 12:22–31, a difficult principle is being taught; however, the Savior helps the learners to understand by giving two concrete, physical examples, which are flagged for our attention by the word *consider* (italicized in the following quotation).

> And he said unto his disciples, Therefore I say unto you, Take no thought for your life, what ye shall eat; neither for the body, what ye shall put on.
>
> The life is more than meat, and the body is more than raiment.
>
> *Consider* the ravens: for they neither sow nor reap; which neither have storehouse nor barn; and God feedeth them: how much more are ye better than the fowls?
>
> And which of you with taking thought can add to his stature one cubit?
>
> If ye then be not able to do that thing which is least, why take ye thought for the rest?
>
> *Consider* the lilies how they grow: they toil not, they spin not; and yet I say unto you, that Solomon in all his glory was not arrayed like one of these.
>
> If then God so clothe the grass, which is today in the field, and tomorrow is cast into the oven; how much more will he provide for you, if ye are not of little faith? [JST]
>
> Therefore, seek not what ye shall eat, or what ye shall drink, neither be ye of doubtful mind. [JST]
>
> For all these things do the nations of the world seek after: and your Father knoweth that ye have need of these things.
>
> And ye are sent unto them to be their ministers, and the laborer is worthy of his hire; for the law saith, That a man shall not muzzle the ox that treadeth the corn. [JST]

Therefore seek ye to bring forth the kingdom of God, and all these things shall be added unto you. [JST]

The principle of depending on the Lord, a requirement placed on all of us but specifically placed on those who were sent to preach the gospel in the beginning of that dispensation, was made clearer to them by the analogies of the ravens and the lilies. The fact that the Savior used those examples apperceptively that is, used something "perceived in terms of previous experience," or substituted "something more familiar," or described "one thing by comparing it with something else"—allowed his disciples to better comprehend the message. Those examples, tangible and real to the learners, helped them understand a principle of dependence that was intangible and abstract.

The Formula for Apperception

Some of the finest instructions on apperception we can read are found in Elder Packer's book *Teach Ye Diligently,* not only the three or four chapters defining and working the process, but the multitude of examples that Elder Packer uses throughout the book showing how he has employed the skill in his talks.

> There is a practical way in which faith or any other intangible ideal can be transposed into something tangible and teachable. In fact, there is a formula we can use. This procedure can help teachers, especially teachers of religion, immeasurably. It can also help parents in teaching some difficult things to children.
>
> At first the formula may seem too simple to be useful. But as we study it a bit and begin to experiment with it, we find it very useful.
>
> I remind you that this method of teaching comes from the New Testament. And I remind you also that Jesus as a teacher taught unlettered audiences about the invisible, intangible ideals of the gospel. In teaching faith and love and brotherhood and repentance, he employed the technique of likening the intangible, invisible ideal to a well-known, ordinary object about which His disciples already knew. That is known as apperception, and here is the formula:
>
> _____ is like _____

(pp. 28–29.)

The Skill of Apperception

In order to help you see the profound nature of this teaching process, let me list several of the subject areas which Elder Packer has addressed over the years, showing you also the way in which apperception was used to clarify the message. Although the simple listing of the subject and the use of apperception will not help you to see the beauty of the method, yet it will begin to help you understand the process of how a teacher comes to use this likening technique.

The gospel	is like	a piano keyboard
Power of creation	is like	a light that kindles other lights
The mind	is like	a stage (with good and bad actors)
Repentance	is like	soap
Resurrection	is like	a glove
Atonement	is like	the creditor and the debtor
Emotional welfare	is like	Church's welfare system and "order of help"
Spiritual danger	is like	crocodiles

Elder Packer is a master teacher himself, not only in the way he proclaims the truths of the gospel and bears his witness, but also by the way he helps his students throughout the Church to understand with greater clarity the gospel message. Let us venture into the thinking process that produced one of the uses of apperception, again from his book *Teach Ye Diligently:*

> On one occasion in general conference I wanted to talk on the subject "The Only True and Living Church" and use as the basic text Doctrine and Covenants 1:30.
>
> And also those to whom these commandments were given, might have power to lay the foundation of this church, and to bring it forth out of obscurity and out of darkness, the only true and living church upon the face of the whole earth, with which I, the Lord, am well pleased, speaking unto the church collectively and not individually.
>
> I did not want to say that all of the other churches were without truth, for they have some truth—some of them a great deal of it. They have a form of godliness. Often the clergy and adherents are

not without dedication, and many of them practice remarkably well the virtues of Christianity. They are, nonetheless, incomplete, and the Lord has declared: "They teach for doctrines the commandments of men, having a form of godliness, but deny the power thereof." (Joseph Smith—History 1:19.)

How could I get the idea across that all churches perhaps have an element of the truth, but there is only one with the fulness of the gospel?

In using the formula for *likening*, I determined that the gospel is like a piano keyboard. After finding something with which to compare the gospel, something that would be familiar to everyone who would be listening, it was much easier to prepare the talk, part of which I quote:

"The gospel might be *likened* to the keyboard of a piano. A full keyboard with a selection of keys on which one trained can play a variety without limits—a ballad to express love, a march to rally, a melody to soothe, and a hymn to inspire—an endless variety to suit every mood and satisfy every need.

"How shortsighted it is, then, to choose a single key and endlessly tap out the monotony of a single note, or even two or three notes, when the full keyboard of limitless harmony can be played.

"How disappointing when the fulness of the gospel, the whole keyboard, is here upon the earth, that many churches tap on a single key. The note they stress may be essential to a complete harmony of religious experience, but it is, nonetheless, not all there; it isn't the fulness.

"For instance, one taps on the key of faith-healing, to the neglect of many principles that would bring greater strength to faith-healing itself.

"Another taps on an obscure key relating to the observance of the Sabbath—a key that would sound different indeed, played in harmony with the essential notes on the keyboard. A key used like that can get completely out of tune.

"Another repeats endlessly the key that relates to the mode of baptism and taps one or two other keys as though there were not a full keyboard. And again, the very key they use, necessary as it is, just doesn't sound complete when played alone to the neglect of the others.

"There are other examples, many of them, in which parts of the gospel are endlessly stressed and the churches build upon them, until alone they sound nothing like they would if blended with the full measure of the gospel of Jesus Christ.

"We don't say that the key of faith-healing, for example, is not essential. We not only recognize it, but we also rely on it and experience it; however, it alone is not the gospel, nor its fulness." (Pp. 41–43.)

The process of apperception follows an order; that is, we first study the principles and doctrines of the gospel of Jesus Christ out of the scriptures. After the study of the principles, then, and only then, do we begin to look for a way to clarify the word. We are not simply collectors of ways to use apperception, amassing object lessons so that we can somehow work them into the lessons that we are teaching. It is not to say that we can't use an analogy for more than one occasion, and have it prepared to be used again, but it is to say that the subject matter needs to be studied and analyzed first, so that the principles which we are trying to clarify actually drive our search to find something familiar to our students from which the lesson will be benefitted.

Again, this process, if approached in the right order, may receive the assistance of heaven by giving us the very analogy that we need. The example of Lehi teaching about the house of Israel and being given the analogy of the olive tree by the Spirit of the Lord, which very use of apperception helped to clarify it, illustrates how we may be aided in this aspect of our teaching (see 1 Nephi 10:12, 15:12). As a second witness, sense the experience of Elder Packer when wanting to give a difficult message to the young people of the Church.

> On one occasion I wanted to explain the resurrection and was having considerable difficulty in doing so. I pondered on it for a time, and then one day as I was putting on a glove, it occurred to me that the glove would make a good visual aid. I used it a few times in talking to young people and finally felt confident enough to employ it in a general conference sermon.
>
> After some practicing, I prepared the talk, in which I likened the physical body to a glove and the hand to a spirit. It was my intention to talk to the five-year-olds and the six-year-olds and the seven-year-olds, knowing full well that if I was successful in teaching them, I would not lose any member of the audience in the older age groups. (*Teach Ye Diligently*, p. 230.)

I can only surmise that the illustration of the glove was an aid from heaven, given to one who cared enough to study and know the principles, given to one who wanted the youth of the Church to clearly understand the message, and given to one who patiently and sufficiently pondered the principles so that ideas would come to his teaching heart. The Holy Ghost is needed as we study the scriptures, needed not only to give us the insights and testimony of the principles but also to help us apperceptively clarify the gospel message.

Appreciation of Apperception

Not only did the Savior give a multitude of parables which make use of apperception, analogies, and metaphors, but the process has been explored by many who are attempting to help us understand different principles of the gospel better. Consider another example of someone from the ranks of the General Authorities who applied the skill of apperception for our benefit, Elder James E. Talmage:

The Parable of the Grateful Cat

A certain English student of Natural History, as I have heard, once upon a time had the experience described below.

Mr. Romanes, in the course of his customary daily walk, came to a mill-pond. At the edge of the water he saw two boys with a basket. They were obviously engaged in a diverting occupation. As he came up to them Mr. Romanes observed that the youths were well dressed and evidently somewhat refined and cultured. Inquiry elicited the fact that they were upper servants in a family of wealth and social quality. In the basket were three whining kittens; two others were drowning in the pond; and the mother cat was running about on the bank, rampant in her distress.

To the naturalist's inquiry the boys responded with a straightforward statement, respectfully addressed. They said their mistress had instructed them to drown the kittens, as she wanted no other cat than the old one about the house. The mother cat, as the boys explained, was the lady's particular pet. Mr. Romanes assured the boys that he was a personal friend of their employer, and that he would be responsible for any apparent dereliction in their obedience to the orders of their mistress. He gave the boys a shilling apiece, and took the three living kittens in charge. The two in the pond had already sunk to their doom.

The mother cat evinced more than the measure of intelligence usually attributed to the animal world. She recognized the man as the deliverer of her three children, who but for him would have been drowned. As he carried the kittens she trotted along—sometimes following, sometimes alongside, occasionally rubbing against him with grateful yet mournful purrs. At his home Mr. Romanes provided the kittens with comfortable quarters, and left the mother cat in joyful content. She seemed to have forgotten the death of the two in her joy over the rescue of the three.

Next day, the gentleman was seated in his parlor on the ground floor, in the midst of a notable company. Many people had gathered to do honor to the distinguished naturalist. The cat came in. In her mouth she carried a large, fat mouse, not dead but still feebly struggling under the pains of torturous capture. She laid her panting and well-nigh expiring prey at the feet of the man who had saved her kittens.

At this stage in the parable—which makes use of apperception, engaging us to consider to what this naturalist and the cat are "likened"—discussion can ensue to help the students articulate some of the relationships and likenings they see. Interestingly, I have yet to be in a classroom, during this preliminary part of the discussion, where someone has made the full connection between the mouse and our tithes and our offerings, which are as totally unnecessary to the Lord as the mouse was to the naturalist. So often we think that the giving of our money is the superlative and supreme gift. How powerfully this parable establishes in our minds the context of our tithes and the Lord's graciousness in even accepting them as our sacrifice. The parable continues:

> What think you of the offering and of the purpose that prompted the act? A live mouse, fleshy and fat! Within the cat's power of possible estimation and judgment it was a superlative gift. To her limited understanding no rational creature could feel otherwise than pleased over the present of a meaty mouse. Every sensible cat would be ravenously joyful with such an offering. Beings unable to appreciate a mouse for a meal were unknown to the cat.
>
> Are not our offerings to the Lord—our tithes and our other

free-will gifts—as thoroughly unnecessary to His needs as was the mouse to the scientist? But remember that the grateful and sacrificing nature of the cat was enlarged, and in a measure sanctified, by her offering.

Thanks be to God that He gauges the offerings and sacrifices of His children by the standard of their physical ability and honest intent rather than by the gradation of His exalted station. Verily He is God with us; and He both understands and accepts our motives and righteous desires. Our need to serve God is incalculably greater than His need for our service. (*The Parables of James E. Talmage*, pp. 37–39.)

This parable is included, not only that you would sense the beauty of the principle in a likened fashion, but somehow to help you sense the nature of apperception, so that you may try this method yourselves.

Having looked at examples of apperception—first from the Savior, and then from Elders Packer and Talmage, each of them developing an extended use of apperception to be the focus or basis of an address—let us consider another master teacher, Elder Neal A. Maxwell, whose style is to include a host of smaller or briefer examples of apperception throughout an address. For instance, in a talk given in the October 1974 general conference, Elder Maxwell made use of apperception in several places throughout the talk, four of which are given here and are emphasized in bold print:

> I should like to speak of and to a particular group of important individuals. These are they who fully intend, someday, to begin to believe and/or to be active in the Church. But not yet! These are not bad individuals, but good individuals who simply do not know how much better they could be. Such individuals often stay proximate to—but do not participate fully in—the Church. **They will not come inside the chapel, but neither do they leave its porch.** . . .
>
> There are reasons for your commitment to be made now, for as the rush of hours, days, and months grows stronger, the will to commit grows weaker. . . .
>
> If, however, you really do not wish to commit *now*, then let me warn of the following: . . .
>
> Do not reflect on the practicality of gospel standards such as abstaining from alcohol; for if you do, **a surf of statistics will wash**

over you, confirming that abstinence is ultimately the only cure for alcoholism that is both preventive and redemptive. You will also see that the living of one protective principle of the gospel is better than a thousand compensatory governmental programs—which programs are, so often, **like "straightening deck chairs on the Titanic.".** . . .

Do not overpack the luggage you plan to take with you when you leave this world, for we simply cannot get most mortal things by **celestial customs;** only the eternal things are portable. . . .

Do not, if you have been offended, recall that while you may have been **bumped by an ecclesiastical elbow, the chip was on your shoulder** long before the elbow appeared. (In Conference Report, October 1974, pp. 14–15.)

Talks by Elder Maxwell are usually laced with these pearls of understanding, which extend the message into our hearts with creativity and insight. Not only do they awaken our minds, but they are very easily called forth in the weeks and years to come. They form a bond with the principle, allowing us to contemplate their meaning perhaps longer and deeper than in ordinary language constructions. Therefore, whether we are utilizing an extended example of apperception that wondrously fills the measure of our lesson, or are using a host of smaller instances of apperception, short and breathtaking, the result is that in the learning of the gospel, using the right kinds of apperception helps the process of teaching.

For emphasis' sake, it is important to remember that we study the gospel message first; then we perhaps search for a use of apperception that will help in the delivery of that message. This process, though exciting when we find appropriate examples of apperception, is a patient, pondering process in which we seek the Lord's help with the likening and clarifying aspects of our lesson as we have already and diligently sought his help in the study and understanding part of our study preparations.

THE LIAHONA AND APPERCEPTION

In the mid-1980s, just a few years after the new editions of the scriptures were introduced to the membership of the Church, it seemed that many of the Saints had a partial difficulty giving up their old scriptures and purchasing a new Bible and triple combination. Three different grades of scriptures were being offered for purchase, starting with the most basic set, which oftentimes was referred to as the "seminary edition." The other two grades accelerated not only in quality but also naturally in price. Although this most economical edition was essentially within the reach of everyone, yet many hesitated, wanting their initial purchase to be the higher quality scriptures, all the while missing out on the beauties of these new treasures of the "words of life."

Sensing this difficulty, and pondering how I could convey this in the most delicate and insightful way, one day for an institute class I devised a presentation that made use of apperception. I hoped it would portray to the students a need to get the most economical scriptures in their hands so that they could be used, and then perhaps later, if necessary, they could purchase the higher quality editions.

Taking an idea from an article on the scriptures in the *Church News*, I altered it so it appeared to be an article about the Liahona. I read it in class with an air of officiality. The statement was as follows:

> The miraculous director, the Liahona, which Joseph Smith in D&C 17 was promised, has been in the care of the succeeding Presidents of the Church since the beginning of this dispensation. As it did with Lehi, the Liahona has served each Prophet as an instrument for revelation.
>
> The President of the Quorum of the Twelve then spoke on how the Brethren had been preparing, over the last several years, to make available for the general Church population the purchasing of liahonas for personal and family use.

An expression of surprise began to develop on some faces, yet not wanting to allow too much time for reaction, I suggested that the most recent Church distribution catalog listed the liahonas that could be purchased. I quickly put the ordering number on the board, and then listed the three styles of liahonas, with the accompanying description of each:

PSI005236

Style A	Style B	Style C
Deluxe	Standard	Economy
20" diameter	12" diameter	3" diameter
Hand-polished brass	Brass, dull finish	Styrofoam, painted brass
Spindles, pointers Pure brass	Spindles, pointers Rugged aluminum	Spindles, pointers High-impact plastic
$1255	$450	$13

Most of those in the class were smiling, some even enjoying it sufficiently to chuckle righteously. They had seen beyond the use of apperception and understood as did Alma when, in Alma 37, he handed over the prophetic instruments to his son Helaman. He told him that the Liahona, "this compass, which would point unto them a straight course to the promised land," was simply a "type" of the "word of Christ, which will point to you a straight course to eternal bliss." The scriptures are in reality a "compass" to us in this day, "prepared" by the Lord, working "according to [our] faith in God," producing a "miracle . . . by the power of God, day by day." (See verses 38–47.)

The point had been made. The Liahona of Lehi's day was no different an instrument than the scriptures for our day. The miracle of the scriptures is that the writing on them, similar to the writing on the Liahona, changes from day to day as we read from day to day, and that by giving heed and diligence to the words, they point us toward the promised land of eternal life. Again, one of the simpler points being made was that even if we could purchase liahonas, the three-inch-diameter, brass-painted styrofoam ball, with high-impact plastic spindles and pointers, which only cost $13—that is, the "seminary edition" of liahonas—would still work, would still give us the course directions for our lives. We needed to get on with the use of the new scriptures, and the "seminary editions" of these new scriptures, which at the time cost only $13, contained the very words of eternal life.

Besides being able to make the point by means of apperception, which perhaps helped to convey a somewhat difficult message, it was important for me as a teacher to experiment with the process of apperception—that is, to sense that something needed to be taught, and to prepare an idea that connected it in a way to help the student. Now, obviously my use of apperception in connection with the Liahona was not of the same caliber as Elder Packer's "keyboard" or Elder Talmage's "grateful cat," but each represents an effort to try to help someone understand the gospel principles better, to help make the living of the gospel more sure, or to help the student see a little more clearly. We do have a responsibility to clarify the gospel message, and apperception is a way of thinking that may produce that clarity.

Conclusion: A Masterpiece of Apperception

In 1978 I listened to a general conference address by Elder Bruce R. McConkie. This talk about the Apostasy and the Restoration thrilled me to the core of my soul. In fact, when the talk was finally printed in the *Ensign,* having been so moved by the beauty of its organization, so moved by the principles of the Restoration detailed in it, and so moved by the language which was used to express it, I went to a place in the house where I could be alone, could read it aloud, could take those very words in my own mouth and declare them. The profound nature of the talk was rooted in a giant use of apperception. I will quote the first six paragraphs, which establish not only a night of darkness but the dawning of a new day:

> "*The morning breaks; the shadows flee;*
> *Lo, Zion's standard is unfurled!* . . .
> *The dawning of a brighter day*
> *Majestic rises on the world.*"
> (*Hymns,* no. 269.)

When the sun goes down and the dusk of day deepens into night, then darkness reigns. During the night, darkness is everywhere and the vision of all is dimmed; none can see afar off. Though the heavens teem with stars—an uncounted host of them—and though the moon—she who rules the night—reflects her rays of borrowed light, yet the darkness is not pierced; the blackness of the night continues.

Deep shadows hide the beasts of forest and field. Wildcats stalk their prey in silence. Packs of hunger-maddened wolves strike terror in their victims as their howling calls draw nearer and nearer. Coyotes are baying in the distance; somewhere a lion roars; and in that deepest shadow a jackal lurks, awaiting his chance to steal the slain game of another. The terrors of the night are real.

But finally a distant dawn is heralded. The morning stars shine forth more brightly than their fellows. A few rays of light part the darkness of the eastern sky, a sky still spotted with clouds. Beyond the mountains, not many leagues away, a new day is gestating in the womb of nature. As the earth turns slowly on its decreed course, the dawn brightens; the light of the morning increases; darkness flees. The stars no longer shine; the moon hides her face; their reflected glimmerings no longer pierce the blackness of the night. The sun rises. The blazing light of heaven covers the earth.

When the dawn comes and the sun shines, the doleful creatures of the night begin to retire. The lions return to their lair and the foxes to their holes; the baying of the coyotes is no longer heard; and the howling wolves are silent. The terrors that lurked in the shadows are now hidden in the rocks and in the caves.

With the new dawn the flowers in the field and the trees in the forest take on new life. The oxen in their stalls and the sheep in their cotes awake from sleep, while the fowls of heaven sing praises to the Lord of Sabaoth, to the Creator of the first day. The blessings of life and light are everywhere seen. It is a new day—a day of joy and rejoicing and light. ("'The Morning Breaks; the Shadows Flee,'" p. 12.)

Having established a mental picture of the darkness of night and the hope of a new day, an experience familiar to all of us, Elder McConkie began to overlay his use of apperception with a description of the long, dark night of apostasy, a night in which the truths of Christ's own dispensation had been lost because of the setting of the gospel sun, a night in which the only light of evening were the stars and the moon representing good people's wisdom, a night in which the jackals and lions and the beasts of hell represented all the apostate creeds, pagan influences, inquisitional tragedies, and wars, plagues, and immorality of these dark ages.

As the night of darkness ceased and the morning stars emerged, so it was that the noble stars of reformational status and the stars of constitutional America emerged to foster the dawning of a new day, in which the preparation of a boy prophet, the distillation of angelic hosts, the uncovering of a treasured book, and the restoration of the gospel principles and covenants produced the gospel sun.

Elder McConkie put eloquent touches to the conclusion of his talk by quoting again the sacred verse of hymn from which he had started, but this time there came a more powerful sense to his delivery, a feeling made more sacred by the profound nature of his use of apperception.

> *"The morning breaks; the shadows flee;*
> *Lo, Zion's standard is unfurled! . . .*
> *The dawning of a brighter day*
> *Majestic rises on the world."*

I love to be a member of the Church, one who has a testimony of the Restoration, a testimony of God once again and clearly in my soul. How I love to be a student of one whose testimony I can feel, whose love of teaching has produced a way to communicate this gospel message into language of compelling means, a language that by way of apperception can drive the message into my mind and my heart.

16

Using Stories to Verify the Scriptures

Stories are an essential ingredient in our teaching philosophy. First of all, scriptural stories house the very precepts necessary for our salvation and are "standard works," conveying the message of an everlasting gospel to each succeeding dispensation. Second, stories outside the realm of the scriptures are clarifying teaching helps for the following four reasons, which are developed in this chapter:

1. Stories house precepts of salvation.
2. Stories of our day verify the stories of earlier dispensations, establishing that God is no respecter of persons.
3. Stories help us to "see" and "feel" the principles and doctrines of the gospel.
4. Stories are a technique of apperception which liken the principles of the gospel to experiences already familiar to us.

Stories House Precepts

William J. Bennett, former U.S. secretary of education, stated in a 1987 article that Americans want their schools to teach thinking, counting, speaking, and writing, and they also want them to help our students develop a moral education. Bennett's premise is that we already have the resources at hand with which to accomplish this purpose. He mentioned several principles of morality—honesty, kindness, faithfulness, and so on—and gave examples of stories from literature and history that illustrate these principles. He concluded: "There are good reasons why we should teach these and other familiar accounts of virtue and vice. First, these stories interest children. Nothing on TV or elsewhere has improved on a good story that begins: 'Once upon a time . . . ' Second, these stories give children specific, common reference points for what is right and wrong. Third, these stories help anchor our children in our culture, its history and traditions. In this way, we can welcome them to a common world and to the continuing task of preserving the principles, ideals and notions of greatness we hold dear." ("What We Must Teach Our Children," pp. 101–2.)

Bennett's recommendation coincides with the premise of this chapter, that stories contain the housing for the precepts that could foster a moral education in the youth of our communities. The use of stories from great literature can establish profound values, but when we use the greatest of literature—that is, the scriptures—we are helped as parents, as Church members, and as teachers to preserve the precepts, the principles, and the values of the gospel of Jesus Christ for the coming generations.

Stories Verify Stories

Elder Bruce R. McConkie, one who always utilized the scriptures in his teaching, offered confirmation as to our need of the scriptural stories, and also as to the use of stories from our own day to confirm the scriptural record. The law of witnesses, the way and the means by which we verify a truth, is also important in the telling of stories. A modern-day story not only can verify the scriptural record but can also act on our students by giving them time for the principle to spiritually register on their souls.

> We have in the Church an untapped, almost unknown, treasury of inspiring and faith-promoting stories. They are the best of their kind and there are thousands of them.
> One reason they are the best and most inspiring faith-promoting stories is because they were selected and edited by the Lord him-

self. They are the ones he had his prophets choose and place in the holy scriptures so that we would have samples before us of how to act and what to do in all the circumstances that confront us in life.

They are stories of real people who faced real problems and who solved them in a way that was pleasing to the Lord. They have been preserved for us so that we will know how to act and what to do in all the affairs of our daily lives. . . .

There is, of course, nothing wrong with telling a modern faith-promoting story, one that has happened in our dispensation, one that occurred in the lives of living people whom we know, whose voice we can hear, and whose spirit we can feel. Indeed, this should be encouraged to the full. We should make every effort to show that the same things are happening in the lives of the Saints today as transpired among the faithful of old. Unless our religion is a living thing that changes the lives of people in whose nostrils the breath of life is now inhaled, it has no saving power.

Unless we enjoy the same gifts and work the same miracles that marked the lives of those who have gone before, we are not the Lord's people. The Lord our King is the same yesterday, today, and forever. A soul is just as precious in his sight now as it ever was. He is no respecter of persons, and anytime any of us exercise the same faith that moved the ancients in their pursuit of righteousness, we will enjoy the same gifts and blessings that attended their ministries. . . .

Perhaps the perfect pattern in presenting faith-promoting stories is to teach what is found in the scriptures and then to put a seal of living reality upon it by telling a similar and equivalent thing that has happened in our dispensation and to our people and—most ideally—to us as individuals. ("The How and Why of Faith-promoting Stories," pp. 4, 5.)

It is interesting to consider that stories of our day confirm the stories of the scriptures; and furthermore, these stories can confirm to our students truths about the nature of God—that he is a being who is no respecter of persons, a being who is the same yesterday, today, and forever. As this insight becomes a part of my teaching philosophy, for instance, then I am "driven" to use stories, for the right reasons. Stories, therefore, can be used to show principles, and can be used to verify other stories by a law of witnesses.

Stories: Seeing and Feeling

Some years ago, in a CES setting, Elder Henry B. Eyring instructed teachers on the value of stories. He quoted an instruction from President David O. McKay, a profound teacher in his own right. Within the context of Doctrine and Covenants 88:77, in which the Lord commands us to "teach ye diligently," President McKay said:

> The great obligation upon a teacher is to be prepared to teach. A teacher cannot teach others that which he himself does not know. He cannot make his students feel what he does not feel himself. He cannot attempt to lead a young man or young woman to obtain a testimony of the gospel of God if the teacher does not have that testimony himself or herself.
>
> There are three things which must guide all teachers: first, get into the subject; second, get that subject into you; third, try to lead your pupils to get the subject into them—not pouring it into them, but leading them to see what you see, to know what you know, to feel what you feel. ("'That You May Instruct More Perfectly,'" p. 557.)

Elder Eyring, taking this excellent teaching quote, had us imagine climbing a steep mountain. As the climber nears the top but is still precariously perched on the side of the mountain, a rope is lowered to assist him to the peak. The rope represents the very doctrines and principles of the gospel that save us, and is, in terms of President McKay's statement, the "know what you know" part of teaching. These saving principles are contained in the scriptures. Elder Eyring then emphasized that "seeing" the object of our ascent and "feeling" that we can actually use the rope and climb to the top are best communicated to our students by stories. The doctrines are there to save us, but the experiences of others, translated into stories, often help us commit to actually live the principles. (See *The Power of Stories in Teaching the Gospel*.)

As an example, I have been married for thirty years, have a family, and have studied the scriptures and the prophets concerning the patriarchal responsibilities that are mine. However, I am often guilty of doing less than I know. A little book written by George Durrant called *Love at Home—Starring Father*, has been a great help to me by illustrating some principles in story form that have helped me to "see" and to "feel" what I "know" I should do. For instance:

> My own father had a hard time saying "I love you." As a matter of fact, I do not recall that I ever heard him say that to anyone. He was good to me and because of all that he did for me I was very suspicious that he loved me; I really knew he did, but he never would say it.
>
> He had been a miner in the silver mines and later he became a poultryman. He was a rough outdoorsman and had expertise in hunting and fishing. He was really a man's man and to me he was a great father. But he never said, "George, I love you." One day he did come close to telling me he loved me.
>
> I was about to depart on my mission to England. I was nearly twenty-two years old. (They didn't go at age nineteen then.) It was in the middle of November and there was snow on the ground. I was to depart in three days. Since I was the youngest of nine children, when I departed all the children would be gone from home. My father must have felt a bit saddened by this. He and I were alone in our big kitchen where we seemed to live our lives (seldom did we go in the front room). He stood looking out the window that was the upper portion of our back door. He suddenly said, "George, come over here." I went to his side and looked out. About a hundred yards beyond our barn was a thicket of brush and trees. There in the snow on the edge of the brush was a beautiful Chinese pheasant. My father spoke again, "George, get the gun."
>
> I replied, "Dad, the season ended over a week ago."
>
> I'll never forget what he said next because it was the most loving thing he ever spoke to me. He said, "I know that. You go get the gun and go out there and shoot that pheasant. And while you're doing it, I'll call the cops and they'll come and arrest you and you won't have to go."
>
> I was by this time much taller than he. I looked down at him and he looked away. I put my hand on his shoulder and then pulled him close to me. Together we cried. My dad, my dear dad, had for the first time said in the best words he could muster, and in the best way he knew how, what I had longed to hear for twenty-two years. He had said, "George, my son, I love you."
>
> It means so much to our children to hear "I love you" from their dads. They don't need to hear it every minute, but they ought to hear it a little more often than once every twenty-two years. We can say "I love you" in a number of ways. When Dwight was six

years old, I took him from Salt Lake City to Provo one day. While I worked at BYU he played with friends in the neighborhood where we had once lived. At the day's end I picked him up and we drove toward home. We stopped for a snack; we took our order from the cafe and walked about twenty-five yards to the bank of the Provo River. There, sitting on a log, we ate. I looked at the river and then at Crow on the opposite end of the log.

I spoke, "I've got a better hamburger than you."
He answered, "Mine's just like yours."
I added, "My milkshake is better than yours."
He replied, "Mine's the same flavor as yours."
"My fries are better," I said.
"I've got ones just like yours," he replied convincingly.
After a pause I looked at him and said, "I've got one thing that you haven't got."
He was certain that I didn't have and asked with a challenge, "What?"
"I've got a son that I call Crow. And I'm sitting on a log with him and I love him with all my heart. And you don't have that."
Crow didn't answer. He just looked at me for a few seconds, then bit into his hamburger and with his other hand threw a rock in the river. I had bested him and he knew it. (Pp. 71–73.)

There is something about this story, and I have read it a host of times over the years, that has helped me to be more expressive to my children, even though I've "known" that I should be. In fact, there is a multitude of stories that I have read from other people's experiences which form in me an ability to see the principles more clearly, and to feel that I could be similarly faithful or diligent, or whatever feeling that would be necessary to live that principle they were teaching. I believe what Elder Eyring has explained, that one of the great values of using stories is to help a person "see what you see" and "feel what you feel." Finding these kinds of stories that produce a way to communicate a feeling about a gospel principle is not only a spiritual boon to me, but it constantly has an effect in the lessons I'm teaching.

A Story "Is Like" a Principle

Just as the teaching method of apperception allows teachers to take an object, a tangible something, and use it to describe an intangible gospel principle, so it is that a story, an actual tangible experience, helps us to sense a principle more clearly. Stories can help a student view a principle clothed in the physical makeup of someone's experience. Again, as was mentioned in the last chapter, the very nature of Paul's treatise on faith in chapter 11 of Hebrews was to first define faith, an intangible principle, and then to illustrate the principle of faith through the lives of the people he subsequently mentioned. In fact, Paul used nineteen specific people, in the form of tangible human examples, to illustrate the principle of faith. In a like manner, Elder Boyd K. Packer, in a general conference address, utilized a story of a handcart group crossing the plains to illustrate a principle about missionary work.

> In the late 1850s many converts from Europe were struggling to reach the Great Salt Lake Valley. Many were too poor to afford the open and the covered wagons and had to walk, pushing their meager belongings in handcarts. Some of the most touching and tragic moments in the history of the Church accompanied these handcart pioneers.
> One such company was commanded by a Brother McArthur. Archer Walters, an English convert who was with the company, recorded in his diary under July 2, 1856, this sentence:
> "Brother Parker's little boy, age six, was lost, and the father went back to hunt him." (LeRoy R. Hafen and Ann W. Hafen, *Handcarts to Zion,* Pioneers Ed. Glendale, California, The Arthur H. Clark Co., 1960, p. 61.)
> The boy, Arthur, was next youngest of four children of Robert and Ann Parker. Three days earlier the company had hurriedly made camp in the face of a sudden thunderstorm. It was then the boy was missed. The parents had thought him to be playing along the way with the other children.
> Someone remembered earlier in the day, when they had stopped, that they had seen the little boy settle down to rest under the shade of some brush.
> Now most of you have little children and you know how quickly a tired little six-year-old could fall asleep on a sultry summer day and how soundly he could sleep, so that even the noise of the camp moving on might not awaken him.
> For two days the company remained, and all of the men searched for him. Then on July 2, with no alternative, the company was ordered west.

Robert Parker, as the diary records, went back alone to search once more for his little son. As he was leaving camp, his wife pinned a bright shawl about his shoulders with words such as these:

"If you find him dead, wrap him in the shawl to bury him. If you find him alive, you could use this as a flag to signal us."

She, with the other little children, took the handcart and struggled along with the company.

Out on the trail each night Ann Parker kept watch. At sundown on July 5, as they were watching, they saw a figure approaching from the east! Then, in the rays of the setting sun, she saw the glimmer of the bright red shawl.

One of the diaries records: "Ann Parker fell in a pitiful heap upon the sand, and that night, for the first time in six nights, she slept."

Under July 5, Brother Walters recorded:

"Brother Parker came into camp with a little boy that had been lost. Great joy through the camp. The mother's joy I cannot describe." (Hafen and Hafen, *Handcarts to Zion*, p. 61.)

We do not know all of the details. A nameless woodsman—I've often wondered how unlikely it was that a woodsman should be there—found the little boy and described him as being sick with illness and with terror, and he cared for him until his father found him.

So here a story, commonplace in its day, ends—except for a question. How would you, in Ann Parker's place, feel toward the nameless woodsman had he saved your little son? Would there be any end to your gratitude?

To sense this is to feel something of the gratitude our Father must feel toward any of us who saves one of his children. (In Conference Report, October 1974, p. 128.)

This story houses a vital principle relating to missionary work. The saving work of the woodsman and the subsequent gratitude of the child's mother "is like" the work we do in teaching and loving the children of God, and his profound gratitude which spills over into our own salvation as well. This story somehow helps us to "see and feel" more poignantly, motivating us to do what we already "know" we should do.

There are powerful stories, simple stories throughout the Church—or, for that matter, the history of the Church—with which we could "clothe" a principle that will help in our teaching.

These stories are found everywhere in our reading; if we are teachers and have already studied the scriptures and are familiar with the principles we will be teaching, then our reading of newspapers, magazines, and books can help us discover a host of stories that will house the principles we are to teach. Preparation, therefore, is more than just studying the specific lesson we are to deliver; it is done in a general and global way by living, learning, reading, and applying what we are experiencing to the lessons we are teaching.

USING OUR OWN EXPERIENCES

There are also simple and important stories from our own experiences which can be used to illustrate our teaching. Let me capture from my own life an experience that houses a principle, and which allows me, at least, to "see" or to "feel" more deeply this intangible precept relating to missionary work.

While our family was living in Seattle and I was serving as a high councilor, I had as part of that assignment the advising of one of the wards in the stake. Although it was a small ward, particularly in the Young Men and Young Women organizations, there was, nonetheless, an energetic group of adult leaders who worked marvelous things with the youth. Inasmuch as I was also serving as the stake Young Men president, there was a profound interest on my part concerning the productivity of this little group. One Sunday the Young Women president invited me to attend a ward activity that was being sponsored by the youth, an event for which these young people had labored intensively. The program was to be held on the following Wednesday, starting at 6:52 P.M. The time intrigued me, but more than that, I just knew I needed to be there as a high councilor, eager and complimentary.

Arriving in my official high council suit, I entered the foyer with the rest of the ward members. We were instructed to sign our names and register ourselves for the event; I didn't have a clue as to its nature. Directed to enter the chapel I noticed that over the door casing was a sign which read, "Premortal Existence," but since I had come that night to be an "observer," and not a "participant," the wheels of my understanding essentially fell off.

Therefore, I quickly moved inside the chapel and took a seat on the back row where I could watch the actions of the youth, and the adults and children who were participating from the ward. At the pulpit were five or six people who were dressed in white, but again, because I was so motivated to be a nonparticipant, I left that initial meeting clueless as to the purpose of the evening.

When the group was dismissed to go downstairs into the cultural hall, a place that was designated as mortality, I was the first person to exit the chapel and the first person to step on the floor of the hall. It was simply amazing. The youth had erected a host of booths around the outside wall of the cultural hall and in the middle of the floor were a number of tables containing all sorts of competitive games, board games as well as a Ping-Pong table and a foosball table. Assuming a position on the floor, I watched the people descend the steps and become participants themselves.

Almost before I could be much of an observer, a ward member greeted me and told me how pleased he was that someone from the stake would come to their ward activity. He also asked me if I would play a game of Ping-Pong with a young man who somehow was already standing by himself at the table with no competitor. I really wanted to watch, but probably because of my love for the game, and the sight of this poor kid standing there alone, I began to play, all the while trying to observe as much as possible. Concluding the games and resuming my observing posture near the middle of the floor, I was again approached by the same ward member to see if I would play a game of foosball, again, interestingly enough, with another lonely and forlorn teenager. After doing that for a few minutes, and winning, I was approached by a woman with a roll of tickets who asked if I had won that game and, for that matter, any previous games that I had played. When I admitted humbly that I had, she reeled off some points with the flair of an amusement park attendant.

Standing now with tickets in hand, I was approached by another ward member who gently asked if I would consider participating in some of the booths that ringed the hall. He pointed specifically to the fishing pond booth and then over to the apple bobbing booth. The first seemed a little juvenile for me that night, especially since I didn't have any of my own children with me. The second one was simply outrageous. I told him, jokingly, that I was a high councilor, dressed in a suit, and I wasn't going to stick my "fool head" in a bucket of water for the entire ward to see. Quietly walking away, he left me to my watching.

Next, a woman approached me, offering a plate of cookies. As I reached for one, she reminded me that I had to purchase them with tickets I had earned. So . . . I traded tickets for cookies, and ate to my heart's content, all the while observing and enjoying the actions of the youth of this ward of whom I was becoming more and more proud.

In an increased state of casualness, and looking around the room, I noticed that one of the booths had no one participating, it being an arm wrestling booth. Perhaps the image of the Scoutmaster, 230 pounds of stature, standing behind the table was enough to ward off any contenders. Nonetheless, at his side, and terribly small by comparison, stood his fourteen-year-old son. As I approached the booth, I asked somewhat facetiously if I could choose whom I would arm wrestle. Learning that it was my choice was the only initiative I needed to engage this boy's arm in the grip and quickly slam it to the table. Proud of how slyly I had queried, acted, and conquered, I asked how many points I had won, inasmuch as I was fresh out of cookies. "None," was the reply, and I walked ignorantly away from the table, again without any understanding of the purpose of the evening.

As I resumed my observing role once again, something happened in that next moment that not only changed the nature of the evening for me but also profoundly affected my whole perspective on missionary work. A woman tapped me on the shoulder and said, "Brother Wilson!" As I turned to acknowledge her statement, she looked me seriously in the eyes and said, "You're dead!" Standing next to her were two individuals wearing warped smiles of chagrin, as if somehow they had recently been given the same message and were now following her to a new destination. Now, I don't know how quickly the mind really works, but in what seemed like a nanosecond I began for the first time to understand what had been taking place that night.

The booths around the hall represented rather important things that needed to be experienced while we are in mortality. For instance, the fishing pond booth had represented missionary work, the apple bobbing booth had represented baptism, and the arm wrestling booth had represented the trials of life. The first individual who had approached me upon my stepping on the cultural hall floor was a man designated as Satan, whose role it had been to keep me occupied in the center of the floor, engaged in activities of no eternal consequence. The other ward member, who gave encouragement to become involved with baptism and missionary work, was playing the role of the Holy Ghost. And so, I had come into mortality that night, accepted the promptings of a man who represented Satan himself, rejected the enticing of one designated as the Holy Ghost, and enlisted all my efforts in useless acts of observing, playing, and eating.

Having a new and profound awareness, I noticed quickly as we were led to the Relief Society room that the sign over the door casing was indeed the "Spirit World." This time, the room's purpose and my role in that purpose were abundantly clear. A powerful sight awaited us as the door was gently opened. Crepe paper hung from the ceiling like a room divider, separating paradise and hell. On the paradise side, the people dressed in white were ministering to those who had been so fortunate as to have entered there. But, on the hell side—and this was the side to which my chagrined cohorts and I were assigned—there were just a few people. They were sitting on small Primary chairs, and from their obviously uncomfortable and embarrassed positions, they took great delight in welcoming any others who had likewise been caught unawares. Their glee was particularly effusive concerning the stake visitor, especially a nonparticipating high councilor, in a suit, who wouldn't consider getting his "fool head" wet. As I sat there, in that part of the room in which the lights had been dimmed, listening to the joy coming from the other side of the gulf, I was more than embarrassed. I began to be deeply contemplative.

The door occasionally opened allowing a woman to announce that temple work in mortality had been accomplished. As people stood whose names were read, they proceeded to the other side of the room, wonderfully received. Perhaps it had been planned for the sake of an uninvolved high councilor, but as everyone else was released from imprisonment, and I sat there alone, I felt as if I were in hell itself, wondering if work would ever be done for me.

Not too many moments later, the lights in the whole building flickered, indicating that mortality—and, for that matter, the spirit world—was over. Walking down the hallways from the cultural hall and Relief Society room, the whole ward converged at the same table at which we had registered earlier, producing for the judges who sat there the fruits of our mortal labors. While some were producing certificates and tickets, I was embarrassed by the fact that I not only had been dismally ignorant of the evening's purpose but also had "eaten" any evidence that I had even been in mortality. We filed into the chapel, sitting according to our celestial, terrestrial, or telestial rewards. As I sat during this concluding meeting, again I was oblivious to what was being said, but this time my thoughts were absolutely captured on ideas and feelings that I had never before experienced.

I was nearly the first person out of the chapel that night, and the drive home was sufficiently contemplative for my wife to notice that something disturbing had happened to me. I could hardly put into words the newness of this feeling, having been a member of the Church all my life, having never had a Protestant or Catholic thought that I had owned. And yet, during that evening I had entered mortal life as an observer, had misunderstood the whole purpose of existence, had played the games of life, and had traded the rewards of temporality for the food of temporality. I had listened to "Satan," resisted the enticing of the "Holy Ghost," and had missed the gospel, the principles, and the entire meaning of the plan of happiness. I had lived that entire existence completely stupid as to its purpose, and—I had never felt that thought with such profound feeling.

The next Sunday was a natural opportunity for me to express compliments for an outstanding ward activity; however, they would never fully understand what that one experience accomplished in the core of my soul as to the reasons for preaching the gospel to our neighbors. I have on occasion used this story with Latter-day Saints who already "know" the commission given us to proclaim the gospel. However, a story like this, or the story of Elder Packer's, can help us to "see" and "feel" more clearly what the principle of missionary work is "like." Furthermore, it may be helpful for some of these personal experiences to be written and preserved so that we don't simply rely on our memories to call them forth.

Conclusion

Listening to a teacher use a story leads me to ask, What is your teaching philosophy that allows you to tell this story? For some it may be employing a change of pace, or utilizing an entertainment technique, or simply a measure to ensure a more secure popularity. However, stories are more than just important; they enhance our teaching of the principles of the gospel from the scriptures. Therefore, consider the following principles relating to the use of stories in teaching.

1. Stories house precepts and principles.
2. Scripture stories particularly house the precepts and the principles of the gospel.
3. Teaching scripture stories helps the principles of the gospel to be fostered in future generations of students.
4. Modern-day stories not only house principles as well, but they verify the scriptural stories, showing that God is no respecter of persons and is the same yesterday, today, and forever.
5. Scriptural stories and modern-day stories form a law of witnesses in establishing the truth of the principles of the gospel.
6. Stories can help the students in "seeing" and "feeling" the principles we are teaching, thereby helping them to actually live the principles.
7. Using stories for the right reasons and motivation surely increases the attendance of the Spirit of the Lord, which Spirit is promised to all those who teach in the way the Lord has commissioned.

I testify that teaching the principles of the gospel out of the context of the scriptural stories and verifying them by the use of stories from our own day and dispensation is a powerful way to help our students trust in the God of heaven and desire to live the gospel. I personally verify that the stories and experiences of Abraham and Joseph, the experiences of Joseph Smith and Gordon B. Hinckley help me to see the gospel principles more clearly, to want to live the gospel more fervently, and to take what I know of our theology and become more faithful.

17

Filing: Establishing a Scriptural Treasure

Filing is a skill, a technique that needs to be developed. It is even a necessity in supporting a teacher in the work he is trying to accomplish. Building a system will bring order to the knowledge he is gaining about the principles and about the scriptures. The more a teacher collects materials, the more important it is to organize those materials, because order, not confusion, must reign.

This skill of filing will be the teacher's constant support, a constant sustaining influence in his teaching, as it was for Elder Bennion in this story:

> We could well be more like Elder Adam S. Bennion, a late member of the Council of Twelve, who could be prepared in just five minutes to give a talk on almost any subject. As his secretary for a few months prior to my marriage, I repeatedly saw this great man select several items from his files, spend a few minutes arranging them, jot down some notes, and be ready with another inspirational talk. It took about five minutes' preparation—plus fifty years of wise filing! (Daryl V. Hoole, "How I Stopped Accumulating and Started Filing in Four Easy Steps," p. 42.)

This is not to suggest that lesson preparation is a five-minute task, no matter how many years of filing; it is to say that an appropriate filing system can be a powerful resource in the preparation of lessons. Those who have learned the value of filing have first learned the value of reading, studying, marking, clipping, copying, and taking the materials of study and making them ready for teaching.

For instance, consider comments by Sterling W. Sill which first reveal the necessity of underlining and marking the things we read, and then organizing those readings:

> I always read with my pen, marking every idea, every phrase, every quote, and every other thing that I think will help me. And then I put these thoughts into my notebooks. One of my most valuable possessions in the world is my collection of twenty-five notebooks. They are just regular 8 ½-by-11-inch page size, three-ring binders with about three hundred pages in each one, so I have seventy-five hundred pages of notes. I think of my reading as a combine harvester sweeping across a field of wheat. It cuts everything before it but throws out the weeds and the chaff and the straw and puts the wheat in the sack. ("Your Four Great Days," p. 44.)

A Box

A starting point for filing may be as simple as gathering what you already have into one spot. Elder Boyd K. Packer, in an article encouraging the members of the Church to get started on genealogy, suggested that we start with ourselves, with the records that would sustain our own life history. Beginning a filing system for teaching materials can be as simple as this:

> Get a cardboard box. Any kind of a box will do. Put it some place where it is in the way, perhaps on the couch or on the counter in the kitchen—anywhere where it cannot go unnoticed. Then, over a period of a few weeks, collect and put into the box every record of your life. . . . Collect . . . everything that you can find pertaining to *your* life. . . .
>
> Don't try to do this in a day. Take your time with it. Most of us have these things scattered around here and there. Some of them are in a box in the garage under that stack of newspapers; other are stored away in drawers or in the attic or one place or another. . . .
>
> Gather all of these together; put them in the box. Keep it there until you have collected everything you think you have. Then make some space on a table, or even on the floor, and sort out all that you have collected. ("Someone Up There Loves You," p. 10.)

I think Elder Packer felt that in this elemental step of faith, the Spirit of Elijah would descend on our efforts, encouraging us to continue in this work, eventually organizing our family history, being more diligent about journal keeping, seeking out the names of our kindred dead, and securing the ordinances for those of our family we have begun to know and understand better. As Alma proclaimed to his son Helaman, "By small and simple things are great things brought to pass" (Alma 37:6), so is the beginning of genealogy brought to pass by something so simple as a cardboard box.

By the same measure, but in the spirit of teaching, a box could be labeled "our filing box," placing it also in the path of our daily labors, finding materials we have collected from our studies in years past, materials which have settled into unusual places in our homes. Like the Spirit of Elijah that permeates the great genealogical work, there may be a Spirit of Mormon or Moroni, the great record keepers, which will descend upon us, causing us to feel the joy of collecting records that will benefit mankind in the teaching years to come.

When Mormon was compiling (see Words of Mormon 1:3, 4), he said, "I searched among the records which had been delivered into my hands, and I found these plates [speaking of the small plates of Nephi]. . . . And the things which are upon these plates pleasing me," he included them for our good. So it is with us as teachers. We search among our "records"—that is, the things we are reading, the things written to help us understand the scriptures and the principles of the gospel—and finding them pleasing unto us, we include them in our filing system. The lessons we are then preparing or that we will prepare for years to come will be constantly benefitted.

Doing Something

The main object in beginning a filing system is to do something, anything, just something that resembles filing. Perhaps you secure a few file folders, and then decide what to put on the tab of each. It may be that as soon as you've labeled ten or twenty of the folders, you decide it isn't what you want to do. That's fine. You'll probably never get the perfect filing system. Never, ever, will it be just the way you want it. Therefore, get started, do something, and in doing something a development will take place, a refinement of the system will happen that may lead to another system, and another, and another. The process may be more important than any specific product.

Once even an elementary file system is in order, you will become a different student and teacher of the gospel. Having a repository for your material, just having it there, will be an impetus or an attraction for you to continue to read, to mark, to study, to copy, and to file, and also to prepare and teach.

I like what Cecil Clark said in his book *Teaching Like the Master*. He mentions a precept closely akin to the simplicity that Elder Packer suggested with his genealogy box:

> The simplest filing system of all is a large cardboard box sitting obtrusively on your desk. A noteworthy article is thrown into the box, as is a book with paper-clipped sections, a 3" x 5" card with a quote on it, and a photocopied story—anything and everything is found in your storage bin.
>
> At least you know where everything is! As you periodically rummage through the box in search of that certain story, you are actually reviewing the contents of the box. You read one quote then another, refresh your memory of an illustration, or come across a story long forgotten. Reviewing your notes places the information in your long term memory. Then when you are preparing a particular lesson, that quote read over several times in the past now jumps out at you. (P. 76.)

Numerical Filing System

After materials have been collected in "the box," you might consider three different ways for filing: a numerical system, a topical system, and a sequential system. The first, and perhaps the simplest, would be the numerical system. When any article, quote, or paper is found that is considered worthy of filing, then copy and number the article. The first article is number 1, the second number 2, and so on up to 100, 1000, or even 100,000. Each article is given an ascending number, and one of the great advantages of the system is that only one copy is made and filed appropriately.

Retrieving the article, on the other hand, requires a further system of organization. In the beginning of filing, it is possible to essentially remember what you store, or to quickly review a contents page listing the titles of each of the articles. However, as you file more and more articles, a better retrieval system must be found. Some use a 3 x 5 or 4 x 6 card box, topically or sequentially organized so that the articles are found quickly, again, without having to read through every article or even a summary sheet with each of the titles listed.

For instance, if one files a talk given by Elder Bruce R. McConkie called "Christ and the Creation" and the number is 423, then a card under the heading of "Creation" is retrieved from the 4 x 6 card box, and on the card it is noted that Elder McConkie's talk is number 423 in the file system. On that same card may be articles 23, 85, and 129, all of which were collected and filed previously to help understand different aspects of the Creation. Perhaps 423 is also noted on a card entitled "Christ," or "Earth"; or if your card box is not topically organized but sequentially organized as to the books of the scriptures, perhaps it is placed on a card entitled "Genesis 1, 2," or "Moses 2, 3," or "Abraham 4, 5," representing the books and chapters of scriptures that regard the creation of the earth.

The numerical system is easy because each article is numbered as it is found and, again, only one article is collected. As the number of articles expands, so does the need to have an organized retrieval system in order to make the filing beneficial to you. One caution would be that since only one article is filed, then when it is used in a classroom setting, it is imperative that the article be placed back into the filing system, an after-lesson discipline that is often tough to develop or to maintain.

Topical Filing System

A number of topical systems could be organized. However, one of the easiest is to go to your Topical Guide and Bible Dictionary, surveying these two areas for the major topics you want to have categorized in your system. Topics cover a range of doctrines (like creation, fall, and atonement) and a host of ethics (like kindness, courtesy, and friendship).

Utilizing a topical system perhaps requires that an article needs to be copied many times and then placed in all the different categories in which it could be used for study and teaching. The realistic humorist who said that filing was simply a way of systematically losing something is speaking some truth. We have to be careful where we file something, because if it doesn't make sense in three months, or in two years from now, we will have "systematically" lost it.

Sequential Filing System

Inasmuch as we are a church studying the scriptures on a four-year rotation basis, a system identifying the books of scripture is very useful. A beginning point is to secure file folders sufficient in number to cover the four standard works, 226 folders:

39 folders	Old Testament
27 folders	New Testament
15 folders	Book of Mormon
5 folders	Pearl of Great Price
140 folders	Doctrine and Covenants, plus two Official Declarations

As you find articles, place them in the areas that will help you teach the specific chapters and books of the scriptures. For instance, in an excellent article printed in the *Ensign,* September 1990, Elder M. Russell Ballard addressed the subject of Church disciplinary councils. The article, "A Chance to Start Over," is concerned with informal and formal Church discipline, the makeup and possible action of disciplinary councils, and the restoration of blessings. It is a profoundly informative and instructive article which I placed easily in my D&C 102 folder, which section contains instruction as to what we used to call a high council court, or stake president's disciplinary council, as it is so named today. It can also be placed in D&C 20, in which verse 80 states that "any member of the church of Christ transgressing, or being overtaken in a fault, shall be dealt with as the scriptures direct." It can also be filed in Mosiah 26, Alma's great cry before the Lord regarding how to handle transgressors; or in Moroni 6, where the basic elements of Church court discipline are recorded in the Nephite Church; or in Alma chapters 30 and 42, in which principles of justice and mercy are discussed.

A Story File

There is an element of the talk given by Elder Ballard, discussed in chapter 16 on stories, which helps us to "see" and "feel" the doctrine in a way that clarifies the scriptural and ecclesiastical matters covering Church discipline. I've included one such story, the story of a man having his blessings restored:

> Some time ago I was asked by the First Presidency to stop and visit a man on my way to a stake conference. This man had been excommunicated, had fully repented, and had been found worthy to be baptized. But baptism did not restore his priesthood and temple blessings. That was my assignment, acting on behalf of the Lord at the direction of the President of the Church.
>
> I found the man lying in a hospital suffering from a disease that left him unable to move or speak. On seeing him, I realized that it would be impossible to conduct the customary interview. Instead, I felt impressed that I should interview his wife, who was there with him. We found a vacant room in the hospital, and I had a wonderful visit with this stalwart woman, the mother of eight. She had stood by her husband, remaining true and faithful through all his struggle and difficulty. Now she, like her husband, greatly desired that he have his blessings restored.
>
> As we walked back into the husband's room, I asked his wife to help me communicate with him. During the two years that his body had deteriorated from disease, he had developed a way to communicate with his eyes. I leaned over his bed and said, "I am Elder Ballard. I have been sent here by the President of the Church. I am authorized to restore your blessings. Would you like that?" I quickly saw I wouldn't need the help of his wife. Tears filled his eyes and ran down his cheeks in affirmative response.
>
> I placed my hands on his head and, using terminology associated with this ordinance, restored to him the Melchizedek Priesthood.
>
> He sobbed—perhaps the first sounds he had made in some time. I restored his office in the priesthood. Then I restored to him, by the power of the priesthood, the holy endowment that he had

received when he went through the temple for the first time. Last, I restored what was perhaps most valuable to him—his sealings to his wife and children.

As the blessing concluded we were all filled with emotion. I looked at his wife and had the impression that I was to bless her also. I said, "Sister, would you like us to give you a blessing?"

She said, "Oh, I would love a blessing, Brother Ballard. I have not had a blessing in a long time."

I asked her to sit down; then the regional representative, the stake president, and I placed our hands on her head. But when I tried to bless her, the words would not come. We took our hands off her head and I said, "Brethren, let's move her chair closer to the bed." We pushed her chair over where I could lift her husband's hand and place it on her head, since he was unable to lift it himself. As we proceeded again with the blessing, the words flowed. Blessings were given; conviction and comfort came. ("A Chance to Start Over," pp. 12, 14.)

Not only would this story, included in Elder Ballard's talk, be filed in the places that I've already mentioned, but this story, on its own merit, might also be filed in a separate "story file." A host of stories which have affected our understanding of the gospel or of the scriptures can be retained and used in clarifying the doctrines we teach. Again, it is one thing to include it in a filing system, but it is quite another to draw it out at the appropriate time for preparation and teaching. Some system of retrieval must be attached to our story file as well.

Filing Examples

Let me use two more examples of filing articles that have meaning for my teaching. I read a book in which the following tender little story affected me. Imagine where you might use it.

Article 1: "Baa-aa"

A little girl so tiny that we could barely see the top of her ponytails over the pulpit told the story in a sacrament meeting. Her mother knelt by her side and coached her gently as she talked. She said, "There was once a shepherd who had a hundred sheep. He loved his sheep, so he counted them every day. One day he counted: '. . .

ninety-seven, ninety-eight, ninety-nine.' A little sheep was lost. The shepherd went to find him. The little sheep was far off in the rocks and bushes. He was frightened and lonely. The shepherd called 'Little she-eep . . . ?' The little sheep heard him and was glad. He said, 'Baa-aa.' The shepherd came and found the little sheep. He picked him up and carried him on his shoulder back to his mommy. Then he counted again: '. . . ninety-eight, ninety-nine, one hundred.' All the sheep were safely home." (Bruce C. Hafen, *The Broken Heart*, p. 38.)

As I read this story, I marked it and then copied it—because it spoke to my soul; it was something I treasured in an instant, and I wanted to use it somewhere in my teaching. In my sequential filing system which reflects my scriptural treasure, it would naturally be filed under Luke 15, the context of the little girl's talk on the parable of the lost sheep, or perhaps under John 10 concerning the Good Shepherd, or even in Ezekiel 34, a chapter showing contrasting shepherds, some who feed themselves and some who care ultimately for the sheep. If I were to file it in my topical filing system, I might place this precious story under "Home and Visiting Teaching" (being true undershepherds), "Missionary Work," "Service," or "Love." This story not only touched my feelings but also caused me to copy and file it as a resource for future lesson presentations.

Article 2: "They Were Awesome"

As the President of the Young Men of the Church, I delight in the story of a fine deacons quorum presidency who sensed the importance of their office in teaching their fellow quorum members.

On a recent Sunday, Mark was ordained a deacon.

When his family returned from Church, the telephone rang. It was the deacons quorum president asking for an appointment for the presidency to visit with Mark and his parents. The appointment was set for Tuesday night at 7:30 P.M. Promptly at 7:30 on Tuesday, the doorbell rang. The members of the presidency stood on the porch, dressed in suits, white shirts, and ties, each one carrying his scriptures.

Sitting down with Mark and his parents, they began with prayer, then handed an agenda to everyone there.

The quorum president then opened the scriptures, having Mark and his father read those references which speak of the power of the Aaronic Priesthood, what it is, and the particular duties of a deacon.

He then spoke about Mark's specific responsibilities and duties, explaining how he should dress as he performed his priesthood duties, where he should be to pass the sacrament, and his duties as a messenger for the bishop. He acquainted Mark with fast offering collection procedures and assured him that a counselor in the presidency would accompany him the first time. Then he asked Mark if he had any questions about his new calling.

At the end of the visit, the deacons presidency welcomed Mark into the quorum and offered help whenever he needed it. As they left, Mark's eyes were as big as saucers as he contemplated the seriousness and honor of his calling. He said to his dad: "They were awesome!" (Robert L. Backman, " 'They Were Awesome!' " p. 8.)

This is a powerful little story because it paints a visualization of a group of young men not only doing good but also specifically responding to their priesthood responsibilities given in Doctrine and Covenants 107:85, which reads: "And again, verily I say unto you, the duty of a president over the office of a deacon is to preside over twelve deacons, to sit in council with them, and to teach them their duty, edifying one another, as it is given according to the covenants." The story is a perfect confirmation of a president who would "sit in council," who would "teach them their duty," all the while "edifying one another."

So that you understand that I'm not collecting just stories, also in my D&C 107 folder is a copy of a quote from Elder David O. McKay which speaks not only of verse 85 but also of the accompanying verses dealing with the other quorum presidents and their responsibility. You can also find this quote in the Doctrine and Covenants student manual, and it reads:

> Presidents of quorums: The Lord has said to you, as you will read in the 107th section of the Doctrine and Covenants, that it is your duty to meet with your quorum. If you are the president of a deacon's quorum, you are to meet with twelve deacons, and preside over them, to sit in counsel with them, and to teach them their duties. O, deacons, throughout the world! respond to that call. Do your duty, Bishops, you who hold the presidency of the Aaronic Priesthood; guide the young men in this activity. Are they slothful? Are they inactive? If they are, some of the results of inactivity men-

tioned before as befalling the idle individual will afflict the quorum in your ward. Mark it, it will not fulfill its place in the councils of the Church, unless it be active as a council, as a quorum. This is true of the Teachers, of the Priests, the Elders, the Seventies, the High Priests, and all. (In Conference Report, October 1909, p. 92.)

EXAMPLES

As an illustration of what could go into a filing folder marked "D&C 107," let me list a few of the articles or materials I have collected that help me to understand and to teach particular segments of that section:

1. I have dismantled the Doctrine and Covenants student manual and placed each part in the corresponding file folder. There are eight pages of quotes from the student manual, statements from the prophets to help me understand a host of different passages in D&C 107.
2. My past lesson plans for teaching section 107.
3. Transparencies I have made showing how I mark and organize section 107 into major categories and subheadings.
4. Elder Backman's *New Era* story on the deacons quorum presidency, already quoted in this chapter.
5. A talk called "Keys of the Kingdom" given by Elder Bruce R. McConkie, *Ensign*, May 1983.
6. A graphic of two circles showing the two priesthoods, offices in those priesthoods, and keys for presidency—a graphic organizer discussed and shown in chapter 14.
7. Article by Boyd K. Packer, *Ensign*, February 1993, entitled "What Every Elder Should Know—and Every Sister as Well: A Primer on Principles of Priesthood Government."
8. Chart listing when Apostles were originally ordained, a list of prophets, seers, and revelators as to seniority, taken from *Mighty Men of Zion*, by Lawrence Flake.
9. My own priesthood line of authority.
10. Three articles on priesthood councils: one by President N. Eldon Tanner (in Conference Report, March 1979),

one by President Ezra Taft Benson (in Conference Report, March 1979), and one by Elder Ronald E. Poelman (in Conference Report, April 1980).

There are also twenty-five to thirty other articles in my folder, all of which help me in some way to better understand this profound section. Each of these articles represents a collection at different times in my life, a burgeoning, ever-growing file folder to help in my teaching.

Computer Filing System

We are living in a world of technology.

Those who have a working knowledge of computers, and easy access to them, will understand that the actual collecting and filing of articles into a physical filing system applies also to the introduction of the same materials into a computer system.

We are living in an age where CD-ROM, filled with hundreds of books, can be explored in examining, organizing, and downloading material that becomes a powerful resource for teaching. With the scriptures on computer, and with countless articles, talks, and books by those who can help us understand the scriptures better, we have access in virtually seconds to the study of words, phrases, and commentary. Utilize these gifts which have come to us in a day of ever-increasing knowledge.

Conclusion

Whether we file in a box, a four-drawer filing system, the computer, or whatever may be introduced in the years to come, the principle of filing is the same. We need materials to help us, and we need them organized into a system by which they can be retrieved and used to teach the principles of the gospel more edifyingly.

You can do as much or as little as you would like by way of filing. However, some organization, even in its most elemental form, will provide a benefit for your teaching. Again, do something.

18

Preparing the Heart and the Lesson

There are two things we need to consider in preparation. One is the actual physical preparation of a lesson, studying and organizing our efforts towards a classroom experience. The second is a preparation of the teacher, manifested by his desires for God and for the salvation of his children.

PREPARATION OF A LESSON

In a burgeoning church which is growing faster than we may even believe possible, lesson manuals correlating the principles and scriptures for teaching are of fundamental importance. Lesson materials are organized and correlated for the use of the whole Church. The teacher, especially if he understands the commission of teaching, then becomes a critical factor in translating the lesson and especially the scriptural materials to the students. He not only needs to make correct decisions about the presentation of the gospel message but also must then prepare appropriately.

Though the next part of this chapter is not intended to be a mechanistic manner of lesson preparation, there are some points I would like to make as to a possible order of preparation. For a moment, let us pretend that we are Gospel Doctrine teachers and I will suggest a method of study which reflects our philosophy:

1. Use the lesson manual to know what chapters in the

scriptures you will be teaching. Open your scriptures to those chapters.

2. Begin your study of the chapters with a prayer thanking the Lord for the opportunity to prepare and teach in the Church, to have a personal experience with the gospel principles. Pray that he will guide you in your efforts to understand the principles, to have a testimony concerning them, to live them, and to help you to be able to teach them edifyingly. We sometimes have the notion that because we are members of the Church, the Lord will simply give us the very spirit of prophecy and revelation that we desire, without once asking for it.

3. Scan the scriptural pages briefly in order to sense the material. Examine the chapter headings and perhaps jot a brief and simple organization or overview of the events or doctrines being covered.

4. Read. Read the chapters. Mark ideas and organizations in your scriptures that come while you are reading. Make notes of ideas and feelings that come to you as you are reading and marking. The Lord can work through you in these beginning stages inasmuch as you have asked for his help and are not only preparing yourself now but also intending to prepare yourself thoroughly before you teach.

5. At this particular stage, after having scanned and then read the scriptural assignment for yourself, go to the lesson manual and read for the first time the lesson material, now that you have had opportunity to feel the beginnings of the doctrines and ways you might teach. The ideas contained in the lesson manual will now be more pointed and more clear as to what needs to be taught because you have taken opportunity to be conversant with the subject matter in the scriptures.

6. Study. Study the chapters. Having read them through preliminarily, having read the lesson and sensed areas of consideration, now begin a study of the chapters. Use the footnotes, the Bible Dictionary, the Topical Guide, and the index. Mark your scriptures as ideas and cross-references come to you. Continue to make notes on ideas and feelings that come to you as you are studying, as they will benefit the lesson organization that you will make later.

7. Research. Research the principles or scriptures that you

studied. Move outside the realm of the scriptures and search out books of commentary, like the CES student manuals, books which will give you clarification as to doctrines and principles needing to be taught or the backgrounds and context of the scriptures. Make marginal notes in your scriptures of the things you are learning. In other words, continually mark your scriptures, and let them be the repository of your learning. Keep notes of the ideas and feelings that come to you as you are researching, inasmuch as the Lord will continue to work through you with the very revelation you have been seeking.

8. Identify the principles contained in the scriptures. At this particular stage, having read the chapters and the lesson, having studied and researched, it is important to make sure you have identified the principles contained in the scriptures that need to be taught, perhaps even making a list of the critical principles. Select the principles that need to be covered, or can be covered in the time period of your class experience.

9. A teacher's role is to clarify and verify the principles; therefore, at this stage of preparation one needs to examine ways in which the scriptural text for that particular lesson can be taught more clearly. Here is an opportunity to develop ways to use apperception, to liken the scriptures to current circumstances, or to utilize stories that will help the process of teaching. Your filing system may serve you effectively.

10. Make a lesson outline, a lesson plan, a lesson organization. Determine what scriptures you will use, how the principles will be taught, discussed, examined, clarified, and verified. Prepare overviews, graphic organizers, stories, and ways that will help the student to understand more profoundly the scriptures and the principles.

11. Prepare with some lead time, so that the lesson plan is not made as you enter the classroom. Remember that the process of revelation which you seek and the feelings of testimony which you desire take time—and if there is sufficient time and a proper attitude, there will be a natural process of thinking, pondering, rearranging, and examining the lesson until it has taken on a more refined stature—a product of the very spirit of inspiration which you need.

Preparation of a Teacher

Although lesson preparation is important in having quality teaching, it isn't the critical factor. Teacher preparation is the critical factor, and teacher preparation is more than lesson preparation, more than just studying, organizing, and presenting. It is the special attitude and demeanor of a teacher whose heart is prepared to teach. In addressing this special topic of teacher preparation, Elder Henry B. Eyring stated:

> You and I have had times in our lives when we consistently made effective preparation for teaching. Other times we were less effective. Everything I have learned from my experience is summed up in a description of the teacher preparation of an Old Testament prophet, Ezra. In chapter 7, verse 10, this is the description given of the way he prepared.
>
> "For Ezra had prepared his heart to seek the law of the Lord, and to do it, and to teach in Israel statutes and judgments."
>
> That not only includes everything I have learned from experience about teacher preparation, but it even gives it in the right order. It starts with preparing your heart. There is a practical reason for that. Ezra was preparing his heart to seek the law of the Lord. Every scripture I know about obtaining the law of the Lord has words in it like *seek, search, meditate, feast, lay hold, ponder, treasure,* or *study*. You and I have read those scriptures. We know they are true. And yet if we look back in our lives to the times we prepared well and the times we didn't prepare as well, the difference was whether or not we acted as if we really believed obtaining the law of the Lord took long, constant, sustained effort." (*Prepare Your Heart,* p. 1.)

It is true that preparing well in our teaching requires "long, constant, sustained effort" and patiently waiting upon the Lord to allow him to grant his gifts in his own time and in his own way. But part of our heart's preparation is evidenced by how naturally our minds turn to the Lord and to the law of the Lord that brings salvation not only to us but also to our students.

Elder Eyring reasoned that only the "humble heart" would naturally seek the law, that only one who was "dependent" on the Lord would have true humility, and that true, "worshipful, grateful prayer" aided us more in being dependent than anything he knew. Second, he suggested that "constant seeking for the Lord's law will always have the effect of making you want to try it." Two things will happen to one who has "tried" it and lived it; first he will know that it is true, and then he will sense the forgiveness of the Lord that will turn his heart "outward to others."

In visually summarizing this formula of Elder Eyring's, we see that the journey that leads a teacher to the law and subsequently to seek salvation for his students, because his heart has turned outward, is perhaps best begun and maintained by prayer—true, worshipful, grateful prayer.

Hearts turn outward
Forgiveness
Know the truth of the law
Do the law (sacrifice)
Seek the law
Prepare heart
Humility
Dependence on Lord
Worshipful, grateful prayer

The order is important, and perhaps the "worshipful, grateful prayer" as a part of our teaching lives will do more for establishing the whole process of preparation than all the books on teaching could possibly do. It is perhaps a confirmation of the passage in 2 Nephi 32:9:

> But behold, I say unto you that ye must pray always, and not faint; that ye must not perform anything unto the Lord save in the first place ye shall pray unto the Father in the name of Christ, that he will consecrate thy performance unto thee, that thy performance may be for the welfare of thy soul.

Nephi's words reiterate the Lord's admonition for teachers to pray the "prayer of faith" given in Doctrine and Covenants 42. Prayer is a critical part of our preparation as a teacher, is really the "manner" or "pattern" of a teacher. It is the prayer thanking the Lord for life, for a plan of happiness, for an atonement, and for the opportunity of salvation. It is the prayer desiring to know the truth of the doctrines and principles, to sense ever deeper the gospel and the scriptures which house the message of salvation. It is the prayer to receive the spirit of prophecy and revelation, to know the certainty of spiritual things, and to receive promptings and insights concerning our teaching. It is the prayer for the students, pleading that their hearts will be softened to receive the knowledge of the truth themselves.

Hearts are prepared to seek the Lord and to teach, by prayer.

> My suggestion is that you and I might pray well before the class, long before the final moments of preparation and before we even begin working on a teaching outline. Rather, my early prayer might be that I would sense my dependence, that I might have a humble heart and that I might then hunger, thirst, search, ponder, and meditate in the moments when I don't have anything else I must think about. When that prayer is answered, you and I will know it as we walk down a street and find that our hearts and minds have turned to the law of the Lord. (Eyring, *Prepare Your Heart*, p. 4.)

Conclusion

Preparing a lesson, at least the physical object of our assignment as teachers, is a wholesome opportunity to study the principles contained in the scriptures, to seek testimony and conversion to those principles, and to find ways to teach the principles in a clarifying manner.

But preparation is also the prayer, the dependence, the humility, the seeking, the living, the knowing, the forgiveness, and the heart turned toward others. It is a task of the Gods, those whose avowed and eternal purpose is to bring to pass the eternal life of others. Teaching, for which we properly prepare, beckons us to be like God himself. True gospel teaching is one of the more exalting works in this mortal, fallen environment.

19

The Grand Fundamental Principles of Teaching

I have thought that the best way to summarize this book would be to review the major points, the important principles undergirding a teaching philosophy. The principles are hereafter listed as they were introduced, chapter by chapter. Hopefully, such conciseness, born of an overview, will reinforce the importance of the principles.

Again, a philosophy of teaching is something which must distill on our hearts, and this takes time, takes repetition, takes experience, and, most important, is based on a dependent trust that the Lord has given us a pattern concerning the teaching we do in this church.

I believe that these principles must be rehearsed often in our teaching hearts. Believing that taking things in our mouths—that is, speaking them aloud—helps the principles to penetrate our minds and our hearts more thoroughly, I encourage you to review these principles, speaking them aloud perhaps to yourself or your fellow teachers with conviction.

THE PHILOSOPHY OF TEACHING

1. A teaching methodology cannot be any better than the philosophy which gives it life.

2. Having a correct philosophy is critical to helping our students toward eternal life.
3. Acquiring a philosophy to teach the gospel is not based on the standards and requirements established by the world.
4. The consistency of teaching principles throughout the scriptural record would seem to indicate that the Lord has a pattern, order, or law concerning the teaching we do to bring about the salvation of his children.
5. There is a "law" of teaching. We are to
    - Teach the principles of the gospel,
    - Teach those principles out of the scriptures,
    - Observe and do the covenants and Church articles,
    - Pray the prayer of faith, and
    - Be directed by the Spirit.
6. The work of God is not frustrated, only the work of men. This principle relates to teaching as well as other work.
7. There are essential principles that form a charted course for education in the Church.
8. There are two fundamental truths that form a context for teaching in this dispensation; one is that Joseph Smith is a prophet, and the other is that Jesus is the Christ.
9. The students in our classes are hungering for the gospel of Jesus Christ, and they need it straight and undiluted.
10. There is a fundamental difference between teaching the principles of the gospel and teaching the ethics of religion. It is not a teacher's charge to be responsible for the gospel behavior of his students. It is, however, his charge to teach the gospel clearly to his students.
11. We have a commission to teach and emphasize the principles of the gospel, the right food for a hungering and spiritual student.
12. Teaching principles of the gospel to students allows them to better use their agency in choosing to govern themselves.
13. The scriptures are the very housing for the principles that are necessary for eternal life.
14. The scriptures contain the Lord's emphasis on the principles for our day inasmuch as the prophets have been divinely assisted in abridging and preparing their writings.
15. A teacher needs to understand the context of the scriptures

by understanding more clearly the original writers' intent.
16. It is important for a teacher to help the students understand the context of the scriptures so that they will be better able to use the scriptures themselves.
17. In presenting the gospel message, teachers should realize that the language of the scriptures better conveys the context and expectations of the Lord than does the language of the world.
18. There is power in the word of God to change lives.
19. The ways of God in teaching—that is, being directed by the Spirit of the Lord—are not the ways of man. There is a fundamental difference in what man can do in the classroom and what the Spirit of the Lord can do. The power of the Holy Ghost far surpasses any power generated by man.
20. The principles of the gospel are ultimately confirmed and conveyed only by the Spirit of the Lord.
21. The power of the Spirit may be diminished by the teacher's inadequate preparation, improper motivation, inappropriate skills, or inadequate lifestyle. The influence of the Spirit in our teaching may be enhanced by the elimination of areas of conflict with the powers of heaven.
22. A teacher must be worthy in order to have the Spirit of the Lord accompany him in his teaching.
23. The Spirit of the Lord is given by the prayer of faith. Implicit in the prayer of faith is the precedent requirement that we do our part in accomplishing the teaching we seek.
24. We cannot force spiritual things; therefore, it is important to prepare early so that the pressures either of life or of the teaching moment do not burden our receptiveness to the influence of the Spirit.
25. Every worthy teacher has the right to secure a witness of the Spirit and to declare that witness in his teaching.
26. The message of the gospel is fundamentally strengthened when we teach such core doctrines as God, the Creation, the Fall, the Atonement, faith, repentance, baptism, the Holy Ghost, and enduring to the end.
27. The prophets have persuaded us to come to God by not only teaching that he exists but also teaching the characteristics and attributes of God.

28. One of the teacher's most important roles is to help the student understand the nature of the God he worships and with whom he has covenant responsibilities.
29. The way we teach the gospel must be worthy of the very gospel itself.
30. The "word of God" is critically important to the presentation of the gospel, and as it is contained in the scriptures, it becomes the way in which we present the principles of the gospel.
31. A teacher's essential responsibilities are to clarify, verify, and testify.
32. It is important to establish and verify gospel principles by utilizing the law of witnesses in our teaching.
33. It is a teacher's obligation to exemplify the word and to be a witness of the truth by receiving the spirit of prophecy and revelation himself.
34. The opportunity to receive the spirit of revelation is commensurate with our diligence in observing our covenants, searching the scriptures, praying the preparatory prayer of faith, and fasting and praying for the witness of heaven to be given.
35. Every teaching opportunity has the potential of establishing the truth by the use of the scriptural witness, the teacher's witness, and, ultimately, the witness of the Holy Ghost.
36. Building faith unto salvation is the fundamental reason we teach.
37. As teachers we are defenders of the faith. We are covenantally bound to defend the Church, the leaders, the principles, and, ultimately and especially, God himself.
38. We are not to teach false doctrines, to modify the doctrines of the Church, or to teach the philosophies of the world. We are to teach the gospel of Jesus Christ, using as our sources the standard works of the Church.

The Methodology of Teaching

39. A prominent part of the study we do as teachers of the gospel should be within the scriptural pages.
40. As teachers, we cannot teach gospel principles in our class-

rooms sufficiently without the currently approved set of scriptures.
41. The scriptures themselves provide fundamental explanation for the scriptures. It is, therefore, important to use prophecy to understand prophecy, revelation to understand revelation.
42. Teachers teach what the prophetic preachers preach.
43. Those who treasure the scriptural word, which is given by the spirit of prophecy and revelation, have a greater occasion to receive the spirit of prophecy and revelation themselves.
44. Marking our scriptures is a thinking, organizational skill which increases abilities to clarify the word.
45. Identifying the organization of the scriptures, and marking them accordingly, allows a teacher and his students to better understand the scriptural originator's intent.
46. Using the organizational strategy of marking the "word of God" in the scriptures (as it comes from the Lord, or from angels, or from previous prophetic scriptural authors) allows a teacher to see how the prophet-teachers in the scriptures used the word to teach the gospel.
47. Marking the characteristics and attributes of God creates a sensitivity to an undergirding purpose for the scriptures. It additionally produces, colored on the pages, an overwhelming testimony of the significance of understanding and teaching the nature of God.
48. Overviewing causes a teacher to sense the organization and beauty of the writings of the original prophets. It provides a teacher with a clearer understanding of themes and purposes of the prophetic writers.
49. Overviewing provides the student with the ability to see a relationship of the parts to the whole. It is the contextual framework for making the principles of the gospel more understandable.
50. Overviewing is a pacing technique which allows the class to see the bigger picture, and yet be able to cover some doctrines in greater detail without losing the wholeness of the chapters being covered.
51. Students need visualizations and graphic organizations to assist their learning and understanding.

52. Pictures with text, or with oral instructions, increase a student's learning.
53. The very process of thinking, pondering, and creating a graphic to clarify a lesson can create in a teacher a greater understanding of the principles, a greater energy about the truth of the principles.
54. It is valuable to help students understand intangible principles by likening them to tangible examples with which they are already familiar; this is known as apperception.
55. We may create examples that make use of apperception after our study of the principles and in an effort to clarify the principles, not the other way around.
56. Stories, both ancient and modern, house precepts and principles.
57. The telling of stories transports vital precepts from one generation to another.
58. Modern-day stories can verify scriptural stories through the law of witnesses.
59. Stories help students to "see" and "feel" the principles of the theology we are teaching.
60. Any kind of filing system, even in an elemental form, will encourage the process of learning and teaching more than no system at all.
61. Order, not confusion, must be brought to bear on the continuing knowledge base we are building for teaching.
62. Retaining material that is considered pleasing to us as teachers, and particularly to God, is a fundamental reason for filing.
63. Preparing lessons must involve the spirit of prophecy and revelation, which is fostered by prayer, reading the scriptural text, studying the scriptural records, researching the prophetic commentary, and by seeking ways to liken and testify concerning the principles of the gospel.
64. Worshipful, grateful prayer has a tendency to make one feel dependent on the Lord, which in turn can cause a humility sufficient to prepare our hearts for seeking and teaching the law of the Lord.
65. A prepared heart causes us to seek the law of the Lord and to live it. The forgiveness which follows the living of the

law helps our hearts to turn outward to others—a necessary dimension of teaching.
66. Using a list of principles derived from the philosophy and methodology of teaching may assist a teacher, or a supervisor of teachers, to more easily review the fundamentals of teaching. Essential to our success in observing the law of teaching is the necessity of constantly renewing our familiarity with the basic principles of teaching.

20

The Power of Teaching unto Salvation

In an address to his people, King Benjamin (see Mosiah 2–4) came to a stage in the development of his talk when he challenged them to act on what he had taught them, on what they believed:

> And again, believe that ye must repent of your sins and forsake them, and humble yourselves before God; and ask in sincerity of heart that he would forgive you; and now, *if you believe all these things see that ye do them* (Mosiah 4:10; emphasis added).

So it is with us. We have been commissioned to teach a certain message, and to teach it in a certain manner. If we *believe* that the Lord has invested us with specific charges related to teaching, then we need to *do* them. There is power in doing what we have been commissioned to do by the Lord and his prophets, even power unto the salvation of man.

A Miracle

Doing what heaven directs brings miracles. Elder Henry B. Eyring, serving as the commissioner of Church Education, started off an area directors convention in Salt Lake City by suggesting that we needed a "miracle." In 1981, when the talk was given, there was not the fervor of scripture study among our young people as there is today. Part of the success we sense in our youth today, in their accelerated feelings for the gospel and the scriptures, would in part have to do with the results of this particularly challenging talk, and with those in the Church Educational System "doing" what they "believed" they stood for:

> I have a hunch that four or five years from now you will see more Latter-day Saint youth in our classes pondering the scriptures, talking about them with each other, teaching each other from them, believing that they really do have the answers to the questions of their hearts. I really believe this, but it is going to take a miracle for young people to do that. It's going to take a miracle. It hasn't happened yet except in a few cases. It's not the rule among our students, not yet. Therefore you are talking about a miracle. . . . I just can't believe the Lord would give us that miracle unless we have faith. I know how you show faith: you do the thing that you would like the students to do. . . . Think of the effect if each of us would say, "I'm going to do it, I think I know what Brother Eyring was talking about, I think I have a picture of a young person reading the scriptures with faith, this will really help me, the answers to my problems are here, directions are here for me, comfort is here for me, and I'm going to read the scriptures." . . . I think we can unify together and say, okay, Heavenly Father, we believe, and we'll show you that we believe! . . .
>
> May I suggest to you what sets apart the religious education programs of the Church, the professionally led religious education programs of the Church. It is a daily, weekday program. Now if that is who we are and if the scriptures are going to be the lever that makes the difference, then if the people sitting in this room are not daily *in* the scriptures, getting comfort and guidance daily, however busy we are, I can hardly believe that God would accept our petition and give us the miracle. And we're going to need a miracle. We need it, and we need it right away. We don't need it in twenty years; we need it now. . . .
>
> I don't see how we can ask for that miracle, and I believe it is a miracle—it's beyond where they are now, unless we do it ourselves. We don't need big solidarity groups to do it; we just need to *do* it. I pledge that I will and warn you a little bit that if you don't all do it, we won't have the power from heaven that we need. (Henry B. Eyring, address to CES area directors.)

Elder Eyring, with the mantle of vision to propose directions and exhortations to the entire Church Educational System, gave us a desire to experience a miracle, one that we all wanted; with the proper combining of our faith, we could pull down the very powers of heaven upon ourselves and our students. Every time I read the talk, I sense a spirit captured in his message—a desire to accomplish our charge, a unity of purpose, and a longing for heaven's help.

The Miracle of Teaching

Teaching is a work of salvation that will require of us the same desires, unity, and longings. We need a miracle as well. We need the powers of heaven showered on our work, in our classrooms, on our students. We need a host of miracles. It isn't the rule yet among our teachers to sense a law of teaching, to have this pattern and manner of teaching written on their hearts. It isn't the rule yet for teachers to study the scriptures intensely, and early, and to search the scriptural and prophetic helps in order to be converted to or deepened in their understanding of the principles of the gospel. It isn't the rule yet for teachers to seek earnestly the gift of teaching and to pay the spiritual price to have the spirit of prophecy and revelation in their lives.

Therefore, we need a miracle to ensure that the teachings of the gospel, the principles of salvation, are taught, and taught in the manner and way prescribed and exemplified by the Lord and his prophets. It will not be sufficient for only a handful of people to be teaching in this manner; it will take an army of Saints, committed to do the Lord's bidding on this matter, committed to study and teach so that the Spirit of the Lord can bring a mighty change and conversion into the hearts of their students.

We need to act as did the Saints at King Benjamin's time, those who had been challenged that if they believed these things, they should do them. The scriptural record evidences their marvelous faith:

> Yea, we *believe* all the words which thou hast spoken unto us; and also, we *know* of their surety and truth, because of the Spirit of the

Lord Omnipotent, which has wrought a mighty change in us, or in our hearts. . . .

And we, ourselves, also, through the infinite goodness of God, and the manifestations of his Spirit, have *great views* of that which is to come. . . .

And it is the *faith* which we have had on the things which our king has spoken unto us that has brought us to this great *knowledge*, whereby we do rejoice with such exceedingly great joy.

And we are willing to enter into a covenant with our God to *do* his will, and to be *obedient* to his commandments in all things that he shall command us, all the remainder of our days. (Mosiah 5:2–5; emphasis added.)

Our Charge

I testify that there is a "law of teaching," a law that outlines our responsibilities and endows us with heaven's approbation if we are compliant. I believe that the Lord's grace does attend those who so diligently teach (see D&C 88:77) by this law:

1. Teach the principles of the gospel,
2. Teach those principles out of the scriptures,
3. Observe and do the covenants and Church articles,
4. Pray the prayer of faith, and
5. Be directed by the Spirit.

The prophets, both inside and outside the scriptural pages, have taught us and witnessed to us that the Lord has commissioned us. There are a legion of principles that form an order of teaching, and inasmuch as we are the agents of the Lord, we are agents of his kind of teaching.

We have a responsibility in this mortal life, granted to us by God himself, to align ourselves with him. This is his plan of happiness, his provisions for an earth, an atonement, and an array of gospel principles and covenants calculated to help us become like him. We are not left ignorant as to the *what* or the *how* of the teaching we are to do.

We have a divine commission to teach. I bear witness that true gospel teaching produces a power unto salvation.

Appendix 1:
Overviewing the Book of Mormon

1 Nephi	1	2—7	8—10	11—15	16—18	19—22
	Lehi's call	Journeys 2-Wilderness 3-4-Plates 7-Ishmael	Lehi's dream & prophecy	Nephi's prophecy	Journey resumed 16-Liahona 17-Ship 18-Ocean	Nephi— Isa. 48, 49, commentary

2 Nephi	1—4	5	6—10	11	12—24	25—33
	Lehi's blessings 2-Opposition 4-Nephi's psalm	Split Nephites and Lamanites	Jacob— Isa. 49–52, commentary 9-Atonement	Nephi, Jacob, and Isaiah saw Christ	Nephi— quotes Isaiah	Nephi's commentary (31–33-Doctrine of Christ)

Jacob	1—3	4—6	7
	Temple sermon Pride & immorality	Written sermon 5-Zenos's Allegory	Sherem

Enos	1	Jarom 1	Omni 1	Words of Mormon 1
	Forgiveness	420–361 B.C. Many prophets labor to help Nephites	361–130 B.C. 5 record keepers	Explains abridgment

Mosiah	1—6	7—8	9————22	23—24	25—29
	King Benjamin discourse 4-Nature of God and man	Ammon	Zeniff—Noah—Limhi 9-10 11——16 17–18 19–22 Zeniff Noah Alma Limhi & Abinadi	Alma release from captivity	King Mosiah 26-Transgressors 27-Alma conversion 29-Government

| Alma | 1——Alma 14 years 4 sons——16 17————28 5-Zarahemla talk 13-Melchizedek & priesthood 22-Aaron & the king's conversion | 29 "O that I were an angel" | 30 Korihor | 31—35 Zoramites 32-Faith 34-Infinite Atonement | 36—42 Alma & 3 sons 36–37-Helaman 38-Shiblon 39–42-Corianton | 43—63 War 46-Moroni & title of liberty 53–57-Helaman & 2,000 warriors |

Helaman	1—6	7—11	12	13—15	16
	Nephite iniquity & combinations 5-Nephi & Lehi & conversions	Nephi— Power Preaching Prophecy	Mormon's editorial | The cycle	Samuel the Lamanite	State of Nephites 6–1 B.C.

3 Nephi	1—7	8—10	11————26	27—28	29—30
	1st 34 years	3 days of destruction and darkness	3 days of ministry 11-Appearance 12–14-Sermon 15-Law of Moses 16-Other sheep 17-Heal children 18-Sacrament 19-Prayer 20–22-Gathering 23–26-Scriptures	Comings and goings of disciples	Mormon's editorial comments

4 Nephi	1
	Rise and fall of Zion society

Mormon	1————7	8—9
	Mormon—account of wars and deterioration	Moroni—instruction and farewell

Ether	1————6	7————11	12————15
	Jaredite beginnings 2 & 3-Brother of Jared	Orihah to Ether	Ether and Coriantumr 12-Faith and examples

Moroni	1	2————6	7————9	10
	Reason to write	Priesthood handbook of instructions	Mormon's epistles 7-Charity 8-Little children	Grand promise and farewell

Appendix 2: Grand Fundamental
Philosophy

HBE "Prepare Your Heart"

Heart turn outward
↑
Forgiveness
↑
Do it
↑
Seek the law
↑
Prepare heart
↑
Humility
↑
Dependence on God
↑
Grateful prayer

Key: We are agents of the Lord. Acquiring a philosophy is not based on the standards and requirements of the world.

BKP
1. Building faith unto salvation is the ultimate reason we teach
2. We have made covenants to protect all that is represented in the gospel of Jesus Christ—the principles, Church, leaders, & God himself

JRC "The Charted Course of the Church in Education"
1. Fundamentals ⟨ Joseph Smith / Jesus Christ
2. Intellectual & moral courage
3. Student—hungers, craves, wants it straight and undiluted

"Law of Teaching"

D&C 42:12–14
Teach principles out of scriptures
Obey & do covenants
Prayer of faith
Directed by Spirit

ETB "The Gospel Teacher and His Message"
1. Language of scriptures conveys Lord's expectations
2. Power of word to change lives

BRM "The Foolishness of Teaching"
1. Teach principles & doctrines, the ethical concepts automatically follow
2. Use standard works
3. By power of Holy Ghost
4. Apply principles to needs of hearers
5. Testify truth of what we teach

ETB "The B of M and D&C"

Words | Way

A teacher's responsibility
Clarify
Verify
Testify
and
Exemplify

(Circle: God — Faith, Repentance, Creation, Baptism, Holy Ghost, Fall, Atonement, Endurance)

Spirit of God

Functions
Strives with man
Fruits & gifts
Power & authority
Discern thoughts
Revelation
Remembrance
Given what to say
Magnifies abilities
Constrains & restrains
Edifies
Validates
Carries to heart

Conditions
Desire
Seek blessings
Contrition & meekness
Walk in virtue and holiness
Seek to build Zion

NF (Neil Flinders) "Curriculum"

1. Scriptures house principles
2. Prophets inspired as editors and abridgers
3. Need to know original writer's intent
4. Help students w/context—know how to use scriptures themselves

Key: Mosiah 4:10 "If ye believe these things, see that ye do them."

Principles of Teaching the Scriptures

Methodology

1. Study scriptures

   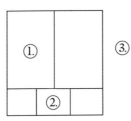

   1. Study text
   2. Study footnotes
   3. Study prophets
   4. Identify principles
   5. Treasure word

2. Mark scriptural text

   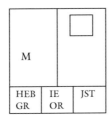

   1. Mark language helps: HEB, GR, IE, OR
   2. Mark JSTs
   3. Mark major organizations (parables, miracles, etc.)
   4. Annotate

3. Overview, outline

1 Nephi						Moses 1			
1	2–7	8–10	11–15	16–18	19–22	1–11	12–23	24–39	40–42
Lehi's Vision	Journeys	Lehi's dream, prophecy	Nephi's prophecy	Journeys	Nephi Isa. 48, 49 Commentary	Vision of God, earth	Encounter with Satan	Vision of God, earth, worlds	Conclusion

   1. Know original writer's intent & themes
   2. Know framework of context
   3. Overviews provide a plan—a "why"
   4. Becomes a pacing technique

4. Graphic focus

   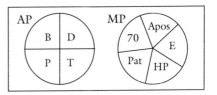

   1. Pictures and text, best medium for teaching
   2. Making a graphic helps a teacher to more fully understand the principles

5. Apperception

   Formula

   _____ is like _____

   1. Intangible principles are understood better by comparing them to tangible things from students' own experiences

6. Stories

   Scripture stories + Modern-day stories

   1. Stories house precepts
   2. Stories help us to "see" and "feel," while principles help us "know"
   3. Modern stories can verify scripture stories; show God is "no respecter…"

7. Filing

   My Filing Box

   1. Any kind of filing will encourage the learning process
   2. Order must be brought to bear on our increasing knowledge

Sources Cited

Backman, Robert L. " 'They Were Awesome!' " *New Era* 13 (May 1983): 4–8.
Ballard, M. Russell. "A Chance to Start Over: Church Disciplinary Councils and the Restoration of Blessings." *Ensign* 20 (September 1990): 12–19.
———. "Small and Simple Things." *Ensign* 20 (May 1990): 6–8.
Bennett, William J. "What We Must Teach Our Children—About Character." *Reader's Digest,* May 1987, pp. 100–102.
Benson, Ezra Taft. "The Book of Mormon and the Doctrine and Covenants." *Ensign* 17 (May 1987): 83–85.
———. *The Gospel Teacher and His Message* [an address delivered to religious educators, 17 September 1976]. Salt Lake City: The Church of Jesus Christ of Latter-day Saints, 1976.
Clark, Cecil D. *Teaching Like the Master.* American Fork, Utah: Covenant Communications, 1994.
Clark, J. Reuben Jr. *The Charted Course of the Church in Education* [an address delivered to seminary and institute teachers, 8 August 1938]. Reprint. Salt Lake City: The Church of Jesus Christ of Latter-day Saints, 1980.
Cook, Gene R. *Raising Up a Family to the Lord.* Salt Lake City: Deseret Book Co., 1993.
Doyle, Brian, and Ben. N. Dunnit. "More Than Just a Pretty Slide." *Training News,* September 1986, pp. 10–16.

Durrant, George D. *Love at Home—Starring Father.* Salt Lake City: Bookcraft, 1976.

Eyring, Henry B. Address to CES area directors, 6 April 1981, Salt Lake City, Utah.

———. *The Power of Stories in Teaching the Gospel.* 20 August 1982.

———. *Prepare Your Heart* [an address delivered to religious educators, 22 August 1987].

Flake, Lawrence R. *Mighty Men of Zion: General Authorities of the Last Dispensation.* Salt Lake City: Karl D. Butler, 1974.

Flinders, Neil J. *Report on Religious Education: Summary of an In-Depth Analysis of Some Fundamental Factors Related to Effective Religious Education in The Church of Jesus Christ of Latter-day Saints.* 1975.

Grant, Heber J. *Gospel Standards.* Compiled by G. Homer Durham. Salt Lake City: Improvement Era, 1941.

Hafen, Bruce R. *The Broken Heart: Applying the Atonement to Life's Experiences.* Salt Lake City: Deseret Book Co., 1989.

Hanks, Marion D. "Changing Channels." *Ensign* 20 (November 1990): 38–41.

Holland, Jeffrey R. "Pitfalls and Powder Sheds." *Growing Edge* 11 (November 1978).

Hoole, Daryl V. "How I Stopped Accumulating and Started Filing in Four Easy Steps." *Ensign* 6 (July 1976): 42–44.

Ivey, Allen E. *Microcounseling: Innovations in Interviewing, Counseling, Psychotherapy, and Psychoeducation.* 2d ed. Springfield, Ill.: Thomas, 1978.

Lee, Harold B. "A Sure Trumpet Sound: Quotations from President Lee." *Ensign* 4 (February 1974): 77–79.

———. *Ye Are the Light of the World.* Salt Lake City: Deseret Book Co., 1974.

Ludlow, Daniel H. *Marking the Scriptures: Suggestions for Understanding and Using the New LDS Edition of the Bible.* Salt Lake City: Deseret Book Co., 1980.

Maxwell, Neal A. "Teaching by the Spirit—'The Language of Inspiration.'" *Old Testament Symposium Speeches.* 1991.

———. "Those Seedling Saints Who Sit Before You." *Old Testament Symposium Supplement.* 1984.

McConkie, Bruce R. "Agency or Inspiration?" *New Era* 5 (January 1975): 38–43.

———. "The Bible—A Sealed Book." *Supplement to the Eighth Annual Church Educational System Religious Educators' Symposium.* Salt Lake City: The Church of Jesus Christ of Latter-day Saints, 1984.

———. "Christ and the Creation." In *Studies in Scripture.* Vol. 2, *The Pearl of Great Price.* Edited by Robert L. Millet and Kent P. Jackson, pp. 77–90. Salt Lake City: Randall Book Co., 1985.

———. *Doctrines of the Restoration: Sermons and Writings of Bruce R. McConkie.* Edited and arranged by Mark L. McConkie. Salt Lake City: Bookcraft, 1989.

———. *The Foolishness of Teaching* [an address delivered to seminary and institute teachers]. Salt Lake City: The Church of Jesus Christ of Latter-day Saints, 1981.

———. "This Generation Shall Have My Word Through You." In *Hearken, O Ye People: Discourses on the Doctrine and Covenants,* pp. 3–15. Sandy, Utah: Randall Book Co., 1984.

———. "The How and Why of Faith-promoting Stories." *New Era* 8 (July 1978): 4–5.

———. *Mormon Doctrine.* 2d ed. Salt Lake City: Bookcraft, 1966.

———. "'The Morning Breaks; the Shadows Flee.'" *Ensign* 8 (May 1978): 12–13.

———. *The Promised Messiah.* Salt Lake City: Deseret Book Co., 1978.

———. "The Three Pillars of Eternity." In *Brigham Young University 1981 Fireside and Devotional Speeches,* pp. 27–32. Provo, Utah: University Publications, 1981.

McKay, David O. *Gospel Ideals.* Salt Lake City: Improvement Era, 1953.

———. "'That You May Instruct More Perfectly.'" *Improvement Era* 59 (August 1956): 557–58.

Packer, Boyd K. *A Dedication—to Faith.* Brigham Young University Speeches of the Year. Provo, 29 April 1969.

———. *The Great Plan of Happiness* [an address to religious educators at a symposium on the Doctrine and Covenants and Church History, 10 August 1993].

———. *The Holy Temple.* Salt Lake City: Bookcraft, 1980.

———. *Let Not Your Heart Be Troubled.* Salt Lake City: Bookcraft, 1991.

———. "Someone Up There Loves You." *Ensign* 7 (January 1977): 8–12.

---. *Teach the Scriptures* [an address to the Church Educational System, 14 October 1977].

---. *Teach Ye Diligently*. Salt Lake City: Deseret Book Co., 1975.

Paramore, James M. "Leadership—Jesus Was the Perfect Leader." In *Brigham Young University 1989–90 Devotional and Fireside Speeches,* pp. 1–10. Provo, Utah: University Publications, 1990.

Parker, Todd. "Teaching with Parables—Matthew 13." CES videotape, part 2, New Testament Symposium, 1988.

Potter, Amasa. "The Lord's Blessings." In *Labors in the Vineyard,* pp. 75–93. Salt Lake City: Juvenile Instructor Office, 1884. *Labors in the Vineyard* was reprinted as part of the 4-vols.-in-1 publication *Classic Experiences and Adventures*. Salt Lake City: Bookcraft, 1969.

Pratt, Parley P. *Autobiography of Parley P. Pratt*. Edited by Parley P. Pratt Jr. Classics in Mormon Literature. Salt Lake City: Deseret Book Co., 1985.

Scott, Richard G. "Four Fundamentals for Those Who Teach and Inspire Youth." *Old Testament Symposium Speeches*. 1987.

Sill, Sterling W. "Your Four Great Days." In *Speeches of the Year: BYU Devotional and Ten-Stake Fireside Addresses, 1974,* pp. 39–52. Provo, Utah: Brigham Young University Press, 1975.

Smith, Joseph. *Teachings of the Prophet Joseph Smith*. Selected by Joseph Fielding Smith. Salt Lake City: Deseret Book Co., 1938.

Smith, Joseph Fielding. Address delivered to seminary and institute personnel, LDS Institute of Religion, Salt Lake City, Utah, 14 January 1961.

---. *Doctrines of Salvation*. Compiled by Bruce R. McConkie. 3 vols. Salt Lake City: Bookcraft, 1954–56.

Stepich, Donald A., and Timothy J. Newby. "Analogizing as an Instructional Strategy." *Performance and Instruction,* October 1988, pp. 21–23.

Talmage, James E. *The Parables of James E. Talmage*. Compiled by Albert L. Zobell Jr. Salt Lake City: Deseret Book Co., 1973.

Tate, Lucile C. *LeGrand Richards: Beloved Apostle*. Salt Lake City: Bookcraft, 1982.

Index

— A —

Aaron (son of Mosiah), 74–75, 81–82
Abinadi, 128
"A Chance to Start Over" (article), 196
Agency, 31
Ahaziah, 104
Alma, gives Helaman "paraphernalia," 126
  on language of the scriptures, 42
  on power, 75
  on "small and simple things," 193
  testifies, 93
  used law of witnesses, 89, 90
Ammon (son of Mosiah), 74–75, 81–82
Amulek, 89, 90
Angelic ministers, 18–19
Anointing woman (biblical story), 82–83

Apperception in teaching, 162–64
  appreciation of, 168–71
  Bruce R. McConkie's masterpiece of, 174–76
  formula for, 164–68
  Liahona and, 171–74
Atonement, as teaching focus, 71–72

— B —

Backman, Robert L., gives story about Aaronic Priesthood holders, 199–200
Ballard, M. Russell, on disciplinary councils, 197–98
  on teaching principles, 75–76
Baptism, as teaching focus, 72–74
Behavior. *See* Ethics, teaching of
Benjamin (Nephite prophet-king), on acting, 216
  on the scriptures, 155

Bennett, John C., 117
Bennett, William J., 177–78
Bennion, Adam S., 191
Benson, Ezra Taft, 75
  on language of teaching,
    42–43
  on the need for Christ, 71–72
  on scriptures of the
    Restoration, 69, 85
  supports J. Reuben Clark address, 24
  on teaching from scriptures, 45
  on teaching the gospel, 101
  on testimony, 100
Bible, Joseph Smith's translation
    of, 113, 123
  reading the, 111
  Sidney Rigdon preaches from,
    21
Book of Mormon, Joseph Smith
    preaches from, 21
  overviewing of, 220–21
  teaching with the, 69
Brigham Young University,
    102–3
Brother of Jared, 61–62

— C —

Cat, grateful (parable), 168–70
Chalkboard, as a teaching tool,
    150–61
*Charted Course of the Church in
  Education, The* (talk), 5, 14,
    24
Clark, Cecil, on filing system,
    194
Clark, J. Reuben, Jr., on mission
    of teachers, 68
  on principles versus ethics, 29
  on pruning, 99–100
  on students, 23, 24–25
  on teaching ethics, 28
  on teaching from the scriptures, 37
  on teaching the gospel,
    100–101
  on testimony, 91
  on Webster-Hayne debate, 14
Colors, marking the scriptures
    with, 127–32
Commission to teach, 4–5
Congregational minister (story),
    34
Context for teaching, 17–21,
    44–45
Cook, Gene R., on the Sabbath
    day, 31–32
Covenants, 60–61
  of teachers, 10
Cowdery, Oliver, 61
Creation, as a teaching focus,
    71–72

— D —

Dispensation concept, 19
Doctrine and Covenants, section
    42, 9–13
  teaching with, 69
Doctrines, false, 101
  interpretation of, 101
  teachers not to create, 11–12
Doorknob, exacting (story), 4–5
Durrant, George, gives story of
    his father, 181–82

— E —

Education, moral, 177–78
Educational methodology. *See*
    Methodology of teaching
Educational philosophy. *See*
    Philosophy of teaching

Index

Elijah, 104
Elisha, 104
Endurance, as a teaching focus, 72–74
Ethics, teaching of, 28
  teaching of, versus teaching principles, 29–32
Eyring, Henry B., on miracle needed in teaching, 217
  on teacher preparation, 206, 208
  on value of stories, 180

— F —

Faith, building in students, 99–101
  case study of building, 104–6
  dedication to, 101–4
  as teaching focus, 72–74
Fall of Adam, graphic demonstration of, 153–54
  as teaching focus, 71–72
"Fault-tree" analysis, 56
Filing, box for, 192–94
  computer system, 202
  examples of, 198–202
  numerical system, 194–95
  sequential system, 196–97
  skill of, 191–92
  of stories, 197–98
  topical system, 195–96
Flinders, Neil, *Report on Religious Education*, 38, 40–41
Focus of teaching, 71–84
Foolishness of Teaching, The (talk), 33
Footnote helps, marking of, 122–23
Fundamentals of Church education, 15–22

— G —

Garden of Eden, graphic demonstration of, 153–54
Glove/body comparison, 167
God, is center of any teaching, 70–71, 73
  marking scriptures about the nature of, 129–32
  teaching nature of, 77–84
Gospel Teacher and His Message, The (talk), 42
Grant, Heber J., on teaching by the Spirit, 49–50
Graphics in teaching, 147–48
  chalkboard and, 150–61
  research studies about, 148–49
  scriptural illustrations of, 149–50

— H —

Handcart company (story), 183–84
Hanks, Marion D., gives story of grieving father and son, 83–84
Heavenly Father. *See* God
Holland, Jeffrey R., on teachers of the gospel, 116–17
Holy Ghost, being taught by, 66–67
  being worthy of, 58–61
  duty and office of, 51–52
  gifts of, 54
  and meetings, 85
  and prayer of faith, 61–63
  scriptures about, 52–53
  stories verifying role of, 63–66
  teaching by, 10–11, 32–33, 48–51, 54–58

as teaching focus, 72–74
Humor, and teaching, 6

— I —

"Iffy" revelation, 117–18
Intent, of scripture writers,
    41–42

— J —

Jacob (son of Lehi), on teaching
    principles, 31
Jared, brother of, 61–62
Jesus Christ, anointed by
    woman, 82–83
    as teaching fundamental, 15–16
    used apperception, 163–64
John the Beloved, on love of
    God, 78
Joseph (son of Lehi), 31
Joseph Smith Translation, 113
    marking footnotes in, 123
Joshua, 154–55

— K —

Kimball, Heber C., 48–49
Kimball, Spencer W., 112

— L —

Lamoni, 74–75
Language of the scriptures,
    42–43
Law of teaching (D&C 42),
    9–13, 58, 219
Law of witnesses, 89–90, 97
    and stories, 178–79
Lee, Harold B., 65
    on cross-references, 114–15
    on "iffy" revelation, 117–18

Lehi, 149–50
Liahona, and apperception,
    171–74
"Line upon line" precept, 96–97
Love at Home—Starring Father
    (book), 180
Ludlow, Dan, *Marking the
    Scriptures*, 122

— M —

"Mantle is Far, Far Greater Than
    the Intellect, The" (talk), 99
Manuals, and lesson preparation,
    203–4
Marking the Scriptures (book),
    122
Maxwell, Neal A., on clarifying,
    verifying, and testifying, 89
    on teachers who live worthily,
    59
    on teaching by the Spirit, 63
    used apperception, 170–71
McConkie, Bruce R., on
    Apostasy and Restoration,
    174–76
    on dispensation concept, 19
    on faith-promoting stories,
    178–79
    on false doctrine, 101
    gives parable of the "unwise
    builder," 35–36
    on the power of the Holy
    Ghost, 66–67
    on prayer of faith, 61
    on reading the scriptures, 111
    on study helps in Bible, 114
    on studying with the scrip-
    tures, 111–12
    on teachers creating doctrines,
    11–12
    on teaching by the Spirit, 57

on teaching from the scriptures, 37
on teaching the gospel, 31
on teaching principles, 33
on testimony bearing, 67
on three pillars of eternity, 71
used graphics in teaching, 151–52
McKay, David O., on his father's mission, 20
on priesthood, 200–201
on a teacher's obligation, 180
on whisperings of the Spirit, 65
Meditating, 119–20
Meetings, and the Holy Ghost, 85
Methodology of teaching, 85–89
law of witnesses and, 89–90
philosophy and, 4
sacrament talk example of, 95–98
summary of, 212–15
testifying and, 90–95
Ministers, angelic, 18–19
Miracle of teaching, 216–19
Miracles, marking in scriptures, 123
Moral education, 177–78
Mormon, on angelic ministers, 18–19
Moroni, on the Holy Ghost, 85
on Joseph Smith, 19–20
Moses, 16
Mosiah, sons of, 74–75, 80–82, 93

— N —

Nature of God, 77–84
Nephi, on the Holy Ghost, 56
Nephi's writings, as overviewing illustration, 140–42
scriptural precepts in, 39–40
Night, Apostasy compared to, 174–76
Noah, 62

— O —

Overviewing, 136–37
of the Book of Mormon, 220–21
of chapters, 143
developing the skill of, 140–42
as pacing technique, 144–45
perspective gained through, 137–39

— P —

Pacing, in teaching, 144–46
Packer, Boyd K., on apperception, 162, 164
apperception in writings of, 165–67
on Brigham Young University, 102–3
on building faith, 99, 100
on context, 44–45
on filing system, 192–93
gives story of handcart company, 183–84
on great plan of happiness, 157
on importance of the scriptures, 112
on overviewing, 137
supports J. Reuben Clark address, 24
on teaching by the Spirit, 57
on true doctrine, 34
on use of the chalkboard, 150–51
"Parable of the Grateful Cat, The," 168–70

Parables, marking in scriptures, 123
Paramore, James M., gives story of wayward man, 78–80
Parker, Todd, on marking the scriptures, 133–34
Pattern of teaching, 7, 94
Patterns, identifying in scriptures, 124–26
Paul, on the body of the Church, 126
  on faith, 183
Perspective, of teacher, 23–27
Philosophy of teaching, 3–4
  developing a, 5–8
  divine commission and, 4–5
  methodology and, 4
  summary of, 209–12
Piano keyboard, gospel likened to, 166
Plan of happiness, graphic demonstration of, 157–61
Pondering, 118–19
Potter, Amasa, 48–49
Pratt, Parley P., gives story about Joseph Smith, 21
Prayer of faith, 61–63
Preparation, of lesson, 203–5
  of teacher, 206–8
Priesthood, graphic demonstration of, 151–52
  instructions in D&C 20, 125
  teaching responsibilities of, 86
Principles, Church instructors' right to teach, 33–34
  Holy Ghost and teaching of, 32–33
  teaching of, 28
  teaching of, from the scriptures, 35–36, 222–23
  teaching of, and stories, 182–85
  teaching of, versus teaching ethics, 29–32
Prophets, commentary of, on the scriptures, 116–19

— Q —

Questioning, as a study skill, 156–57

— R —

Raising Up a Family to the Lord (book), 31
Rector, Hartman, Jr., gives story of Congregational minister, 34
Red shawl (story), 183–84
Repentance, as teaching focus, 72–74
Report on Religious Education, 38, 40–41
Restoration, as teaching context, 18–21
  as teaching fundamental, 16–17
Revelation, "iffy," 117–18
Richards, LeGrand, 17
  on teaching fundamentals, 18
Rigdon, Sidney, preaches in Philadelphia, 21

— S —

Sabbath day, 31–32
Sacrament talk example, 95–98
Scott, Richard G., on being spiritual, 58–59
  on teaching by the Spirit, 55–56
Scriptures, as context, 44–45
  helping students mark, 132–34

identifying large patterns in, 124–26
knowing the, 41–42
language of, 42–43
lesson preparation and, 204–5
marking footnote helps in, 122–23
marking JST footnotes in, 123
marking of, 121–22
marking parables and miracles in, 123
power in, 45–47
precepts in, 39–41
principles of teaching (chart), 222–23
prophetic commentary on, 116–19
reading the, 111–12
of Restoration, in teaching, 69–70, 85
study aids to, 114–16
studying the, 109–11
teaching principles from, 35–36, 37–38
treasuring the, 119–20
using colors to mark, 127–32
using the right, 112–14
Sheep, lost (story), 198–99
Sill, Sterling W., on marking what we read, 192
Smith, Joseph, on correct principles, 34
  on Holy Ghost, 51
  on nature of God, 77
  preaches in Philadelphia, 21
  prepared basic curriculum, 38
  as teaching context, 18–21
  as teaching fundamental, 16–17
  testimony of, 124
  translated Bible, 113–14
  on the work of God, 55

Smith, Joseph F., 50
Smith, Joseph Fielding, on the Fall, 153–54
Spirit, the. *See* Holy Ghost
Standard works. *See* Scriptures
Stories, example of use in teaching, 6
  help seeing and feeling, 180–82
  house precepts, 177–78
  teaching principles through, 182–86
  using our own experience for, 185–89
  verify stories, 178–79
Students, 23–27
  marking their scriptures, 132–34
Study aids, 114–16

— T —

Talmage, James E., "Parable of the Grateful Cat," 168–70
Taylor, John, 50
Teacher, preparation of, 206–8
Teaching focus. *See* Focus of teaching
Teaching Like the Master (book), 194
Teaching methodology. *See* Methodology of teaching
Teaching philosophy. *See* Philosophy of teaching
Teach Ye Diligently (book), 164
Terminology of teaching, 42–43
Testifying, 90–95
  sacrament talk example of, 95–98
Tree of life, as a graphic teaching, 149–50

— U —

"Unwise builder," parable of the, 35–36

— W —

Webster-Hayne debate, 14
Wells, John, 65

Wilson, Kathy, 26
Witnesses, law of. *See* Law of witnesses
Words, power of, 45–47

— Z —

Zeezrom, 89

About the Author

Jerry A. Wilson was born and reared in Ogden, Utah. After serving full-time in the Central British Mission, he returned to Utah and graduated from Weber State University with a bachelor's degree in psychology. He later received master's and doctorate degrees in educational psychology from Brigham Young University.

The author has worked in the Church Educational System for many years, during which time he has been a seminary teacher, an institute teacher and director, and an area director. He is currently an instructor at the Logan Institute of Religion at Utah State University.

His callings in the Church have included stake Sunday School president, stake Young Men president, and bishop. He is presently a high councilor in the North Logan Stake.

The author is married to the former Kathleen Williams. They are the parents of four children, and the family resides in North Logan, Utah.